BETWEEN DIXIE AND ZION

RELIGION AND AMERICAN CULTURE

BETWEEN DIXIE AND ZION

Southern Baptists and Palestine before Israel

WALKER ROBINS

THE UNIVERSITY OF ALABAMA PRESS
Tuscaloosa

The University of Alabama Press
Tuscaloosa, Alabama 35487-0380
uapress.ua.edu

Typeface: Caslon and Arial

Cover image: Detail of "Dome of the Rock with graceful century plants," G. Eric and Edith Matson Photograph Collection, Library of Congress Prints and Photographs Division
Cover design: Todd Lape / Lape Designs

Cataloging-in-Publication data is available from the Library of Congress.
ISBN: 978-0-8173-2048-5
E-ISBN: 978-0-8173-9279-6

To my KP, who loves books.
Here is one for you.

Contents

Acknowledgments

Much of what historians do simply involves looking at what others have found and gathered. I want to start, then, by thanking those who found and gathered the materials that I mined for this study. At the top of the list are Taffey Hall and Bill Sumners of the Southern Baptist Historical Library and Archives (SBHLA) in Nashville, Tennessee. This project would have been impossible without their work. I am also grateful to the helpful archivists and librarians at the American Jewish Archives (AJA), the Central Zionist Archives, and Southwestern Baptist Theological Seminary, as well as the anonymous many who scanned the books, periodicals, and other documents I have used online—from the Z. Smith Reynolds Library at Wake Forest, to the International Mission Board's Archives and Records Services, to the Harry S. Truman Presidential Library, and, again, to the SBHLA and AJA. Finally, I would like to thank the interlibrary loan services at the University of Oklahoma and Brandeis University.

I am also grateful to those who provided material support for this project. Much of the original research was funded through the Anne Hodges and H. Wayne Morgan Fellowship, awarded through the Department of History at the University of Oklahoma. My sister, Ashton, and regional tastemakers Will McDonald and Mark Salvie provided research support in the form of couches. An Israel Institute Fellowship at the Schusterman Center for Israel Studies at Brandeis University allowed me important time and funding to refine the manuscript. Having studied and worked at two Schusterman Centers while working on this project, I am particularly indebted to the Charles and Lynn Schusterman Family Foundation for its support throughout my education and career.

I would also like to thank the journals that have published essays derived from this project. Portions of chapter 4 ("Missionaries") dealing with W. A. Hamlett appeared in "The Forgotten Origins of the Southern Baptist Convention's Near East Mission: W. A. Hamlett's Month in the Holy Land," which was published in the summer 2017 issue of the *Baptist History and Heritage Journal*. Portions of chapter 10 ("Cyrus") appeared in "American Cyrus? Harry Truman, the Bible, and the Palestine Question," published in the September 2017 issue of the *Journal of Church and State*. Sections of chapter 5 ("Jew") appeared in "Jacob Gartenhaus: The Southern Baptists' Jew," which was published in the 2017 issue of the *Journal of Southern Religion*.

I must also thank those who have had a direct hand in improving this work and bringing it to publication. At the top of the list are my mentors, Noam Stillman and Alan Levenson, who have guided and supported me at every step of my career. Their influence on this book goes far beyond its contents. Ben Keppel's impact on my scholarship likewise goes beyond the specific ways in which he helped me improve this work. David Chappell and Charles Kimball provided helpful critiques and suggestions at early stages of the project. Kevin Butterfield showed me how to put a manuscript proposal together. David Ellenson and Rachel Fish allowed me to present my work in a variety of forums during my time at the Schusterman Center for Israel Studies at Brandeis. Particularly valuable was the feedback from students and faculty that I received in the Schusterman Scholars Seminar, organized by Yehuda Mirsky. Of course, I am deeply grateful to the University of Alabama Press, including series editors John Giggie and Charles Israel and, most especially, editor-in-chief Dan Waterman, for their interest and support in bringing this work to press. I am thankful, too, for the hard work of Joanna Jacobs and Jessica Hinds-Bond in refining the text. I must also express my sincere gratitude to the anonymous reviewers whose suggestions and critiques have strengthened this work in significant ways.

Finally, this book would not have been possible without the love, support, and encouragement of my family. This includes Callahans and Parrys in Oklahoma and beyond, and Martins and Hawks in Texas. Above all, it includes my parents, Gregg and Liz Robins, and my sister, Ashton Hawk. And it includes my wife, Kate, who is a very good dresser. I love you all.

Abbreviations

ACPC	American Christian Palestine Committee
ADL	Anti-Defamation League
AJA	American Jewish Archives
APC	American Palestine Committee
AZEC	American Zionist Emergency Council
BWA	Baptist World Alliance
BWC	Business Women's Circles
CHM	Chicago Hebrew Mission
DPs	Displaced Persons
JG	Jacob Gartenhaus Papers
FMB	Foreign Mission Board
HCAA	Hebrew Christian Alliance of America
HMB	Home Mission Board
NBC	Northern Baptist Convention
PAE	Palestine Arab Executive
SBC	Southern Baptist Convention
SBHLA	Southern Baptist Historical Library and Archives
SBTS	Southern Baptist Theological Seminary
SWBTS	Southwestern Baptist Theological Seminary
URL	Una Roberts Lawrence Papers
WMU	Woman's Missionary Union

Introduction

On May 14, 1948, David Ben-Gurion proclaimed from the Tel Aviv Museum that the State of Israel would come into being at the midnight expiration of British rule over Palestine. Eleven minutes after midnight—6:11 p.m. in Washington, DC—the United States became the first government to grant de facto recognition to the newly formed state as the following statement was issued: "This Government has been informed that a Jewish state has been proclaimed in Palestine, and recognition has been requested by the provisional Government thereof. The United States recognizes the provisional government as the de facto authority of the new State of Israel."[1] The signature on the statement belonged to US president Harry Truman, a member of Grandview Baptist Church and a Southern Baptist from the age of eighteen.

The following week, messengers from across the South gathered in Memphis, Tennessee, for the ninety-first Southern Baptist Convention (SBC) Annual Meeting.[2] The meeting promised to be unusually tense, as notorious fundamentalist gadfly J. Frank Norris had decided to hold a counter-convention of sorts at the city's famed Peabody Hotel.[3] Though his primary focus was on castigating SBC president Louie Newton for being too friendly to Soviet Communism, Norris also held a May 17 address in the Peabody's Continental Ballroom on the Palestine question. The pastor had planned the occasion for months, and he had even made inquiries about holding the talk in the "largest synagogue in Memphis," something that he believed would "certainly draw large attention."[4] Norris had long believed that the Jewish people had a God-given right to Palestine and that the Zionist movement—the movement to create a Jewish state in Palestine—was a fulfillment of biblical prophecy. He had even written to President Truman the previous year in support of the movement, prompting a response that Norris had proudly published in his periodical, the *Fundamentalist*.[5] When May 17 arrived, Norris called on SBC delegates to send a telegram of congratulations to Truman for recognizing Israel.

Within the meeting, Norris ally E. D. Solomon of Florida proposed a motion to send the congratulatory telegram on the morning of Wednesday, May 19. It was referred to the Resolutions Committee. Solomon again raised his motion in the afternoon session. It was overwhelmingly voted down. The following day, S. G. Posey of California moved that the convention's messengers convey their appreciation to the United Nations in recognition of its role in the creation of Israel, as well as extend congratulations to the "people of Israel in this partial restoration of their dreams and the partial answer to their prayer for over 2000 years."[6] This motion, too, was referred to the Resolutions Committee, which recommended its rejection the following day. The SBC, it was clear, would not be congratulating anyone on the creation of the Jewish state.

That Southern Baptists would repeatedly and overwhelmingly shoot down resolutions expressing support for Israel would shock most observers today. It has become common knowledge that Christians—particularly the white evangelical Protestants that populate the SBC—are now the largest pro-Israel constituency in a US population that is very supportive of the Jewish state generally.[7] It has become a common assumption, too, that evangelicals have always supported the idea and reality of a Jewish state. To find that the denomination that has become effectively synonymous with conservative evangelicalism could not even muster the votes to send a congratulatory telegram to the president—himself a Southern Baptist—is to find an unexpected past, almost unimaginable from today's perspective.

Between Dixie and Zion recovers that past. It explains both how conservative evangelicals could be so hesitant in celebrating Israel's birth in 1948, and how the roots of their eventual support were already taking hold. It does so by examining the variety of ways in which Southern Baptists encountered the land, the peoples, and the politics of Palestine during the years leading up to the creation of Israel. In particular, this study focuses on what is known as the Mandate era. Between the defeat of the Ottoman Empire in World War I and the creation of Israel in 1948, Great Britain governed Palestine through a League of Nations mandate that called on the British to prepare the region (known from 1923 to 1948 as Mandatory Palestine) for eventual self-government. What this government would look like was a matter of public debate that was frequently referred to as the Palestine question. Would it favor the Zionists, who wanted to establish a Jewish state in Palestine and were immigrating in increasing numbers? Would it favor the Palestinian Arabs, who were the majority of the population and wanted Palestine to form part of a larger Arab kingdom or an independent Palestinian Arab state? Or would it strike a balance between these competing—even contradictory—interests?

In looking at how Southern Baptists engaged the Palestine question, I found that the tempting categories of pro-Zionist (the pre-1948 analogue to pro-Israel) or pro-Arab simply do not fit the sources. Though there were exceptions, most Southern Baptists writing about Palestine did not prioritize the political questions raised by the conflict between Arabs and Zionists. Rather than engaging *the* Palestine question, Baptists developed their own queries when writing about the region. Examining the sources, I found that the ways in which Baptists encountered Palestine tended to determine the shape of these Palestine questions—each of which had its own answers. A foreign missionary had different concerns than an editorialist. A travel writer passing through Nazareth had different priorities than an Arab Baptist living in it. A Jewish convert and missionary had different responsibilities in 1948 than did Harry S. Truman.

Because of this varied engagement, *Between Dixie and Zion* is organized according to the types of encounter rather than particular political or religious perspectives. This framework stands in contrast to most studies of the relationship between evangelicals and the Zionist movement or State of Israel. Since the 1990s, as evangelical support for Israel has become more overt and more organized, scholarship on what is loosely termed Christian Zionism has proliferated.[8] Much of it has focused on evangelical Christians who root their support for Israel in particular interpretations of the Bible, with several scholars having demonstrated the pivotal role of "Judeocentric" biblical hermeneutics in inspiring some of the most fervent Christian support for Zionism and the Jewish state. These interpretations hold that biblical covenants between God and the Jewish people have not wholly transferred to the church—that Jews remain God's chosen people and Palestine remains their promised land—and that prophecy indicates the return of the Jewish people to their land. Scholars have fixed particular attention on a system of interpretation and eschatology known as premillennial dispensationalism, which anticipates the ingathering of Jews to the land of Israel as part of a series of cataclysmic events that will precede the return of Christ and the establishment of his millennial kingdom on earth.[9] Such beliefs have certainly been an important part of the Southern Baptist story. However, *Between Dixie and Zion* shows that they are only one part. Biblical interpretation, in other words, offered one way of encountering the Holy Land that bumped up against and, often, intermingled with others.

Prioritizing encounters, rather than political or religious perspectives, has allowed me to both better contextualize what Southern Baptists had to say about Palestine and better recognize the broader patterns that emerged across different types of encounters. Most prominent among these patterns is that Southern Baptists almost universally identified the Zionist movement with Western civilization, modernity, and material progress over and against the Arabs, whom they saw as quaint or even backward. In doing so, Baptists trafficked in what scholars call Orientalism: common modes of representation in Europe and the United States that broadly divided the world into halves between "the West" (seen as the realm of civilization, progress, Christianity, and modernity) and "the East" (seen as a backward and superstitious realm in need of the civilizing influence of the West).[10] This view was true of travelers, of missionaries, of premillennialists—and of premillennialists' opponents. It was true of those who supported Zionism on prophetic grounds and those who condemned it on political grounds. Repeated throughout all manner of Baptist writings on Mandatory Palestine were allusions to Isaiah 35—the Zionists were making the land once again "blossom as the rose." At times these references were suffused with prophetic significance. At others, they simply made for colorful allusion. Either way, even as most Baptists refused to engage political questions or explicitly endorse the Zionist movement, their words painted images of Palestine that could have fit nicely on Zionist posters.

Such images were not idle. They suggested that the Zionists were fulfilling long-expressed hopes that the Holy Land would one day be revived and regain the prosperity that it had held in the biblical era (examined in chapter 1). In the decades leading up to the British conquest, Southern Baptists had shared with other Western Christians in lamenting the degraded state of the Holy Land under the Ottoman Empire. Although they celebrated its sacred associations, they decried its seeming backwardness, viewing Palestine as a benighted land brought low by Turkish misrule, Islamic fanaticism, Jewish impotence, and Eastern Christian idolatry. At the same time, Southern Baptists expected that God would redeem the land and its peoples. For some, this redemption was a matter of prophetic fulfillment or a signal of Christ's second coming. For most, however, redemption would come through the spread of Protestant Christianity, which they ultimately understood as intertwined with Western values, modernity, and material progress. After World War I, Southern Baptists would find in Zionism shades of this redemption. It was not Protestant; but it was Western, it was modern, and it was progress. For almost all Southern Baptists, these things were good. For many—believers in God's perpetual immanence—they were godly. The Baptists who did overtly support Zionism seized onto these often-vague impressions in making their case for the movement. None did this more effectively than J. Frank Norris, who interwove his premillennial interpretation of the Bible with the language of civilizational clash in calling on Christians to support the Zionists, offering a foretaste of the "marriage of religion and geopolitics" that Stephen Spector identifies in contemporary Christian support for Israel.[11]

The overarching lesson of this study, though, is that there was no single Southern Baptist approach to Palestine, that the diverse ways in which Baptists encountered the Holy Land shaped how they thought about it, even as they articulated those thoughts in the common language of Orientalism. Baptist travelers during the Mandate era, for instance, necessarily saw the region in passing (chapter 2). Their postcard impressions of Palestine highlighted its material transformation—long-awaited modernity was finally coming to the Holy Land. While some emphasized the role of the British in modernizing the region, more focused their attention on the Zionists, whose settlements looked familiarly Western and thus modern, especially when compared to Arab cities and villages. Few Baptist travelers expressed support for Zionism, but their images offered a sort of postcard Zionism to readers in the States.

Missionaries, of course, encountered Palestine as a mission field. That field, though, could look quite different depending on the missionary. Indeed, the Woman's Missionary Union, which was tasked with providing Southern Baptists with mission study materials, sometimes struggled to synthesize missionaries' diverse perspectives on Palestine (chapter 6). For some, the Holy Land was home. The first Southern Baptist missionary to Palestine was an Arab from Safed named Shukri Mosa, who had converted to Baptist Christianity while peddling Holy Land souvenirs in Texas. Above all, Mosa and other Arab Baptist leaders prioritized winning material support for their budding mission in Nazareth (chapter 3). These priorities guided their communications with stateside Baptists and shaped their depictions of the Holy Land. Arab Baptists criticized Zionism, for instance, but they did so in terms of practical implications for their mission. They criticized Arab life and culture, too, using Orientalist language in an attempt to convince Southern Baptists to invest in Arabs' salvation. These criticisms had broader implications, of course, but Arab Baptists' immediate goal was to stir support for their mission.

The American missionaries who began arriving in 1921 quickly eclipsed so-called native workers as the primary spokespeople for Palestine as a mission field (chapter 4). Less focused than their Arab colleagues on concrete communal goals, American missionaries celebrated the dramatic transformations reshaping Palestine. Often, they shared Baptist travelers' understanding that Zionism was bringing progress to a blighted region and presented their mission as part of this redemption. Several missionaries were also inspired by premillennial biblical interpretations to believe that the Zionist movement was somehow the fulfillment of prophecy, even as they were divided on the terms of that fulfillment. Among the questions that most vexed and inspired Baptist missionaries was whether the movement presented a missionary opportunity or hindrance. Some, like H. Leo Eddleman, came to view Zionism as inimical to the gospel. Others, like Robert L. Lindsey, believed that it presented a historic evangelistic opening and sought to adapt the Baptist message to Zionist forms.

Back in the American South, a very different missionary in a very different mission field was also shaping Southern Baptist perceptions of Palestine. That missionary was Jacob Gartenhaus, an immigrant and convert from Judaism (chapter 5). During a tenure that roughly coincided with the Mandate era, Gartenhaus served as the SBC's only missionary to the Jews of the American South. Though hired to evangelize Jews, he spent the majority of his time teaching Southern Baptists about Jews and Judaism in order to stir interest in Jewish evangelism, becoming in the process Southern Baptists' leading spokesperson on Jewish issues—including Zionism. Gartenhaus was a firm supporter of the movement, his support rooted both in his identity as a Hebrew Christian (a convert who maintained a Jewish identity) and in his premillennial understanding of the Bible. In books, in lectures, in articles, and in sermons, Gartenhaus conveyed to Baptist audiences for nearly three decades that Jews were a nation whose conversion, restoration, and revival were intertwined parts of God's plan for history.

Gartenhaus was not alone in this belief. Growing numbers of Baptists were being drawn to premillennial dispensationalism and encountering Palestine through prophetic passages in their Bibles (chapter 7). While few Baptists adhered to the system as of World War I, it soon spread, its popularity alternately aided and checked by its association with J. Frank Norris. A radical fundamentalist and born controversialist who had once shot and killed a man (he claimed self-defense), Norris repeatedly tried to split the SBC by organizing rival denominational bodies around adherence to premillennialism. While Baptists often disagreed on the interpretive system, premillennialists themselves argued over its implications for Palestine. Norris, of course, led the charge for Zionism, synthesizing a dispensationalist interpretation of the Bible with a heightened sense of civilizational clash between Arabs and Jews that was informed by his many trips to Palestine (chapter 8). Other premillennialists, however, including former Norris disciple John R. Rice, rejected the notion that the movement was part of God's plan.

Baptist political commentators were likewise divided (chapter 9). Virtually every Baptist periodical had an editorial section, though the extent to which they focused on Palestine varied from editor to editor—as did the lenses through which they viewed the region. Some could not help but view events in Palestine through a scriptural lens. Others argued forcefully against mixing prophecy and politics. Especially prominent in making this case was a trio of professors at the Southern Baptist Theological Seminary (SBTS): J. McKee Adams, H. Cornell Goerner, and W. O. Carver. Not only did these professors inveigh against premillennial dispensationalism as an interpretive system, they argued in political and humanitarian terms against Zionism as an unjust imposition on Palestinian Arabs. Still others argued for the movement on ostensibly secular terms, sometimes for surprising reasons. L. L. Gwaltney of the *Alabama Baptist*, for example, supported the establishment of Israel in 1948 not because he felt any real interest in the Zionist movement or concern for the Jewish people, but because he believed that it would strengthen the newly formed United Nations, which had voted to divide Palestine into a Jewish state and an Arab state. Even those Baptists who did encounter Palestine as a political question, in other words, could not agree on what the question was.

Of course, no Southern Baptist's encounter with Palestine was of greater consequence than President Harry Truman's (chapter 10). Truman did not believe that the establishment of Israel was a fulfillment of biblical promises to the Jewish people (although some scholars have argued that he did), but his Baptist faith did make him amenable to the arguments of the Zionists and their supporters as he struggled to define his Palestine policy. An independent thinker when it came to religion, the biblically literate Truman believed that moral action was the defining purpose of faith. The plight of Jewish refugees in the wake of the Holocaust spoke both to Truman's sense of moral duty and to his sense of global responsibility as president, eventually helping to convince him that supporting the creation of a Jewish state was a moral solution to the refugee crisis. Truman was an unconventional Southern Baptist, and his encounter with Palestine was utterly unique, but his exceptional case nonetheless speaks to two of *Between Dixie and Zion*'s overarching arguments—that *how* Southern Baptists encountered Palestine was crucial in shaping *what* they thought about the region, and that Orientalist assumptions nonetheless framed all varieties of encounter. For while Truman came to his decision in part out of concern for Jewish refugees, that decision was bolstered by the belief that the "whole region waits to be developed"—and that the Zionists would make the best use of it.[12]

When delegates to the 1948 SBC Annual Meeting debated whether to send a congratulatory telegram to Truman, they brought to the floor a number of shared assumptions about Palestine. However, they also brought with them more questions to consider than whether they agreed with Truman's policy. Each question came with its own context. Each context came with its own tangle of associations. Above all, my goal with *Between Dixie and Zion* is to recapture those contexts, to follow each thread of each tangle in hoping to understand the diversity of concerns, experiences, and impressions that shaped Southern Baptist attitudes toward the land that they all agreed was holy. It is to encounter Palestine as Southern Baptists did, to understand what lay for them between Dixie and Zion.

I

Before the Palestine Question

It was the British conquest of Palestine in World War I that raised the Palestine question. However, once Baptists began confronting the issues surrounding the question, they found themselves engaging and employing ways of thinking about the land, the peoples, and the politics of Palestine that had already been circulating among Southern Baptists—and American Protestants more broadly—for decades. Palestine, after all, was the Holy Land for Southern Baptists and occupied a special place in their *imago mundi*.[1] It was where their God had walked, their faith had begun, and their sacred stories had taken place. For every Baptist, the Scriptures provided the starting point for engaging the region and, for most, the end point, too. In some sense, then, Southern Baptists encountered Palestine anytime they cracked open their Bibles or sat for a Sunday sermon. The few Baptists who did engage contemporary Palestine sought to explain and understand the region with reference to its biblical past and, often, its biblical destiny. For them, Ottoman Palestine was a place between. The Holy Land had fallen from its biblical glory and was now mired in an Eastern, Islamic backwardness. But it would be reborn, whether through the civilizing influence of the Christian West or the arrival of Christ himself.

Backgrounds

The Ottoman Empire had ruled Palestine since the early sixteenth century. The Ottoman sultans, regarded as the caliphs of the Sunni Islamic world, had initially invested much in the region. Sultan Suleiman the Magnificent, who pushed the polyglot empire's boundaries to the gates of Vienna, funded the construction of the walls that still surround Jerusalem's Old City and refurbished the Dome of the Rock. Over time, however, the Ottomans' investment in the region declined as the empire itself weakened. The empire's military and administrative bureaucracy, formerly the envies of the world, withered. Still, while Baptists would find Ottoman Palestine a stagnant land whose rebirth lay in the future, the region was already undergoing something of a transformation by the time that Southern Baptists organized their own convention in 1845. Napoleon's 1798 invasion of the Levant had stirred the ascendant European powers to assert greater interests within Ottoman territory. In 1831, Egyptian khedive Muhammad Ali rebelled against the Ottomans and conquered Palestine, ruling it until the Ottomans turned to Europe to help pressure his withdrawal in 1840. In the ensuing decades, the Christian nations of Europe raced to assert their presence in the Holy Land, building churches and institutions and establishing a number of consulates in Jerusalem.[2]

After the restoration of Palestine to Ottoman control, the Ottomans themselves began taking greater interest in the region. Formerly, most of the Holy Land had come under the administration of the Vilayet of Damascus. In 1841, however, the sultan took steps to bring the territory surrounding Jerusalem and Jaffa under more direct administration, eventually forming the independent Sanjak of Jerusalem in 1874 (the rest of the Holy Land fell under the administration of the Sanjaks of Acre and Nablus).[3] As more and more pilgrims poured into Palestine, the Ottoman government took steps to build the region's infrastructure, investing in a series of carriage roads connecting Palestine's major cities. In 1892, a French company completed a rail line between the port of Jaffa and Jerusalem. This increasing investment in Palestine came alongside broader efforts to reform the Ottoman government (Tanzimat). European pressure had combined with the push of internal reformers to yield two important imperial edicts, the 1839 Khatti-Sherif of Gulhane and the 1856 Khatti Humayun, which established basic rights for Ottoman subjects and proclaimed the equality of religious minorities. While these edicts were unevenly implemented, they nonetheless signaled a change in the relationship of Ottoman subjects to the state.

The religion and ethnicity of those subjects varied.[4] The majority in Palestine were Arabic-speaking Sunni Muslims, most of whom lived in rural areas, while small communities of Shia and Druze also dotted the region. Arabic-speaking Christians composed the region's largest religious minority at about 10 percent of the population. Most were Orthodox, but a significant number were Melkite (Greek) or Latin Catholics. They were joined by Christians of smaller ethnic and ecclesiastical groupings—Armenians, Maronites, Ethiopians, Syriacs, and Copts, among others. Jews also composed a small but significant minority, with the community particularly concentrated in Jerusalem. At the beginning of the nineteenth century, most of Palestine's Jewish population was Sephardic (descended from Iberian Jews expelled from Spain and Portugal in the fifteenth century) or Mizrahic (from longstanding Jewish communities in the Middle East). However, increasing numbers of Ashkenazi (European) Jews began settling in the region throughout the century. Most of the earlier Ashkenazi settlers came as a matter of piety. From the 1880s onward, though, more and more Jewish settlers came through involvement with what would come to be termed Zionism.

Zionism is most easily understood as Jewish nationalism.[5] It developed as both an ideology—a way of thinking about how Jews fit into the world—and a movement. Though there was ideological variety within Zionism, at its most basic it proclaimed that Jews constituted a distinct nation and so required a state or other political framework wherein they could articulate their national destiny. Zionism thus also became a movement—a movement to invigorate Jewish nationhood and, in its mainstream form, create a Jewish state. While the movement drew on the millennia-long Jewish attachment to the land of Israel, it was more immediately the product of nineteenth-century Europe. Over the long nineteenth century, the spread of Enlightenment liberalism had resulted in new attempts to integrate Jews into wider European society, particularly in central and western Europe, a process often shorthanded as "emancipation." In fits and starts, Jews won increasing civil, political, and economic rights as subjects and citizens of the various European states, with many expecting and hoping that political and legal equality would prepare the way for broader social integration. The so-called Jewish question or Jewish problem—the question of the status of Jews as a minority—would soon be resolved.

Zionism emerged from somewhat contradictory responses to this process. More cultural forms of Zionism (such as that advocated by Ahad Ha'am) developed out of fears that emancipation might work too well, that Jews were losing their distinctiveness under the pressures of assimilation, secularization, and modernity, and that they needed to take positive steps to protect their national identity. More political forms of Zionism, on the other hand, developed from a sense that emancipation had failed, that anti-Semitism was indestructible, and that Jews would always be a distinct and despised minority. Both forms drew on the national movements then stirring throughout Europe, which sought to reorganize the continent's political structures around people groups bound by language, culture, and history. Though there were important predecessors, the first significant stirrings of Zionism came in western Russia after the assassination of Czar Alexander II in 1881 led to an outbreak of pogroms and the imposition of repressive legislation targeting Jewish communities. While Russia had taken hesitant steps toward emancipation, the wave of persecution that the assassination unleashed convinced many Russian Jewish thinkers that the promise of emancipation was illusory. In 1882, Leon Pinsker published

Auto-Emancipation, which argued that "Judeophobia" was incurable—the only answer to the Jewish question was for Jews to recognize their distinct nationhood and emancipate themselves by creating their own state. Though far more eastern European Jews would flee to the United States than to Palestine, a trickle of settlers inspired by these early Zionist stirrings did make their way into the Ottoman Empire, establishing small agricultural settlements. Over a decade after Pinsker, a far more westernized, assimilated Jew—Theodor Herzl—separately reached the same conclusion. In 1896, Herzl published *Der Judenstaat* (*The Jewish State*), which echoed Pinsker in arguing that anti-Semitism would never go away and that Jews could only solve the Jewish problem by creating their own state. Though he did not invent Zionism, Herzl brought it to the world stage through his diplomatic efforts, and the institutions that he created, including the Zionist Congresses and the World Zionist Organization, provided the eventual basis for the creation of a Jewish state.

At the same time that Jewish nationalism was gaining adherents, an Arab national identity was emerging within the Ottoman Empire.[6] Though initially a cultural identity claimed by small numbers of Christian and Muslim intellectual elites, this Arabism began to have political consequences in the first decades of the twentieth century.[7] Within the Ottoman Empire, Arabs pushed for greater political autonomy in Arabic-speaking regions through the appointment of Arabs to local governmental posts and the usage of Arabic as the language of administration. After the Young Turk Revolution in 1908 led to the opposite—greater Turkification of the Ottoman administration—Arab national consciousness intensified, with small numbers even calling for the creation of an independent Arab state. These ideas, of course, made their way to Palestine, where they intermingled and overlapped with existing layers of identity—communal, religious, familial, tribal, and even Ottoman.[8] Even as most Arabs in Palestine (like Ottoman Arabs more broadly) remained loyal to the empire into World War I, local elites increasingly identified as part of the Arab people and mobilized the growing Arab national consciousness against the emerging threat of Zionism.[9] As early as 1905, a Christian Arab nationalist named Najib Azouri could see a conflict emerging: "Two important phenomena, of the same nature yet opposed, which have still not drawn anyone's attention, are emerging at this moment in Asiatic Turkey. These are the awakening of the Arab nation and the latent effort of the Jews to reconstitute on a very large scale the ancient kingdom of Israel. Both these movements are destined to fight each other continually until one of them wins."[10] The end of Ottoman rule in World War I would begin that fight in earnest.

Few Southern Baptists writing about Ottoman Palestine apprehended these developments. Those who did only captured their dim outlines. For most, these developments remained unknown, unnoticed, or at least unmentioned, submerged in an Orientalist gaze that saw a largely immutable East. However, it must be remembered that Southern Baptists during these decades were not setting out to write comprehensive studies of the contemporary Holy Land, the Jewish question in Europe, or the first stirrings of Arab nationalism. Baptists had specific interests in writing about contemporary Ottoman Palestine. Their impressions of the region reflected those interests. In the nineteenth and early twentieth centuries, three stood out in particular—interest in the region as a potential mission field, interest in its place in biblical prophecy, and interest in the Holy Land as a pilgrimage destination.

The Holy Land as a Mission Field

From the very beginning of the Southern Baptist Convention itself, Southern Baptists had expressed lukewarm missionary interest in the Holy Land. For the most part, that interest was intertwined with interest in the evangelization of Jews. At the inaugural triennial convention of the Southern Baptists in 1846, the Committee on New Fields of Labor for Foreign Missions haltingly suggested "the propriety of making enquiries . . . as to the practicability of establishing, at some future, yet not far distant time, a mission in Palestine, with reference, at least in part, to the spiritual benefit of the Jews."[11] Committee chairman C. D. Mallary asserted that Jews remained God's beloved people and were assured by prophecy of future salvation. He noted that increasing numbers of Jews were returning to Palestine, although he refused to speculate whether this indicated a broader national restoration. Whether or not it did, Mallary claimed that the traditional Jewish interest in the land meant that Jews would always remain a significant portion of the region's population and would likely outlast the Muslim majority—for this practical reason, they presented a tantalizing missionary target.[12] He also argued that the successful evangelization of Jews in Palestine could provide a foothold for expanding work among populations in Asia Minor, Egypt, Arabia, and Persia. "Have Baptists, have *Southern Baptists* nothing to do, instrumentally, for their salvation?" he asked the gathered delegates.[13] The answer in 1846, it seems, was no. Nothing came of the committee's recommendation.

The testimony of Abraham Jaeger (a Jewish convert to Christianity) at the 1873 annual meeting in Mobile briefly revived Baptist missionary interest in Jews and Palestine.[14] A Kentucky delegate was so moved by Jaeger's story that he immediately offered a resolution calling on the Board of

Domestic Missions to hire the convert as a missionary to his people. The resolution died, though, by referral to committee. In its place, the convention adopted a resolution offered by Thomas Miller of Alabama that endorsed the idea of Jewish evangelism in general and pledged vague support for Jaeger's work.[15] Though Miller had not been inspired to support the Kentucky delegate's bolder resolution, he had nonetheless been inspired. Before the convention closed, he submitted a letter to the Foreign Mission Board (FMB) containing a gold dollar to be set aside for the eventual creation of the First Baptist Church of Jerusalem. The board soon opened an account dedicated to that purpose. The Alabamian would continue to donate small amounts in fits and starts over the next several years, even organizing a "Friends for church at Jerusalem" group at his Mobile congregation to encourage further donations.[16] His efforts did not get far. By the 1890 convention, the account held $5.20. That year, Miller wrote a second letter to the board, noting that he had received "no response—no intelligence of any effort to favor my wishes or carry out my views" over the years.[17] He enclosed another dollar, again in hopes of kicking off interest in an actual missionary program in Palestine. The board replied that the $6.20 was being held in trust.

Though Miller's modest donations would not be utilized for another thirty years, the secretary of the FMB, Henry Allen Tupper, was himself sympathetic to opening work in Palestine. It was Tupper who publicized Miller's efforts in an 1890 article in the *Foreign Mission Journal*, perhaps hoping that news of Miller's token gesture would spur other Baptists to add to the $6.20. Ten years prior, Tupper himself had included two open letters to rabbis in his history of Baptist missions, *The Foreign Missions of the Southern Baptist Convention*—an odd step given that Southern Baptists had no mission to Jews at the time.[18] His first letter, addressed to "Rabbi E. S. L. of A. G.," not only called on the rabbi to convert and be baptized, but noted, "A noble friend of Foreign Missions sends statedly a gold piece of money for the First Baptist Church of Jerusalem. We must have that church. Would that you, honored sir, might be prepared to be our missionary to establish that church in the City of David!"[19] Tupper republished these lines in his 1890 article on Miller. Like Miller, when Tupper thought of Jews—even American Jews—his mind leaped to Jerusalem.

In the following months, the *Foreign Mission Journal* published two brief articles by Texan A. J. Holt, who had recently traveled to Palestine and wanted to offer his assessment of its potential as a mission field. Holt lamented that American Christians had largely failed to establish a missionary presence in Jerusalem.[20] Such lack of effort, he thought, might lead some to wonder "whether Mohammedanism were stronger than the gospel of Christ." Holt argued that the ascent of Islam in the Levant had been the result of "degenerate and effeminate forms of Christianity" and that the "Mohammedan of to-day will never be won by either the Greek or Latin Catholic." Only a "pure Christianity" could overcome it.[21] While Holt recognized the difficulty of this task, he laid out several reasons that it could be accomplished—Muslims were ignorant of true Christianity, Islamic countries were in decline, Protestant Christianity had begun to penetrate the Middle East, and Muslims themselves held Jesus in high esteem. Adding a prophetic tinge to his assessment, Holt averred that the "'fullness of time' seems about here."[22] Jews were coming to the region in large numbers. The Middle East was modernizing. Amid this change, Holt had somehow intuited "a feeling on the part of the Mohammedans that they were only in temporary possession of the country"—by which he meant the entire Middle East. Islam was weakening. Christianity was strengthening. Baptists needed to take advantage by planting a mission in Jerusalem.[23]

Corresponding Secretary Tupper and *Foreign Mission Journal* editor T. P. Bell continued to raise the topic of the Jews and Palestine over the next several years. In 1891, Bell published part of the Blackstone Memorial, a petition circulated by premillennialist Methodist William Eugene Blackstone that called on President Benjamin Harrison to facilitate the restoration of Jews to Palestine.[24] Three times in 1892 the *Foreign Mission Journal*'s Scraps Picked Up, a recurring column that shared tidbits of news from around the globe, noted the increasing numbers of Jews coming to the region.[25] This increased attention did stir some Baptists to action. In 1891, J. H. Devotie of Cass Station, Georgia, donated fifty-four dollars to the FMB for the evangelization of Jews in Palestine.[26] Tellingly, this amount was far more money than Devotie set aside for missions in China, Mexico, and South America that actually existed. In summer 1892, Philip Hough of Mississippi added four dollars to Thomas Miller's Jerusalem church fund. Again, though, nothing came of these efforts. Despite Tupper's own interest, the increased attention, and the small number of donations, the FMB would not send a foreign missionary to Palestine until after World War I—when Thomas Miller's son, E. C., offered the board $15,000 to fulfill his father's dream.

Palestine in Prophecy

Other Baptists looked to Palestine in anticipation of the fulfillment of prophecy. While most held only dim expectations of the restoration of the Jews or the triumph of Christianity in the land of its birth, some elaborated complex hermeneutical and eschatological systems. Those who did tended to hold a premillennial eschatology, anticipating that Christ would return to earth prior to establishing the millennial kingdom alluded to in Revelation 20. This view was in contrast to the postmillennialist perspective (popular among Baptists in the nineteenth century), which argued that Christ would return after Christians built a heavenly kingdom on earth, and the amillennialist perspective (popular among Baptists in the twentieth century), which held that biblical references to a millennial kingdom were either metaphorical references to the church or uninterpretable. Though far from widespread, premillennial thought and the biblical hermeneutics underpinning it had been present among Baptists since the birth of the convention. The most influential Baptist premillennialist of the nineteenth century was James Robinson (J. R.) Graves, who edited the *Tennessee Baptist* (later *Baptist and Reflector*) from 1848 to 1889.[27] Indeed, Graves's position as editor of the *Tennessee Baptist* (which at times during Reconstruction was the official Baptist paper of Arkansas, Louisiana, and Mississippi, in addition to Tennessee) and father of the Landmark movement, which held that the Baptist church (with its congregational polity and full-immersion baptism) was the only true church, made him one of the most singularly influential Southern Baptists of the late nineteenth century.

Graves's premillennialism was underpinned by a system of biblical interpretation that drew a hard distinction between Israel (understood as the Jewish people) and the church. In other words, Graves held that God's biblical promises to Israel were still promises to the Jews—they had not been transferred to the church, as traditional Catholic and Protestant hermeneutics maintained. In this belief he followed a strand of Judeo-centric interpretation of prophecy that stretched back to early seventeenth-century England and echoed aspects of the contemporary teachings of John Nelson Darby, the father of premillennial dispensationalism, a system that would contribute to the development of the fundamentalist movement in the American industrial North.[28] Darby-style dispensationalists believed that God's covenantal relationship with the Jewish people would reach its culmination in a series of prophesied events that would attend Christ's second coming. Broadly, they anticipated that the Rapture of the church—the taking up of Christian believers from the Earth—would precede the unfolding of a seven-year tribulation, during which Jews would be gathered to Palestine and undergo great suffering before recognizing the returning Christ as their messiah and playing a leading role in his millennial kingdom on earth. While the spread of Darby's interpretive system and this corresponding eschatology in the United States is usually traced to a series of visits that the Englishman made to the States beginning in 1862, Graves had published a series of articles promoting a similar system before Darby ever set foot in

North America. In this 1854 series, Graves specifically tied his method of biblical interpretation to the expectation that the Jews would be restored to Palestine prior to Christ's return, mobilizing nine proofs.[29] His first proof, "the Covenant made with Abraham," was the centerpiece of his argument, reflecting the crucial distinction that God's covenant with Abraham had not wholly transferred to the church but remained with the Jewish people. This promise, he argued, was reiterated by the prophets, Christ, and the apostles—and confirmed by the "ancient Christians," "Reformers," and the "ripest biblical scholars."[30]

As Graves pushed his interpretations in the South, a transdenominational movement was beginning in the northern churches among evangelical Protestants who wanted to affirm the traditional authority and authenticity of the Bible in response to an increasing number of threats—chief among them Darwinism and higher criticism (interpretive methods that presumed that the Bible was a human product).[31] More than merely reacting to these threats, though, many in the nascent transdenominational movement found positive inspiration in Darby's dispensationalism, which figured prominently at the increasing number of Bible and prophetic conferences that were bringing the movement together. If Graves shared much with this movement—which eventually coalesced into the fundamentalist movement in the 1910s—he was not committed to it. The protofundamentalists defined themselves by doctrinal emphases that transcended denominational barriers. While Graves was interested in non-Baptists' approaches to biblical prophecy, in general he was utterly devoted to the Baptist distinctives. Alongside—and far outnumbering—his articles on premillennialism were his broadsides against "pedobaptists" and Methodists. As the guiding spirit of the Landmark movement, Graves was exceptional in his Baptist exceptionalism.[32]

As the century turned, premillennialism (especially its dispensationalist variety) became increasingly intertwined with the emerging fundamentalist movement. After the death of Graves in 1893, Atlantan Len Broughton emerged as the leading premillennialist in the SBC.[33] To a much greater extent than Graves, Broughton was involved with northern protofundamentalists, having attended Dwight Moody's Northfield Bible Conferences in the 1890s. Broughton's own Bible conferences, modeled after Moody's, brought fundamentalists like A. C. Dixon (a Southern Baptist who had gone on to pastor the Moody Church in Chicago and edit *The Fundamentals*, a collection of essays that articulated the intellectual bases of the emerging movement), William Moody, James Gray, R. A. Torrey, and Cyrus Scofield to the pastor's Tabernacle Baptist Church in Atlanta.[34] As in the North, these conferences were transdenominational affairs that helped spread premillennialism. In 1914 the *Christian Workers Magazine* published an editorial titled "Eminent Exponents of Premillennialism" that listed notable premillennialists alive and dead. Of the 132 living premillennialists on the list, there were eight Southern Baptist pastors.[35] M. E. Dodd, a Southern Baptist preacher in Shreveport, Louisiana, included an appendix that listed nine SBC premillennialists in his 1917 tract *Jesus Is Coming to Earth Again*.[36] That same year, J. B. Gambrell, who was sympathetic to premillennialism, was elected president of the convention. It would only spread further—and grow more controversial—among Southern Baptists from there.

Palestine through Pilgrimage

The primary way in which Southern Baptists encountered contemporary Ottoman Palestine was through travel and travel literature. Middle-class travel to the Holy Land exploded in the late nineteenth century, made possible by the increasing ease and affordability of steam travel, the expansion of a Western diplomatic and missionary presence in the region, the increasing openness of Ottoman rulers to the West, and the consequent development of a travel infrastructure linking Europe and America to the eastern Mediterranean.[37] Put simply, it was easier, safer, and cheaper to travel to the Holy Land than it had ever been. By 1867, Missourian Samuel Clemens—better known as Mark Twain—could make his way through an all-inclusive recreational trip to the cultural capitals of Europe and the Levant, something that would have been impossible only a few years before.[38]

Many Southern Baptist leaders followed in Clemens's wake, both traveling and writing about their experiences in the Holy Land. Travel to the region was especially attractive to the educated and upwardly mobile Baptist ministers of the South's cities, offering as it did a pious manner to flaunt growing status and learning.[39] Among the earliest and most notable Baptist travelers was Rev. John Broadus of South Carolina, one of the founding faculty members of the Southern Baptist Theological Seminary, who traveled eastward in 1871. While in Jerusalem, Broadus purchased a mallet hewn from a local olive tree, which he later presented to SBC president James Boyce to use as a gavel. The Broadus gavel, as it came to be called, has been used by every SBC president since.[40] Beyond souvenirs, Broadus also brought back his impressions of Ottoman Palestine. Shortly after returning he published a series of articles in the *Christian Herald*, a Baptist periodical out of Richmond, Virginia. Broadus's biographer A. T. Robertson also included extended sections from his trip diary in *Life and Letters of John Albert Broadus*, which the American Baptist Publication Society published in 1901.[41] Others followed with book-length travelogues.[42]

Among them was Rev. Henry Marvin Wharton of Baltimore, whose account of his 1891 trip to the Levant was published as *A Picnic in Palestine*.[43] Rev. Tupper, corresponding secretary of the FMB, also traveled to the region after leaving the board. The energetic Tupper published accounts of his 1895 trip in several forums, including the newspaper *Baptist and Reflector* (1896), the travelogue *Around the World with Eyes Wide Open* (1898), and the partially fictionalized narrative of a family journey to the Holy Land, *Uncle Allen's Party in Palestine* (1898).[44] Thirteen years later, W. A. Hamlett published *Travels of a Father and Son*, an account of a 1910 journey taken with his ten-year-old son that eventually led to his nigh-disastrous appointment as superintendent of the FMB's Near East Mission.[45] Still more individuals published brief episodic travelogues in Baptist periodicals. State Baptist papers like the *Biblical Recorder* of North Carolina, *Baptist and Reflector* of Tennessee, the *Messenger* of Oklahoma, and the *Baptist Standard* of Texas—among many other state publications—intermittently featured the travel writings of local notables.

Most voyages to the Levant followed itineraries established by travel agencies. The two leading agencies during the Ottoman era were the British outfits Thomas Cook & Son and Henry Gaze & Sons.[46] The majority of Baptist travelers visited Palestine as part of a broader European or Mediterranean tour. Tour parties would depart by steamer from New York City and visit the cultural capitals of Europe—London, Paris, Berlin, Rome, and so forth—before continuing on to Egypt, Palestine, and Anatolia. Travelers were expected to draw contrasts between Christian Europe and the Islamic world. As Edgar Folk, editor of the *Baptist and Reflector*, noted while promoting an upcoming trip, "It is quite attractive to see some of the continent before reaching the Bible lands; the contrast in the customs, manners of living, etc., are very valuable."[47]

Besides their own experiences, Baptist travelers drew on a number of sources in shaping their impressions of the Holy Land. Many travelers had read earlier travel narratives from the region.[48] Most were at least familiar with Twain's *The Innocents Abroad* (1869); both Henry Wharton and W. A. Hamlett clearly tried at times to ape the Methodist skeptic. Two other popular works were Edward Robinson and Eli Smith's *Biblical Researches in Palestine* (1841) and *Sinai and Palestine in Connection with Their History* (1856) by Arthur Stanley, the dean of Westminster.[49] Travelers' impressions were shaped not just by these literary influences but also by local contacts. Perhaps most influential was the American dragoman Rolla Floyd, who was employed by the Cook and Gaze agencies.[50] Even when Floyd did not individually lead tours, he hired local dragomans and developed the agencies' itineraries. In the late nineteenth century, some travelers made contact with Yohanah El Karey, a local who ran a mission at Nablus that was affiliated with English Baptists. Tupper borrowed stories about the bedouin from both Floyd and El Karey for his two 1898 publications, *Around the World with Eyes Wide Open* and *Uncle Allen's Party in Palestine*. Though El Karey's mission disappeared, by 1911 a new mission had been established at Nazareth by Shukri Mosa (then employed by Illinois Baptists, but later brought under the FMB). At least one Baptist tour party met and attended services with Mosa prior to World War I.[51] Some Baptists, too, made connections with Anglican clergy through attending Protestant services at Christ Church in Jerusalem.

Without fail, Baptist travelers emphasized that Palestine was the Holy Land—that it was essentially different from other stops on their journeys. Nearly every writer included a breathless aside describing their feelings upon arriving at either the port of Jaffa or Jerusalem itself. Broadus thanked God "that the hopeless dream of many a year has become a reality. I am at Jerusalem."[52] Wharton expressed the difficulty in capturing his feelings in words: "It is utterly impossible to describe the feelings of the pilgrim Christian when he first sets foot upon the Holy Land; the land which is the cradle of Christianity; the land of which we read in God's word, where those wonderful men and women lived whose record is given us in the Book which is a lamp to our feet and a light to our path."[53] In Wharton's words can be found the themes that shaped Protestant approaches to the Holy Land: the land was the birthplace of his faith and the setting of the Bible. While these points are perhaps obvious, they need to be kept in mind when looking into other aspects of the texts. Baptist travel writers—especially in the Ottoman era—were first and foremost concerned with Palestine as the Holy Land. The bulk of their accounts concerned the relation of their experiences to the Bible. Baptist readers, for their part, primarily sought to vicariously join the pilgrimages or illumine their own faith.

Largely middle-class, educated, and urban, the Southern Baptists who were able to travel to Palestine and write about it were keenly focused on matters of material and social progress, which in Palestine they interpreted according to the prevailing Orientalist assumptions of their day. Baptist writers generally understood Ottoman Palestine as economically, socially, and intellectually backward, and in need of the civilizing influence of the Christian West. Especially relevant in terms of later discourse surrounding the Arab-Zionist conflict was the writers' understanding of Palestinian agriculture. Almost every writer who took up the topic noted that the coastal plain and the Jezreel Valley (or Plain of Esdraelon) were quite fertile.[54] Several remarked on the successful crops.[55] Yet most Baptist writers viewed local agriculture as quaint.[56] Wharton described "an old mill . . . grinding a little yellow corn; a rude and peculiar paddle-wheel turned the upper stone and the meal fell out in an odd kind of way which made it seem more like children at play than men at work."[57] Of frequent comment was the single-handed plow used by fellahin (Arab peasants).[58] Tupper described seeing "the single-handed plow, used from time immemorial, drawn through the rich soil by an ox and an ass, and driven by the bearded Syrian."[59] His *Around the World with Eyes Wide Open* included two separate pictures of Palestinian farmers behind the plow.[60] Hamlett saw the plow as more backward than quaint, signaling that fellahin were deliberately opposed to modernity.[61] Walter Andrew Whittle joked that a "camel . . . a forked stick, and a half-naked Arab, make a first class plow team for Palestine."[62]

Baptist travelers likewise depicted Palestinian cities and villages as premodern, invariably describing them as crowded and filthy.[63] Wharton noted of Jaffa, "It is a fair sample of all Eastern towns; the streets are narrow and exceedingly filthy, the houses small, most of them one story high with flat roofs."[64] He even expressed surprise that Shunem (now Sulam), a small village in the Galilee, had been mentioned in the Scriptures, given that it was so small and dirty.[65] Though Wharton was genuinely impressed with the many soap factories of Nablus, he felt obliged to comment, "If they had a soap factory every hundred yards from one end of Palestine to the other, I should think they would find ready use for the whole business in washing these miserable, dirty wretches that throng every highway, pack the streets and crowd the houses."[66] Hamlett found Jerusalem magnetic for its religious associations, though he could not help but mention the "many cases of pious poverty, of unmistakable suffering" and "abhorrent filth."[67] Indeed, the way that he reconciled the Jerusalem of his expectations with the Jerusalem that he found was, basically, to delude himself into seeing the ancient city. "Then the Turk no longer troubles," he wrote, "nor the awful conditions chafe, for one is not living in the to-day."[68] Decades earlier, Broadus had likewise recorded the disappointment that could come with seeing the "wretched hovels in which most of the people live" and "the narrow, filthy, and disgusting streets which are universal." He, like Hamlett, urged that travelers "by effort of imagination sweep away these disagreeable actualities and reproduce what once was here."[69]

Broadly, Baptist travel writers felt that Palestine was simply behind. They identified so-called Mohammedanism as the main culprit, which worked its injurious influence both through the government of the "cruel Turk" and through the local inhabitants themselves.[70] Though Wharton did at times have positive things to say about Islam, he criticized the Ottoman government as "Mohammedanism at its worst."[71] Hamlett found Turkish soldiers to be both incompetent and dangerous.[72] Elsewhere, Baptist writers decried the religion's effect on the native populations. "Mahommedanism does nothing for the education and raising up of the poor and ignorant," wrote Wharton. "The Moslem peasant lives more in the fear of his superiors than he does in the sense of accountability. He cannot read or write; [he] goes through his prayers or counts his beads, but it all means nothing to him."[73] Tupper lamented that the majority of the population was "for the most part extremely illiterate, fanatical, and indolent."[74] Hamlett viewed Muslim men as particularly indolent, claiming that they spent all their time drinking coffee while the women worked.[75] Rev. Millard Jenkens perhaps best summed up Baptist attitudes toward the region in a 1903 article: "The cities are filthy, the land barren, the people largely a low class of Arabs and Bedouins, are an indifferent good-for-nothing lot. The foot of the Turkish tyrant has mashed what little life remained out of the land. The curse of God is upon the land, and the only hope is the return of the blessed Christ."[76]

When Jenkens spoke of the return of Christ, he had a Protestant Christ in mind. Baptists did not view Levantine Christians as their coreligionists. Or, at the very least, Baptists viewed them as followers of a degraded or "effeminate" form of Christianity (to borrow A. J. Holt's phrasing). Paired with long-standing Protestant critiques of the dominant Catholicism and Orthodoxy of Palestine, Baptists tended to view the Eastern churches as tainted by Islam. "The Greek Church has existed for a long time in the Turkish empire side by side with Mohammedanism," noted Wharton, "and has sunk so low in piety and zeal that there is no religious principle set forth by its light."[77] Hamlett likewise viewed local Christianity as similar to Islam "in spirit, though differing in creed."[78] Joseph Marstain Fort described Jerusalem's Christians as being "as far from . . . Christ-like . . . as the Mohammedan or the heathen; yea, farther."[79] Many focused their criticisms on the Church of the Holy Sepulchre (jointly maintained by the Greek Orthodox Church, the Roman Catholic Church, and other Eastern churches). Broadus was especially disgusted by the Orthodox Pascha events there, which included the annual Miracle of the Holy Fire: "No devoutness, no seriousness—frolic for the crowd, ridiculous to the persons officiating. It is ceremony run in the ground, utterly defeating its own object. I have never in my life beheld a spectacle so humiliating. This is Oriental Christianity."[80] Tupper's semifictional family visited the church but "turned away sick at heart to think that such folly and superstition should be associated with the most sacred events of the world's history"—even as they admired the earnestness and seriousness of Russian Orthodox pilgrims.[81] Baptist writers frequently suggested that Catholic and Orthodox priests cynically manipulated the piety of their flocks. Wharton claimed of the Catholic Church,

"It is a pity that one of the largest and strongest ecclesiastical organizations in the world should live and fatten upon the credulity of its members by a system of humbuggery and rascality."[82] Hamlett viciously derided Eastern Christianity as "hatched in hell," declaring that "none but a child of hell would deal it out to ignorant, hungry souls."[83]

Baptists viewed local Jews as sharing the deficiencies of local Christians and Muslims in the Ottoman era. Just as descriptions of native Christianity revolved around the Church of the Holy Sepulchre, descriptions of local Jews and Judaism tended to center on the Western Wall (generally referred to at this time as "the Jews' wailing place"). "It is a pitiful sight to look upon these old Jews," wrote Wharton, "with their wives and daughters, clad in the worst clothing, their long hair streaming down their backs, as they place their heads against the stones and mourn and weep until the tears run down their cheeks."[84] Tupper described the site as the most pathetic in Jerusalem.[85] According to Hamlett, the Jews who gathered at the wall plainly showed their long persecution.[86] "I have seen mothers cling to their dead babies. . . . I have stood by while bereaved hearts rained their tears on the glass top of a coffin, and in all cases I have been touched." He added, "But I declare these cases were no more sad than the sight of those poor, outcast Jews, tenderly patting the walls, kissing the stones, crying with deep and genuine sorrow, refusing to be comforted, until Jehovah comes with restoring power."[87] If Baptists frequently saw all of Palestine as stagnated, they saw the Jews as particularly inert, even backward. Perhaps the greatest illustration of this view was a bizarre 1906 report by Sarah Hale, a missionary on vacation from her post in Mexico, that offered a drastic and perniciously inventive misunderstanding of what was likely the death and burial of Sephardi Chief Rabbi Yaakov Shaul Elyashar in Jerusalem. Beyond noting the presence of "few Saduccees" and "many Pharisees," Hale claimed that Jerusalem's Jews had dragged the dead body of their "high priest" across rocks "until the skull was crushed and part of the brains came out." She reported that the priest himself had apparently requested this treatment on account of his sins. Hale took this event as evidence that the Jews' "opposition to Jesus of Nazareth, as their Messiah, seems to be as great as ever."[88]

Prior to World War I, few Baptist travelers mentioned the Zionist movement. Tupper noted in 1896 that Jews were colonizing the region in greater numbers, however he made no effort to analyze the movement.[89] Later, in *Around the World*, Tupper did mention that the "Rothschilds and other wealthy Hebrews" had established an agricultural school near Jaffa that was struggling because "these sons of Abraham are so intuitively biased toward commercial life that when a few pounds have been accumulated at the school, they bid good-bye to the hoe and plow and go forth as traders."[90] Even those travelers who believed that Jews were prophesied to return to the land did not draw connections between prophecy and the Zionist movement itself. Unlike later writers, they made no clear distinctions between Zionist Jews and Jews of the Old Yishuv (the preexisting, non-Zionist Jewish community in Palestine). Hale lapsed into a dispensationalist synopsis of the anticipated eschaton after describing the practices of religious Jews at the Western Wall.[91] Though she never mentioned the Zionist movement itself, she foresaw the impending conflict between Jews and Arabs, even recalling a conversation with an Arab Orthodox Christian in which she declared to him, "It is sad, I know, to give up your country. But the Lord only lent it to you, you know, until his time should come to restore it to his people."[92] God had prepared a place for the Arabs in America, she argued.

With the exception of Hale, Baptist travel writers did not anticipate the possible displacement of Arabs as key to the region's future or as part of God's plan. To Baptists, the region was essentially stagnant. Wharton wrote of a Galilean hillside that "there is nothing to remind us of the civilization and progress of our own busy land."[93] There were, though, signs of change. A single telegraph line served as a "herald of better days" and would "prepare the way for the thundering steam-engine."[94] To Wharton and others, it was clear that such "better days" would only come through Western, Christian influence. Where modern improvements—agricultural or otherwise—were to be found, they were positively identified as European. Tupper's fictionalized account of arriving in Jaffa depicted his nieces' and nephews' excitement as they pass through orange, lemon, and pomegranate orchards maintained by German Templers. "What is done with all this fruit," the children ask, "and what nationality are the people in the gardens?" "They are Germans," Uncle Allen replies, "I am told that eighty thousand pounds is realized annually from these fruit farms, which were formerly a barren plain."[95]

The land, even if somewhat successfully farmed already, held immense potential that could be unleashed by the innovation of the Christian West. The same was true of the cities and the people. After mentioning that Nazareth was "well built" and noting that "the houses have a better appearance than the towns and villages generally," Wharton went on to explain why that was: English Christians "have services here; a large orphanage, and an excellent school; so that the people look better, live better, and are better than perhaps in any other town in Palestine."[96] Only a Protestant Christian modernity could redeem the people and the land. Wharton, after discussing ongoing missionary efforts in Palestine, offered this assessment: "I cannot tell what progress has been made by these different missionary efforts in the Holy Land. To the inquiring observer the whole people seem steeped in sin and wretchedness, and not only the people as individuals, but the government; the very land itself will have to be born again before ever the wilderness shall blossom as a rose, the mountains and the hills break forth into singing, and the people become the happy people whose God is the Lord."[97] Wharton wove in the language of Isaiah 35 in hoping for a Protestant Christian rebirth of the people, government, and land. References to this passage would become commonplace in the years after World War I. As will be seen, though, the meaning of the allusion would change. Whereas Wharton offered it in defining Christian hope for the future, post–World War I Baptist writers would increasingly use it to describe the achievements of those "New Jews"—the Zionists.[98]

2
Travelers

Southern Baptist travelers would find a very different Palestine after World War I. The four-hundred-year reign of the Ottomans had ended. The British were now in power.[1] Their Foreign Office had thrown its support behind the Zionist movement with the 1917 Balfour Declaration, which committed the British government to facilitating the creation of a Jewish national home in Palestine—a commitment confirmed at the 1920 San Remo Conference and written into international law with a League of Nations mandate in 1923.[2] Besides hoping to secure a strategic position in the Middle East, Britain sought to develop Palestine economically as a colonial holding, with Zionists serving as its agents.[3] Under British rule, the process of economic development haltingly begun under the Ottomans intensified rapidly, aided by Zionist investment.

With British protection, the Zionists developed a number of institutions that transformed Palestine and prepared the way for a future Jewish state—even as that state had not been guaranteed by the deliberately ambiguous Balfour Declaration.[4] The most important institution was the Palestine Zionist Executive, restructured into the Jewish Agency in 1929, which functioned as a sort of protogovernment for the Yishuv (the Jewish community in Palestine). Led initially by Chaim Weizmann, the agency helped coordinate development and Jewish immigration. Between 1918 and 1946, the Jewish population of Palestine would grow from sixty thousand to nearly 550 thousand, going from less than one-tenth of the population to nearly one-third of it.[5] Most of these immigrants settled in cities, including the newly created Tel Aviv, but the more ideologically motivated Zionist pioneers gravitated toward socialistic agricultural communities established on collective land purchased by the Jewish National Fund. These halutzim sought to "build and be built in the land" as "New Jews." Over the course of the Mandate era, Labor Zionists who mixed their Jewish nationalism with a socialistic commitment to building a workers' society in Palestine would become the dominant political force within the Yishuv, led by David Ben-Gurion.

Arabs, too, stirred politically. World War I had stoked Arab national consciousness and brought Arab nationalism to the world stage through a revolt led by the family of Sherif Hussein of Mecca. The British had encouraged that revolt, promising Hussein an Arab kingdom in Arabia and Greater Syria in exchange for his support against the Ottomans.[6] Arabs' hopes for a united Arab kingdom were thwarted, however, as the Great Powers carved the former Ottoman territories into mandates administered by the French (Lebanon and Syria) and the British (Palestine, Iraq, and after 1922, Transjordan). Sherif Hussein's son Faisal had briefly rebelled against the powers' determination, proclaiming an Arab Kingdom of Syria from Damascus in 1920 before being deposed by the French and installed by the British as the king of Iraq. Meanwhile, Muslim and Christian Palestinian Arabs grew increasingly sure-footed in their identity as both Arabs and Palestinians.[7] Broadly united against Zionism, the Arabs of Palestine were torn between the pan-Arab impulse and the push for Palestinian self-determination, with the latter winning out after the failure of Faisal's kingdom. Though rival factions struggled for control of the Palestinian national movement, its leadership was primarily concentrated in two bodies: the Palestine Arab Executive (PAE), led by Musa Kazim al-Husseini until his death and the PAE's dissolution in 1934, and the Supreme Muslim Council, led by the grand mufti of Jerusalem, Hajj Amin al-Husseini.[8] A fierce opponent of Zionism, the mufti would walk a fine line until 1936 between cooperating with the British to achieve Arab goals and avoiding any accommodation with British support for Zionism.

As many Baptist travelers recognized, there was a Palestine question that had not been apparent or urgent before the war. At its most basic, that question was whether the Zionists or Arabs would eventually control the country. Until World War II, Zionist leaders sought to develop the Yishuv through immigration and colonization under the protection of the British, in anticipation of eventually building a Jewish majority and a Jewish state. The Arabs sought the repeal of the Balfour Declaration, the cessation of Jewish immigration and Zionist land purchases, and a transition to majoritarian self-government. At several points during British rule, these colliding interests exploded in violent conflict.[9] In 1920, Arab Muslims rioted against Jerusalem's Jewish population during the pilgrim festival of Nebi Musa. The following year, Arab mobs attacked Jewish sections of Jaffa. Though most of the 1920s would be calmer, the end of the decade saw unprecedented violence break out over controversies surrounding Jewish access to the Western Wall. The situation only grew more tense from there. Between 1936 and 1939, Palestine's Arabs revolted against British rule. After World War II, the Zionists initiated their own rebellion against the mandatory power. Ultimately, the British would recognize the insolubility of the Palestine question that they had helped create, referring its resolution to the United Nations in 1947. The mandate itself would end amid civil war between Arabs and Jews.

Altogether, the seeming Ottoman stasis depicted by pre-war Baptist travelers was obliterated under British rule: the Holy Land was now a land of conflict and dramatic change. Baptist travelers recognized both, interpreting each according to the same Orientalist framework of their Ottoman-era predecessors. Believing Western Protestant rule to be inherently salutary, none questioned British rule in Palestine, even as several came to retroactively question the wisdom or legitimacy of Britain's divergent wartime promises. Unlike earlier travelers, though, post-war Baptist travelers came to draw distinctions between Jews and Arabs, viewing the Zionists as the agents of Western civilization and progress—if also, often, of conflict—in the Holy Land. In part, these shifting impressions were a reaction to very real changes on the ground. The Zionists were indeed draining swamps, irrigating deserts, and building modern cities. The shifting understandings were also, though, a product of the transitory nature of travel, which privileged visual impressions that easily accorded with existing Orientalist cultural assumptions. Though Jewish and Arab communities alike were undergoing dramatic transformations, Zionist development *looked* familiarly Western and thus familiarly modern to Baptist travelers quickly passing through. And while these Orientalist impressions did not on their own translate to political support for Zionism, they did leave many Baptists convinced that the Zionists were establishing—as one traveler put it—"a little patch of our Western civilization" in the Holy Land.[10]

Changes in Travel and Travel Writing

Though pilgrimage remained the main impetus for travel to the Holy Land, the Mandate era saw Baptists traveling to Palestine for increasingly diverse reasons, particularly missions. In 1919, the Foreign Mission Board (FMB) of the SBC brought the Nazareth mission of Palestine native Shukri Mosa under its purview (examined in the next chapter). That same year, J. F. Love (corresponding secretary of the FMB), Z. T. Cody (editor of South Carolina's *Baptist Courier*), and Everett Gill (FMB missionary in Rome), set out to "make a general survey of the economic, social and religious conditions in Europe with a view to recommending to the Baptists of the South where and how they can aid most effectively in the reconstruction of that continent."[11] On their itinerary, too, was the new mission station in Palestine. Similar official delegations would follow from that point forward, as the Near East Mission was formalized in 1921 and expanded up until World War II.[12] Especially important was the mission survey undertaken by J. McKee Adams in 1933, which resulted in *The Heart of the Levant*, effectively a full-length treatment of the Palestine question that was published as part of the FMB's graded mission study series in 1937.[13]

The growth of the Baptist World Alliance (BWA) after World War I likewise boosted the number of Baptist journeys to Palestine. Many delegates to the 1923 Stockholm and 1934 Berlin BWA meetings tacked on visits to the European and Middle Eastern mission fields, in trips that paired pilgrimage and denominational business.[14] Extended study visits also became more common under the British. Before performing his mission survey in the 1930s, Adams had spent months in the region studying archaeology for his work *Biblical Backgrounds*.[15] Wake Forest graduate Percy Upchurch wrote in the *Biblical Recorder* about his time with the American Schools of Oriental Research.[16] Before becoming a missionary, Oklahoman Robert L. Lindsey spent a year studying at the Hebrew University. In the end, though, most reasons for traveling to Palestine blurred together. A pilgrimage could easily lead to engaging with Baptist missionaries. A missionary survey could not avoid becoming a pilgrimage.

Baptist travelogues also took on new forms. Though pilgrimage narratives predominated, more and more travel writings involved self-conscious reporting or editorializing. Travel became the occasion for writing about the region rather than the subject matter itself. Many of these reports dealt with the status of the mission stations. Others engaged with political questions. Z. T. Cody of Richmond, who had traveled to the Levant as part of the postwar missionary survey, published an article evaluating Zionism in 1920. Adams tackled both mission and politics in his articles. Upon his return from a 1937 tour of the region, W. T. Halstead penned a brief history of the conflict for readers of the *Florida Baptist Witness*, as did James Day one decade later.[17] Overall, Baptist travelers in the Mandate era were much more concerned with contemporary Palestine than their forebears had been. Part of this concern, of course, related to the war and its aftermath. World War I had thrust Palestine onto the world stage. Its status was a matter of global discussion, with the country counting in the present. The presence of an actual Baptist community in Palestine, however small, also made for a different travel experience.[18] In a sense, Southern Baptists now had a home. They could worship with the Nazareth congregation and share meals with the missionaries. Though some still used their imaginations to slip back to the first century, for most Baptist visitors the presence of Baptist work in the region meant a necessary encounter with the contemporary.[19] Baptists also expressed new thoughts about travel itself. Coleman Craig, who in the late 1940s would become an active member of the pro-Zionist American Christian Palestine Committee (ACPC), pondered what bound and divided humanity as he walked through the crowds of Jerusalem's Old City: "I felt the isolation that everyone feels where the people are so different, and one finds himself asking the question, Are we really after all kin? Do they have the same loves, the same hatreds, the same emotions that we do?"[20] While reflecting on his journey to Palestine aboard an Austrian steamer, J. M. Dawson noted that "one of the effects of travel is a broader humanism."[21] Though Craig, Dawson, and many other Baptist travelers in the Mandate era held and broadcast the same preconceptions as their predecessors, such statements reflected an increasing sense that challenging preconceptions was an important aim of travel. With such aims, the present necessarily became more important.

With a renewed appreciation for the contemporary among Baptist travelers, the role of local interpreters and informants was as important as ever.[22] In the Mandate era, the Baptist missionaries eclipsed the travel agency dragomans in this regard. Nearly every traveler who reported their experiences in North Carolina's *Biblical Recorder* explicitly mentioned making contact with the missionaries or locals involved with the mission churches.[23] Of course, the extent of the contact between travelers and missionaries could vary. Missionary Shukri Mosa actually complained in a 1924 letter to the *Baptist Standard* that "very few [Baptists] stopped over-night at Nazareth" after the BWA meeting in Stockholm, adding that "tourists nowadays travel by motor cars and they pass the country in such a rush that they hardly have time to see anything."[24] Some, however, took a deep interest in local life. J. J. Wicker, a Baptist minister and the director of a Richmond travel agency, recorded several instances of Baptists (and non-Baptists) sponsoring the education of local children—including Mosa's daughter, Hilda.[25] Many improvements to the Nazareth and Jerusalem missions were funded by donations from travelers.[26]

The Travelers' Impressions

As Baptist travelers engaged a more contemporary Palestine, they tended to focus their writings on three topics: the modernization of the region, the burgeoning conflict between the Arabs and the Zionists, and the growing Baptist mission. They marveled that a new modernity had come to the Holy Land. In contrast to John Broadus, who in 1871 could complain that the carriage roads "were merely bridle paths," many postwar travelers were struck by the quality of the paved roads.[27] R. T. Bryan was so enthusiastic about the roads that he mentioned them three separate times in a three-page travelogue.[28] Several were jarred by the sight of automobiles in the land of the Bible.[29] Writing of Jerusalem outside the Ottoman walls, Walter Alexander noted, "the modern city is modern indeed, and, although built entirely of stone and native rock, possesses all the comforts and conveniences [that the traveler] is accustomed to at home."[30] Palestine had a new economic and technological vitality. A power plant was being built on the Yarmouk River.[31] The minerals of the Dead Sea were being excavated and processed.[32] Perhaps most impressive to Baptist travelers, a modern port and harbor were being built at Haifa.[33] The Holy Land was born anew; the desert blossoming as the rose.

Many credited the salutary reign of the British in bringing about these improvements. More striking, though, was the number of Baptist travelers who attributed the modernization of the region to the Zionists, often specifically juxtaposing Zionist modernity with Arab or Muslim backwardness (many travelers used the terms "Arab" and "Muslim" interchangeably). A recurring symbol of this divide was the difference between the majority-Arab Jaffa and Jewish Tel Aviv. E. Norfleet Gardner's 1935 description of the two is worth quoting in full: "The old city [Jaffa] is marked by dirty, narrow streets of bad smells. It has a population of 60,000. Adjoining it, however, is Tel-Aviv, the Zionist city, with 72,000 inhabitants, built since the war. You may drive from one into the other, but are able to observe almost immediately the difference. Clean, paved streets, nice homes, good places of business, a long beach lined with bathers, whom we joined, and pleasant citizens made our brief visit here another happy step along the way."[34] R. T. Bryan, who was sympathetic to the Arab political cause, likewise remarked that Tel Aviv offered "a striking contrast to the Moslem cities." This disparity was also clear in the realm of agriculture, where Bryan found "a very striking contrast between the Jewish farmer's crops and up-to-date methods and implements, and those ancient ones of the Moslems." The implications of these differences seemed clear: the Arabs "must certainly wake up, change and progress, otherwise their fears of being displaced by the Jews will be realized."[35]

Even the most outspoken critics of Zionism were impressed by Zionist modernity. After making the case for Arab opposition to the movement in a 1920 article, Z. T. Cody suggested that there were nonetheless "many very fine things that can be said of Zionism as it is seen in actual operation here": "These Jews are bringing with them a far higher civilization than they find in Palestine and a better religion. They buy the large tracts of land they occupy, and turn them from a waste into a garden. Wherever you find a Jewish colony, and you find many here and there, you find a little patch of our Western civilization set up here in the dead and dirty East."[36] Cody's phrasing makes explicit what other Baptists implied. The Zionists were part of a civilization superior to that of the Arabs, the same Western civilization ("*our* Western civilization," as Cody put it) as the Baptists themselves. This was a significant change from prewar writers. For travelers in the Ottoman era, civilization and Protestant Christianity had gone hand in hand—Jews in Ottoman Palestine had lacked both. Writers such as Cody, though, showed that for Mandate-era travelers, the Zionists were demonstrating that a Jewish modernity could transform Palestine for the better and vivify "the dead and dirty East."

While their images of Jews changed, most Baptist travelers continued to view Arabs as premodern. As did their Ottoman-era precursors, they depicted Arab men as especially lazy and exploitative of female labor.[37] Writing of the fellahin, John Bunn noted, "The men ride donkeys, and with one stick urge the donkeys along and with another stick urge the women along."[38] Echoing prewar travelogues, Bunn lamented that the women worked all day while the men drank coffee and told tall tales. He attributed this exploitative arrangement to Islam, noting, "Womanhood has no freedom where Jesus is not served."[39] When Bunn did observe Arab men working in building the Naharayim power station, he found it "interesting and pathetic": "Some were digging with picks," he noted, "some were using shovels, filling the little baskets of those who came to bear the dirt away. What a process of work; but it was very well for all the people to have something to do."[40] Even as Arabs helped build a modern hydroelectric power plant, their methods were, to Bunn's eyes, quaint.

Besides being impressed by the country's new modernity, Baptist travelers found Palestine increasingly defined by the Palestine question in its various forms. Most were aware of the burgeoning conflict between Arabs and Zionists, as well as the untenable position of the British. For many, the question was strictly a matter of Zionist success or failure. A 1924 report from J. M. Dawson in the *Baptist Standard* is illustrative: "The recognition of Zionism by the British government under its mandate over Palestine, the huge national fund being raised for Zion in all lands, the improved quality of the colonists, and the intense anti-Semitic spirit in America since the war, favor the realization of the Zionist hopes. On the other hand, the extreme poverty of the land, the division in Zion's own ranks, and divine retribution on the Jews as a people for rejecting Christ, discourage the prospect of the restoration of Zion."[41] For Dawson, Arabs did not appear as a complicating factor in the success or failure of the Zionists. Even those like Z. T. Cody, who were supportive of the Arabs, tended to view the Zionists as the region's primary actors. Cody had been sympathetic toward the Zionist cause, before his travels led him to reconsider. "I have been learning some other new things since I came here," he wrote in 1920.[42] While Cody found much to admire in Zionism, he saw it as inevitably leading to the displacement of the Arabs. He insisted that opposition to the movement was "not merely another manifestation of anti-Jewish prejudice. . . . The seven hundred thousand natives are looking on a movement whose avowed purpose is to supplant them. It is not difficult to imagine how they feel."[43]

At times, specific political events worked their way into travelers' reflections. In 1929, controversy over Jewish rights at the Western Wall brought simmering tensions between Arabs and Jews near the boiling point. In August, those tensions erupted into unprecedented violence, with Arab mobs attacking Jewish communities in Jerusalem, Safed, and Hebron, leading to the deaths of 133 Jews and 116 Arabs.[44] In response to the violence, the British temporarily imposed restrictions on Jewish immigration and land purchasing, soon reversing them after Zionist protests.[45] Writing in the aftermath of the disturbances, J. McKee Adams blamed the region's troubles on Britain's support for Zionism, arguing that the "general disaffection in Palestine can be attributed definitely to the implications of the Balfour Declaration . . . and to the alleged radical changes effected in the Zionistic organization by that pronouncement."[46] The vague language of the declaration had empowered "the aggressive wing of Zionism" to push for the creation of a Jewish nation-state.[47] These developments had justifiably aroused Arab fears of dispossession, made more urgent by Jewish immigration, land purchasing, and economic competition. Adams believed that Zionism needed to be redefined "in terms more acceptable to Arab sensibilities" and that the word *national* needed to be removed from the Balfour Declaration. If the Zionists and British took these actions, Adams was certain that "the Arabs would fold their tents and as silently steal away, while the Jews would settle down to an era of blessedness in peace."[48]

Peace, though, was not in the offing. Tensions between Jews and Arabs only increased in the 1930s, as growing numbers of Jews fled to Palestine from escalating persecution in Europe. In 1935, sixty-two thousand Jews came to the region, a migration that was roughly the same size as Palestine's total Jewish population at the end of World War I. Increasingly, Arab leaders were pushed toward the realization that cooperation with the British would not lead to the achievement of their goals. The following year, Arabs initiated a general strike to protest British support for Zionism, a strike that soon escalated into an outright revolt against the British.[49] Amid the revolt, Britain dispatched a royal commission to investigate its causes and make policy recommendations. Ultimately, this Peel Commission concluded that Jewish and Arab ambitions were irreconcilable and recommended the partitioning of Palestine into Arab and Jewish territories, with a corridor connecting Jerusalem and Jaffa remaining under British administration.[50] The commission's report only stirred further outrage among Palestinian Arabs, who saw the partition plan as confirmation of their worst fears—that the British sought to give over their country to the Jews. The revolt intensified until being harshly put down by the British, only ending in 1939.

Britain's struggle to quell the revolt caused Baptist travelers to revisit the divergent promises that the British had made to Arabs and Jews during World War I. Ruth Collie, whose numerous travel articles rarely engaged the political, reported a conversation with her guide, an Arab Christian named Mr. Jamel, who told her that "his people are quite disturbed about the English Mandate Commission which was published three or four days ago relative to the dividing of the Holy Lands." Despite her warmth for Jamel (she noted of her party, "we already love him"), Collie nonetheless seems to have favored partition. After noting that travelers to the Holy Land would require three visas under the plan, she remarked, "Quite a situation for a country this size, but of course you realize it has come about through the promises of England to both Jews and Arabs that they may have a home here."[51] W. T. Halstead used the occasion of his 1937 trip to Palestine and the publication of the Peel Commission's report to lay out his basic understanding of the conflict to readers of the *Florida Baptist Witness*. Though he did argue that "it is Arab discontent that is causing trouble in Palestine," Halstead also sympathetically laid out Arab claims and fears. More than anything, Halstead felt that it was the tangle of "misunderstanding, unfulfilled hopes," and "unkept promises" that had spurred the increasingly violent conflict.[52]

In 1939, the British issued a white paper that severely restricted Jewish immigration and land purchasing and called for the creation of an independent Palestinian government within ten years.[53] Zionists condemned the new policy as an abandonment of the Balfour Declaration and a death sentence for European Jews fleeing Nazi persecution. Amid the unfolding Holocaust, Zionist and non-Zionist Jews alike were soon convinced that only Jewish sovereignty could secure a needed safe haven for Europe's Jews.[54] In 1942, Zionist leaders adopted the Biltmore Program, which called explicitly for the creation of a "Jewish commonwealth" in Palestine after the war.[55] As the war ended, underground Zionist paramilitary forces initiated their own insurgency against the British. As British efforts to reach a settlement between Jews and Arabs failed, the Palestine question was handed over in 1947 to the newly formed United Nations. After conducting its own investigation, the UN Special Committee on Palestine followed the Peel Commission in recommending the partition of Palestine into Jewish and Arab states, with Jerusalem remaining under international administration.[56] The

Zionists accepted the plan. The Arabs rejected it. Nonetheless, with American support, the UN General Assembly voted in favor of partition in November 1947.[57] The vote was a huge victory for the Zionists, who above all had sought international recognition of their right to independent statehood. It was a disaster for the Palestinian Arabs, who refused to recognize the decision of the assembly.

Florida Baptist James Day had been in Palestine as the UN Special Committee on Palestine held hearings. Amid deliberations of the partition resolution later in the year, he gave his impressions of the conflict to readers of the *Florida Baptist Witness*. More than any other Baptist traveler in the Mandate era, Day expressed wariness of his position as a traveler-observer, noting that "one should be very careful in writing about a country where one has been for only two weeks and the problems have existed for over two thousand years." He explained his wariness in terms that would appeal to his fellow white southerners, noting that he wanted to avoid "the mistake of those who have visited the South for two weeks or two months, and then have gone home to write 'expert' articles on the 'Negro problem in the South.'"[58] Over the course of three articles that straddled the United Nations' vote on partition, Day laid out Jewish and Arab claims to the land, as well as five possible solutions to the Palestine question. The first two solutions were what each side wanted—total control for Jews or total control for Arabs. The third was binationalism, the formation of "a united Jewish-Arab State in all of Palestine, with a legislative body composed of an equal number of Jews and Arabs," which Day noted was only supported by a small but active minority of Jews.[59] The fourth was the United Nations' partition plan, which Day found to be reasonable since it gave "the Jew most of the farm land (for in Palestine he is primarily a farmer)" and the Arab "most of the grazing land (for he is primarily a herdsman)." That the plan was reasonable, though, did not mean that it would work. "All Arabs with whom I talked in Palestine," Day noted, "stated that they would fight to the last Arab, to keep the Jews from having even a part of Palestine." In the end, Day concluded that no "man-made" solution would work. "The only permanent abiding peace on this sin cursed earth," he was certain, "can come only through the Prince of Peace."[60]

Day's concerns over partition proved correct. As he wrote his last article, Palestine was already descending into civil war between Zionist and Arab forces, with the Zionists attempting to secure the territory promised by the United Nations, the Arabs working to thwart the implementation of partition, and the British seeking to minimize their losses as they maneuvered to exit the country.[61] By late April, the Zionists had largely succeeded in securing their territory. Already, hundreds of thousands of Arabs had fled or been expelled. On May 14, the last day of British rule, David Ben-Gurion proclaimed that the State of Israel would come into being at midnight.[62] The following day, the surrounding Arab states—Transjordan, Egypt, Syria, Lebanon, and Iraq—began a promised invasion of the territory. When the fighting ended in 1949, Palestine had indeed been partitioned, albeit not on the terms of the 1947 UN resolution. Transjordan had seized the West Bank of the Jordan River. Egypt had secured control of the Gaza Strip. Israel had survived, even extending its borders in the process. SBC executive secretary Duke McCall, who traveled to the region shortly after the war, celebrated the fact that the Jewish people "have at last made a national home." At the same time, he found himself seeking "justice for adequate recompense for the displaced Arabs." The birth of Israel, to McCall, had been an "immoral miracle."[63]

Conclusion

Almost every Southern Baptist traveler would have agreed with the Floridian James Day that only Christ could bring true peace to Palestine. Though he had claimed that the rescinding of the Balfour Declaration would allay tensions, J. McKee Adams was likewise certain that "warring factions in the Holy Land will never cease from struggle until Christ is brought again into the midst of their relations."[64] Day, though, had meant something different. A premillennialist, he believed that the ultimate end of conflict would come through Christ's second coming. Most Southern Baptists, including Adams, imagined a subtler intervention, hoping that the spread of the gospel would help pacify the increasingly war-torn Holy Land. In this way, many travelers in the Mandate era looked to the growing Baptist mission as the region's greatest hope.[65] "I have seen Jews and Arabs sitting together in the only place in Palestine where Jews and Arabs come together without fighting," Claude Broach wrote of the Jerusalem mission amid the Arab revolt. His stirring visit had led him to wonder why Baptists should "not be done with the note of despair and sound the note of hope and victory!"[66]

Baptists had long hoped to sound the note of Protestant victory in the Holy Land, believing that it would herald the rebirth of Palestine as a more modern, more Western, and—of course—more holy land. When Broach called for Baptists to announce this victory in 1938, though, he meant more a celebration of the eternal victory of Christ than the victory of Christianity in Palestine—a victory that, if still hoped and worked for by the Baptist missionaries examined in the next two chapters, remained distant. Nonetheless, postwar Baptist travelers did find a Holy Land undergoing many of the changes for which their precursors had hoped. It was modernizing. It was westernizing. It was, despite the deepening conflict, progressing. While some travelers praised the British for remaking the region, more focused their attention on the Zionists, drawing Orientalist distinctions between Zionist progress and Arab backwardness that stood in clear contrast to views in the Ottoman era, when Baptists had often seen Jews as a particularly backward portion of the benighted East.

This change was not simply a matter of shifting impressions. Baptists saw real changes on the ground. Demographically, the rapidly growing Yishuv was largely European, largely educated, more familiarly Western, and more apparently modern than the Old Yishuv had been. Zionists were building new cities and new agricultural communities, as Jews from around the world, particularly the United States, poured money into the development of the Yishuv.[67] Acting on its own Orientalist presumptions, the mandatory government granted crucial economic concessions to Zionist entrepreneurs, believing that European Jews would make better use of these concessions than would Arabs.[68] All these developments led the Yishuv to one of the highest sustained economic growth rates in the world over the course of the Mandate era.[69] Baptists could see these changes. While the Arab community of Palestine underwent its own rapid social, cultural, and economic transformation during these decades, too, Baptists were simply not conditioned to see this transformation. Their Orientalist presumptions were encouraged by the transitory nature of their travels, which privileged the easy apprehension of visual contrasts. While those presumptions did not necessarily translate into support for Zionist political goals, they nonetheless offered a sort of postcard Zionism—pictures of a Holy Land reborn by the movement—in the pages of the Baptist papers.

3
Arabs

During and after World War I, Protestant missionaries and Arab Christian émigrés educated in Levantine mission schools served as leading voices in presenting Arab perspectives on developments in the Middle East to American audiences. Especially prominent were Presbyterians and Congregationalists, who had long-standing ties to the region. Though these groups were few in number in the Arab world, they had an influence far beyond their numbers, particularly in what is now Lebanon and Syria. Beginning in the first half of the nineteenth century, Presbyterian and Congregationalist missionaries had built an educational network throughout the Levant in an effort to peel off "nominal" Christians from the Eastern Churches.[1] It was largely out of this network—which most notably included Syrian Protestant College (later the American University of Beirut)—that an Arab Christian intelligentsia had emerged in the late nineteenth century, concerned with both the revival of Arabic as a modern language (the *nahda*) and the formation of modern identities that transcended religious division.[2] It was such educated Syrian Christians (as Arab Christians from the region were most often referred to in the United States) and their missionary associates who spoke up for a variety of Arab interests in the United States during and after World War I.[3] Among those interests were greater Arab self-determination and opposition to Zionism.

As with American Protestants more broadly, Southern Baptists' most direct connections to the Arabic-speaking world would be through missions. However, Baptists had far weaker ties to the region than did the Presbyterians or Congregationalists. As noted in chapter 1, beyond abstract hope and sentimental attachment to the Holy Land, Southern Baptists had no substantial ties to Palestine at all until the 1910s. Though Baptists had expressed missionary interest in the Holy Land since the founding of the Southern Baptist Convention, it took the serendipitous arrival of an Arab named Shukri Mosa in Texas in 1908 to actually draw them into the region.[4] Mosa developed a close relationship with the most important Texas Baptists of the day and, along with his wife, Munira, established the first Baptist mission in Palestine in 1911, which the FMB took over in 1919.

In the years following World War I, Shukri Mosa and his nephew Louis Hanna were effectively the only Arabs whose voices penetrated Baptist discussions of Palestine. The Arab Baptists, though, never became spokespeople for Arab political causes in the way that many Arabs affiliated with other American missions did. In part, this was because their voices as spokespeople for their own mission and mission field were quickly drowned out by the American missionaries who began arriving in 1921. In part, too, it was because Mosa and Hanna simply did not prioritize politics in their communications with Baptists in the United States. This is not to say that they were apolitical, but rather that their leading priority—securing resources for the development of their mission and their community—circumscribed their presentation of the peoples and the politics of their native land, guiding both critiques of Zionism and critiques of Arab life and culture that appealed to the Orientalist assumptions of their fellow Baptists in the States. To that end, their marginal voices, in the long run, had an impact.

Building the Mission

Shukri Mosa was born to a Greek Catholic (or Melkite) family in Safed in 1870. His father served on the Safed municipal council as the representative of the Christian community in the city. Shukri's own first career was as a civil servant, working for the postal service in Jerusalem and Safed. In 1905, he married Munira Youssef Badr, who was born in the village of Shweir near Mount Lebanon.[5] Munira had grown up in the aforementioned missionary milieu, her parents having converted to Presbyterianism from Greek Orthodoxy in the 1870s under the influence of American missionaries. Her father, Youssef Badr, had served as the first Arab pastor of the National Evangelical Church in Beirut. As a young girl, Munira had attended the British Normal Training School for girls, where she studied English, among a host of other subjects.[6]

It was three years after Shukri wed Munira that he left with his nephew Youssef for the United States, hoping to win riches and return to his family. Like many others among the tens of thousands of Arabs who came to the United States from the Ottoman Empire between the 1880s and 1920, he found his opportunity in peddling. Mosa's route took him through Texas, where he sold Holy Land souvenirs door-to-door. It was likely one of these souvenirs that led to a conversation on faith with Dr. L. R. Scarborough, who was then a professor of evangelism at the new Southwestern Baptist

Theological Seminary (SWBTS) and soon would be its president. Scarborough, along with George Truett, the pastor of the First Baptist Church, Dallas, took an interest in the ambitious peddler, soon guiding him to accept conversion and baptism as a Baptist. Reborn, Mosa dedicated himself wholly to religion, seeking to become a missionary to his people. After securing an appointment with the Illinois Baptist Missionary Convention, he returned to Safed in 1910. The following year he moved his family to Nazareth—"the Lord's home city," as he would note in his letterhead—where he and his wife began to build their mission. Shukri baptized his first convert, his nephew Louis Hanna, who himself soon headed to Texas to study for the ministry at SWBTS in Fort Worth.

Though Mosa was officially sponsored by the Illinois Baptists, he maintained his connections with the Texans. They sent him copies of the *Baptist Standard*, and he replied with reports on the mission's progress.[7] Southern Baptist travelers to the Levant, particularly Texans, sometimes sought out the missionary and attended the services that he held in his house. J. W. Graham, who traveled to Nazareth in May 1913, reported that the Mosas kept a portrait of Truett in their home.[8] Shukri had also developed a relationship with Dr. James Marion Frost, the secretary of the SBC's publishing house (the Sunday School Board), during his time in the States. He used this connection to obtain Sunday School Board materials, the most important of which were the picture cards that he gave to young Sunday school attendees as a reward for good attendance.[9] He also repeatedly pleaded to Frost to help bring the mission under the aegis of the FMB. As early as one year in, it was clear the Illinois Convention would be unable to uphold its financial commitments.

A 1914 status report by Shukri gives some insight into the functioning of the early mission.[10] By then, the Mosas were holding five meetings per week with an average attendance of twenty-six. Munira had begun her work among women, which would remain one of the mission's strong points into the late 1920s. The five meetings were in addition to Sunday services, as well as boys' and girls' Sunday school classes (Munira taught the girls), which had 313 students on their rolls (fewer attended).[11] Shukri reported having given 148 sermons in 1913. Munira played the organ for their services. They had baptized twelve individuals since the work had begun in 1911, though three were then in America (including Shukri's nephew Hanna, by then attending seminary). Shukri reported that the group, though small in number, was stirring active resistance in the community, particularly among the native Christian communities that the mission targeted. Their rivals—chiefly the Orthodox—hung "papers in the streets in which were written very bad names, cursing us, our doctrines, baptism, etc."[12] The Orthodox bishop was concerned enough to thwart attempts by Shukri to purchase land for a cemetery by pressuring local Christians not to sell to the Baptists. The missionary noted that, though many "of the enlightened folk say that we have the very purest doctrine of the Bible," the question of rebaptism was keeping many inquirers away.[13] This distance was likely because rebaptism would be seen as a social breach with the Orthodox Christian community. Still, they were making progress.

This small progress, though, was almost totally wiped out by World War I. Palestine was thrown into general chaos.[14] The Ottoman military governorship under Jamal Pasha (known as the Blood Shedder) was extremely brutal and repressive, particularly toward local Arabs. The economy ground to a halt as the fighting interrupted trade and men were drafted into the Ottoman forces. Mosa himself was conscripted and posted to Riyaq (in modern-day Lebanon). After the British and Arab forces pushed the Ottomans from Palestine, Mosa returned to Nazareth and began rebuilding the mission. Of the eighteen that he had baptized prior to the war, only ten remained. Among the rest, he noted in a letter to Secretary T. B. Ray, "1 died, 1 backed, 1 because of the great tribulation of the war sheltered himself in the Roman Catholick's convent . . . & the rest 3 are in different parts of America."[15] However, on August 1, 1919, one of the missionary's long-standing hopes was fulfilled as the FMB officially took over control of the mission from the Illinois Baptists.[16] Immediately, Mosa expressed to the board his highest hopes—the establishment of a church and a school.

The Mosas steadily built the mission over the next several years. By the mid-1920s, they were holding seven meetings each week in addition to their Sunday service and Sunday school.[17] Though there is not much record detailing these meetings, a 1919 letter to Isaac Jacobus Van Ness (Frost's successor with the Sunday School Board) sheds some light on the Sunday schools. Each Sunday, Shukri and Munira would teach their respective classes two stanzas of a hymn, explain the day's lesson "in a very simple way," teach the golden rule, pray, and give out picture cards as rewards for attendance.[18] Another mission staple was Munira's Thursday night meeting for women, which in 1923 drew an average of sixty to eighty attendees. This meeting was apparently part Bible study, part workshop. To draw in local women, Munira provided thread for needlework, which she then purchased and attempted to sell herself, sometimes reaching out to Baptist women in the United States.[19] In 1923, Shukri began a night reading and writing class for young men. By 1925 he was able to organize a Baptist Young People's Union.

Beyond the expansion of the Mosas' own efforts in Nazareth, the FMB enacted a more general expansion of what was known as the Near East

Mission in the first half of the 1920s. The main feature of this expansion was the placement of a superintendent from the United States over the regional missions (the Near East Mission included the stations at Nazareth, Kfarmichky, and Beirut, which had already been established by local Baptists) starting in 1921. Although he had started the mission on his own, Shukri was categorized as a "native worker" subordinate to the rotating cast of "foreign missionaries" (i.e., Americans) that the FMB sent. Also classified as a native worker was Mosa's nephew Hanna, who had graduated from SWBTS and been sent by the FMB in 1921 to work among Arabs in Jerusalem. While the Mosas and Hanna were technically subordinate, they were supported and given relative autonomy by J. Wash Watts, who served as the mission's superintendent from 1923 to 1928.

The crowning achievement of the Mosas' mission came in 1927 with the dedication of Bottoms Memorial Baptist Church. Shukri had long pleaded to the officers of the FMB that Baptists needed to establish a permanent presence in the city as an act of good faith.[20] The matter of Baptist honor had become especially urgent after the failed tenure of the first mission superintendent, W. A. Hamlett, who almost destroyed the mission in one disastrous month of work (examined in chapter 4). Concrete steps toward establishing a permanent presence were not taken until 1923, when a tour group of Texas Baptists, including Truett and Scarborough, visited the mission and pledged $2,500 for the purchase of land.[21] To that gift was soon added a ten thousand dollar donation from the Bottoms family of Texarkana, Arkansas, a donation that paid for the construction of the church building near Mary's Well. The Bottoms Memorial Baptist Church was dedicated on May 3, 1927. As Mosa had predicted, the dedication of the church boosted the confidence of inquirers. Thirteen new members joined in 1928.

Nazarene Baptists' excitement over the dedication of Bottoms Memorial Baptist Church soon turned to despair with the unexpected death of Shukri Mosa in August 1928. His death was only the first challenge of many that would beset the small community over the following two decades. The congregation, though, did not die with their pastor. Munira continued her work as a rotating cast of local Protestant ministers and laypeople shared preaching duties over the following months. In September, the congregation penned a letter to the FMB, calling Louis Hanna as their next pastor.[22] Hanna, who was completing his bachelor's degree at Howard Payne College in Brownwood, Texas, at the time, wrote to Watts that he felt "like Elisha when he saw Elijah taken away in the storm." He promised that when he and his wife, Velora, completed their studies the following spring, they would be "ready to go anywhere the Board points the way for us, whether to return to Palestine or go to any other place."[23]

Though Hanna was the obvious choice to replace his uncle, his appointment was not without difficulty. Hanna had spent much of his life in the United States and had become thoroughly Americanized. He had attended SWBTS in the 1910s before joining his uncle in the mission field and had spent the previous several years in Brownwood. His wife was from Texas. Their marriage challenged the FMB's formal distinction between native and missionary workers, between which lay a significant gap in pay and authority. T. B. Ray expressed his frustrations over the Hannas' status in a 1928 letter to Watts:

> I must confess to the standing question I have about these young foreigners who are educated in America and who marry American wives. My observation has been that the largest percentage of them are failures. They become so Americanized, and have so many American connections, that it is hard to keep them on their fields. It is almost impossible for them to accept the status of regular native workers, and, when they assume a different classification, discord is aroused amongst the native working force. Furthermore, they have cultivated American taste and habits of living which increase the problem. In Hanna's case in particular, he has been in America so long that he perhaps is more American than he is Syrian. That raises the consideration that if we are going to send a native who is practically an American out there, why would it not be better to send an upright American.[24]

Just as Ray feared, the Hannas did request to be sent to Palestine as foreign missionaries. Ray adamantly refused the designation. The Hannas nonetheless agreed to go to Nazareth the following year as native workers, where they would remain until 1938.

Hanna returned to his native Palestine on February 10, 1930. He and Velora set to work immediately, holding a women's meeting and a prayer service in Nazareth the following day.[25] They began restructuring the church facility, installing folding doors that divided the building into classrooms. Soon, their Sunday school was averaging 150 students divided between six classes. Though the loss of Shukri Mosa had been devastating to the small congregation, Hanna's long experience with the mission ensured a measure of continuity. Also helpful was that Munira Mosa had remained employed by the FMB as a "Bible woman," something of a mission assistant and lay instructor. Munira, though, was much more than that: she had effectively kept the Nazareth mission running for two years and remained in charge of the women's work even for a short time after the Hannas' arrival.

The Hannas sought incremental, steady growth of the mission. Their early priority was to cultivate study groups among young adults, something that had already been attempted by Louis during his earlier tenure in Jerusalem but that was new to Nazareth. In 1933, the Hannas began a Daily Vacation Bible School.[26] The first week they had twenty-two pupils. By the second session, enrollment had grown to fifty-six. The success of the Bible school made it clear to the Hannas that Shukri Mosa's unfulfilled dream of a Baptist day school in Nazareth was both possible and necessary. In 1935, they created the day school that would evolve into the Nazareth Baptist School, which would become one of the most important and lasting contributions of Baptists to the community, despite being forced to shut down between 1941 and 1949. As had occurred during the mission's first decade, though, war again brought the Baptists' progress to a halt in the 1940s. The Hannas, who had gone stateside on furlough in 1938, were forced to extend their stay in Texas after Velora fell ill in 1939.[27] They remained in Texas as hostilities broke out in Europe and the Middle East, and the rest of the Near East missionaries were recalled in 1941. The Hannas never returned as missionaries. Louis joined the US Army as a chaplain during the war before settling down in Bryan, Texas, with Velora. They remained in Texas the rest of their days.

Arab Baptists as Spokespeople

Shukri Mosa and Louis Hanna were among the few Arabs whose voices penetrated the SBC in the Mandate era. Though subordinated as native workers after 1921, both had connections to the FMB and to the Texas Baptist elites that had brought Mosa to the faith. The high point in this relationship was the 1923 visit of the Armstrong Party to Palestine. Led by Dr. Andrew Joseph Armstrong, Baylor University English chair and tour guide, the tour reunited Mosa with the men who had led him to conversion: Truett and Scarborough. By then, Truett had become the most influential Southern Baptist in Texas (three years later he would be elected president of the SBC), and Scarborough had already spent a decade as president of SWBTS. The visit also opened up new connections. Among them was J. B. Tidwell, then the head of the Bible department at Baylor, who had gathered the party's $2,500 gift to the mission. That money went to the purchase of the lot on which Bottoms Memorial Baptist Church was built. In 1925, the Texans had also helped secure the Mosas' eldest son, Munir, a place at the San Marcos Academy in San Marcos, Texas, with Truett serving as his caretaker in the States. As mentioned, Louis Hanna had married a Texan, Velora Griffin, and he had also studied at two Texas schools: SWBTS in Fort Worth and Howard Payne College in Brownwood. Whereas his uncle had connections to the Lone Star State, Hanna had sprouted roots there.

Mosa and Hanna also connected with stateside Baptists through intermittent articles in Baptist periodicals. They published a small handful of articles in the *Baptist Standard*, the main outlet of their Texas connections, and *Home and Foreign Fields*, the main outlet of their FMB connections, between 1911 and 1938. These writings were mere drops in a bucket of articles about the Near East Mission within the ocean of Baptist periodicals. From 1923 onward, foreign missionaries took the lead in writing about the mission. Between 1923 and 1942 (when the foreign missionaries left the field), *Home and Foreign Fields* published twenty-eight articles from workers at the Near East Mission, about 1.5 articles per year. Among those twenty-eight, only one was written by Louis Hanna. Mosa never published a full article in *Home and Foreign Fields*. In contrast, Jacob Gartenhaus (examined in chapter 5), the SBC's domestic missionary to Jews (and a supporter of Zionism), published over thirty articles in the journal during the same time period.

This mixture of strong personal and weak public connections to stateside Baptists never added up to a prominent Arab voice in Baptist discussions of Palestine. To the extent that Mosa and Hanna did have a voice within the SBC, they used it to win material support for the mission. Mosa's main priorities from his return to Palestine in 1910 until his death were ensuring a livelihood for his growing family and building Baptist institutions in Nazareth—in particular, an actual church and a school. He raised these issues when he wrote to individual Baptists in the States, when he published his infrequent articles in the *Baptist Standard*, and when he encountered travelers in Nazareth. Hanna's few published articles likewise focused on winning support for the mission. This goal circumscribed both Arab Baptists' depictions of the land, the peoples, and even the politics of Palestine.

Mosa, for example, expressed opposition to Zionism, albeit in terms of practical consequence for the mission. In 1920, he warned the FMB that the influx of Jews was sending rents higher and would make it more difficult for Baptists to lease property.[28] The following year he cautioned that the Zionists were likely to open a boarding school in Nazareth. "Of course the people hate it," he noted, but they would attend if it was the only school in town.[29] The board needed to act quickly, lest the field be left to the Zionists (the Zionists, it should be noted, had no presence in Nazareth at this point in time). The only time that Mosa was directly negative toward the Zionists was in a 1922 article in the *Baptist Standard* calling on stateside Baptists to support the expansion of work throughout the Galilee. After touring the area, Mosa noted the dramatic expansion of Zionist settlements, particularly in Tiberias and Safed. He warned that the majority of "these new Jews" were "irreligious people" and "immoral," adding that "they are very proud, their noses are very high up thinking that they are coming to be kings over the inhabitants."[30] Mosa went on to recount an episode in which he had seen a Zionist Jew spit on an egg that had been decorated with an image of Christ: "I don't believe in pictures, but it made me angry because he did spit on the picture, he meant to despise my God and Saviour. It came to my mind what a hatred this Jew had against Christ and Christianity. Such deeds they do make the people hate them. Yes, they are hated by all the inhabitants, even the ancient Jews themselves. They are more Bolshevist than Jew."[31] While many Southern Baptists celebrated Zionist modernity, Mosa believed that it was a vehicle of irreligion, inimical to Christ, that was putting pressure on existing missionary institutions. Southern Baptists needed to push back by sending additional workers to the Galilee, "that it may be turned to the Great Galilean."[32]

If Mosa exceeded other Baptists in questioning Zionist modernity, he and Hanna nonetheless echoed many of their criticisms of Arab life and culture, intermingling American Protestant Orientalist assumptions about religion, gender, and culture with their own personal experiences. As with Mosa in his warnings about Zionism, Mosa and Hanna shared these criticisms with American Baptists in order to stir up support for the mission. They shared with their American counterparts a Protestant distaste for Orthodox and Catholic Christianity, though they were often more temperate in their critiques. In a 1924 article, Mosa described giving the gospel to the "nominal Christians" of Cana who felt that they were "driven as animals by the priests."[33] Hanna likewise referred to the Christians of Cana as being "tightly held in their Catholic chains" in a 1932 article.[34] The Mosas and the Hannas were both especially concerned with the status of Arab women. As described in her granddaughter Jean Said Makdisi's memoir *Teta, Mother, and Me* (2006), Munira Mosa expressed her identity as a Protestant woman by transgressing local gender norms.[35] She was educated. She did not cover her face in public. She favored simple clothing over the often-elaborate Palestinian female dress and considered herself liberated from the traditions and superstitions that bound Arab women. For the foreign missionaries and Velora, her American niece, Munira was a model of Protestantism's potential in the Levant. Velora even devoted a chapter of the 1937 mission study manual *Questing in Galilee* to Munira's life story, hailing her as "an inspiration, a counselor, and the mother of us all."[36] Most of all, Munira stood in contrast to the unconverted women of Nazareth. Describing the attendees of the mission's women's group, Louis Hanna noted that "the majority are entirely illiterate, old, superstitious, and blinded by an abundance of tradition. . . . They are treated like animals by their husbands, the lords of the households."[37]

For the most part, Arab Baptist leaders celebrated the modernization and westernization of Palestine. In Hanna's most detailed survey of the region, a 1930 article in the Oklahoma *Baptist Messenger*, he acknowledged that there was "a great deal of filth, squalor, ignorance and unpleasant sites in Palestine," but that the region was undergoing changes that were "very marked and real, and, therefore, very encouraging." Palestine now had "hard-surfaced highways" and "modern automobiles." Palestinian women were beginning to adopt "dresses fashioned after American and Parisian styles," while men were "wearing the same sort of suits worn by any American or European gentleman." The government was expanding access to education at all levels, and "scores of young men" were leaving Palestine "to enter European and American colleges."[38] Young people were breaking free of the "awful tyrannical chain of formalism, as represented by the religious leaders of Catholicism, the followers of the Arabian prophet, and the descendants of the Pharisees and the scribes," and they were "earnestly seeking for something satisfying" to take its place.[39] Still, the arrival of modernity had its dangers. Hanna warned of "materialistic evolution and the encroachment of many isms," even among the missionary community of Palestine.[40] To ensure a godly modernity, Hanna called for Southern Baptists to support the development of Baptist educational institutions in Palestine.

Hanna published his 1930 article only months after the Wailing Wall riots, which brought unprecedented violence to the Zionist-Arab conflict, including in his hometown of Safed. It is telling that in an article that was preoccupied with the dangers of *isms*, Hanna completely omitted the *ism* that was most dramatically transforming his homeland—Zionism. In the context of Palestine in early 1930, it is a striking omission. In the context of Arab Baptists' priorities in communicating with Baptists in the United States, however, it makes sense. Hanna, like his late uncle, wanted to win Baptist support for the establishment of a school in Nazareth. Having spent several years in Texas, he knew that raising the threat of "materialistic evolution . . . Russellism, Eddyism and Mormonism"—threats familiar to Southern Baptists—might well stoke the generosity of Baptists unwilling to lose the Holy Land to atheists, Christian Scientists, or Mormons.[41]

That Arab Baptists never developed a political voice in the vein of the Presbyterians or Congregationalists during the Mandate era does not mean that they ignored politics. As functional as his infrequent nods to Zionism were, Mosa clearly opposed the movement. The recollections of the Mosas' children, as relayed in Jean Said Makdisi's memoir, likewise suggest that Mosa held broader political concerns over the Zionists. What is not clear is whether he ever translated these concerns into outright political advocacy—be it through support for Faisal's stillborn Arab kingdom or for the nascent Palestinian national movement.[42] If Mosa saw any good in the Muslim-Christian committees that sprouted in the postwar years or in the PAE, he never made it clear to the Baptists.[43] It must be remembered, though, that Mosa was an outsider even within the Christian community of Nazareth, which was overwhelmingly Orthodox and Catholic, in a region in which communal identity was inextricable from religion.[44] Mosa was not only a Protestant: he was a peculiar, unfamiliar type of Protestant lacking the political heft and social standing of the Syrian or Lebanese Presbyterians or the Jerusalem Anglicans. "I cannot forget how lonely I felt most of the time," recalled his daughter, Hilda. "People found us very strange in Nazareth."[45] In an age in which many Arab Christians were seeking to transcend their religion in pursuit of new national identities and political horizons, Shukri Mosa had staked his own identity on being first and foremost a Baptist.[46] He was to Nazarenes *al-qassis*—the Minister.

Conclusion

To the extent that Southern Baptists were directly implicated in the changes sweeping the Holy Land under British rule, it was through the Arab Baptist community of Nazareth. That community's leaders, the Mosas and Louis Hanna, were the most direct link that most Baptists (outside the missionary corps itself) had with local Palestinians. Southern Baptists' investment in and connection to this Arab community, though, did not lead many to identify with the Arab cause in the context of the unfolding Palestine question. One possible exception to this pattern was Z. T. Cody, who visited Nazareth as part of the 1920 missionary survey mentioned in the previous chapter. Cody had been initially supportive of Zionism but became critical of the movement after "learning some other new things" while visiting the country.[47] Whether he learned those new things from the Baptists whom he visited in Nazareth, though, he left unmentioned. All told, Southern Baptists did not cite their connections with Arab Baptists in articulating either support for the Arab cause or criticism of Zionism.

Of course, the Mosas and Hanna had their own priorities. Even though they represented the Arab perspective insofar as it existed in Southern Baptist discussions of Palestine, their writings on the region were not mere expressions of their Arab identity. They were missionaries and community leaders with tangible and urgent goals—sustaining their Baptist community and building its institutions. They wrote to Baptist leaders and published articles in the Baptist press in pursuit of those goals. At times, these goals called for warnings against Zionism. At others, they called for ignoring it. And sometimes these goals called for criticizing Arab culture in terms that both drew on and confirmed the Orientalist assumptions of the Arab missionaries' Baptist interlocuters. Though their voices were marginal and were quickly drowned out by those of the American missionaries dispatched to the region only two years after the FMB took over the mission, their message did eventually find an audience among stateside Baptists. That there remain Baptists in "the Lord's home city" is a testament to the vision and effectiveness of these "native workers."[48]

4
Missionaries

On June 8, 1921, a recent Episcopalian convert to Baptist Christianity named E. C. Miller addressed the Foreign Mission Board of the Southern Baptist Convention in Richmond. The title of his address, later published in a pamphlet, made clear the occasion of his speaking: "The proposal to establish the First Baptist Church at Jerusalem, together with a College, a Hospital and an Orphan Asylum."[1] Though Miller had spent twenty-five years as an Episcopalian and had lived most of his life in New York City, he had been born in the South to Southern Baptist parents. Indeed, it was Miller's father, Thomas, who had been inspired in 1873 to give the initial gold dollar to the FMB for the eventual establishment of a Baptist church at Jerusalem. Over four decades later, E. C. Miller appeared with $15,000 to add. Having already taken over financial responsibilities for Shukri Mosa's mission in Nazareth and having initiated plans for a massive expansion of its global missions, the board was eager to add a foreign missionary in Jerusalem who could oversee an expansion of the work.[2] Within months it sent its first appointee, W. A. Hamlett, to Palestine.

Though Shukri and Munira Mosa had effectively built the Southern Baptist mission in Palestine on their own, they were—as "native workers"—considered subordinate to the handful of American missionaries who began to arrive in 1921.[3] From the moment that the FMB took over responsibility for Mosa's mission in 1919, the plan had been to send an American superintendent to oversee the ongoing missions at Nazareth, Rasheya, and Kfarmichky, and to expand the work into other Levantine cities, especially Jerusalem.[4] With the arrival of American missionaries throughout the 1920s, Mosa's voice began to be crowded out in SBC circles. The publication of his articles in SBC periodicals slowed as the American missionaries began writing home. His letters to SBC personnel tapered off as he was encouraged to communicate with the FMB and other SBC bodies through the superintendent.

By the mid-1920s, American missionaries had become the primary representatives of the Southern Baptist mission in Palestine as well as some of the SBC's foremost interpreters of events in the region.[5] They communicated their perspectives to Baptists back home through articles in state Baptist periodicals and *Home and Foreign Fields* (the SBC's missionary digest, later renamed the *Commission*), circular letters petitioning support for the mission, informational pamphlets, full-length books, personal letters, and mission study materials produced by the Woman's Missionary Union. Also important was the deputation work that missionaries performed while on furlough, which involved visiting churches, associational meetings, and conventions in order to drum up interest and support for the FMB's initiatives. Deputation work necessarily involved describing the progress of the mission and informing audiences about the ever-shifting state of affairs in the region. Missionaries also communicated with the Southern Baptist laity through direct interaction with Baptist pilgrims to the Holy Land.

For the most part, the missionaries drew the same Orientalist distinctions between Arabs and Jews as did Baptist travelers, while emphasizing both peoples' need for Christ. Missionaries both thrilled at the dramatic changes reshaping the Holy Land and worried at its deepening conflict, understanding their work as part of the region's revival and their gospel message as its only hope for true peace. Several were inspired by premillennial interpretations of the Bible to believe that the revival of the land, the successes of the Zionist movement, and their own missionary task might be part of God's plan for history. At the center of the missionaries' interest in Zionism, though, was a question rooted in their evangelistic priorities: was Zionism a help or a hindrance to the spread of the gospel? Throughout the Mandate era, Baptist missionaries alternately voiced hopes and frustrations toward the movement as they weighed whether it was a complement or a stumbling block to their mission. While their perspectives on this and other questions varied, what was consistent—if unsurprising—about the missionaries' understandings of the region was that they remained inextricable from the priorities, successes, and failures of the Near East Mission itself.

The Failure: Dr. W. A. Hamlett

The FMB's first attempt to place an American in Palestine was nearly a disaster.[6] In 1921, the board selected William Alexander (W. A.) Hamlett of Austin, Texas, as its first superintendent of the Near East Mission. Educated at Baylor University, Hamlett had pastored several churches in Oklahoma and Texas prior to his appointment, including the First Baptist Church of Austin. He was a popular figure among Texas and Oklahoma Baptists, as well as one of the more prominent premillennialists in the SBC.[7] Although not experienced in foreign missions, he had worked as a transport secretary for the military in France during World War I. He had also previously traveled to Palestine. That 1910 trip, taken with his ten-year-old son, had resulted in the 1911 travelogue *Travels of a Father and Son* (examined in part in chapter 1), which had been publicized and reviewed favorably in state Baptist periodicals. Although the work shared a number of characteristics with other Baptist travel writings from the era, it was distinguished by its acerbic tone and frequent attempts at wit. More significant to Hamlett's later role as a missionary, though, was that the work displayed an aggressive imperialist mentality toward the Near East. An example can be found amid an extended paean to imperial Britain, written while Hamlett reflected on his time in the British protectorate of Egypt: "'twere better to resort to the sword that an entrance might be effected for the Bible and for education, than never have them enter at all. Suppose a few thousand natives are slain in their fanatical opposition to the coming of modern ideas. Better kill them and enlighten the remaining millions than have a nation lie in darkness forever." "The enlightened portion of the earth," he added, "is responsible for the benighted."[8]

A future leader within the revived Ku Klux Klan, Hamlett was a firm believer in Anglo-Saxon superiority and had a low opinion of Arabs, be they Muslim or Christian. At different points in his travelogue, he described Arab men as childlike, monkey-like, murderous, menacing, fanatical, and most often, indolent.[9] He described Arab Jericho as filled with "dirty degenerates and as many howling dogs."[10] Hamlett found local religion empty at best and pernicious at worst, describing the religion of Jerusalem as "a religion of sadness, whether Mohammedan, Jewish or the local interpretation of Christianity."[11] His thoughts on Jews mixed racial anti-Semitism, traditional Christian anti-Judaism, and premillennial expectations of future glory through conversion and restoration. The "Jew is sad," Hamlett wrote, "for in his hardness of heart he still continues to kick against the pricks, and carries on the fruitless rebellion against his brother, Jesus of Nazareth, which is only prolonging a warfare of inevitable defeat."[12] While many Southern Baptists of the era shared Hamlett's prejudices toward the region, few shared this gleeful disdain for its inhabitants.

If, in the postcolonial era, Western missionaries have often been criticized as aggressive, insensitive, racist, imperial destroyers of native cultures —something Hamlett, in all honesty, aspired to be—Hamlett's experience as a missionary perhaps shows the degree to which a measure of tact, sensitivity, and genuine interest in the well-being of others was required to be a success. Hamlett, with all his certainties, was a total disaster as a missionary. The pastor and his family arrived in Palestine in September 1921. They were accompanied by Louis Hanna, who was returning from Texas. Along the way, Hamlett had stopped to visit E. C. Miller in New York and clearly imbibed the benefactor's vision for the mission. "I hope we shall soon be reinforced by many American helpers," Hamlett wrote to the *Baptist Standard* en route to Palestine, "for we shall need schools and hospitals to make entrance for and augment our evangelistic endeavors."[13] He also hoped to develop a Bible school at Jerusalem.

Hamlett lasted slightly over a month. No one was more upset than Mosa, who had hoped that Hamlett's arrival would herald a long-desired expansion of the work. "It seems that Bro. Hamlett's coming to this country is a blessings [*sic*]," Mosa had written to FMB corresponding secretary J. F. Love after his initial meeting with the missionary. He was particularly excited that Hamlett had "noticed our immediate need to the schools."[14] By the time that Love received Mosa's letter, however, Hamlett had already decided to leave Palestine in order to return to his pastorate in Austin. With his departure, the high expectations that he had cultivated among local Baptists and inquirers began to backfire on the mission. Mosa noted that local Baptists had "heard [Hamlett] talking and assuring them of having a fine church building, schools, & their buildings etc. & etc." When Hamlett bolted after making these promises, "they now began to doubt our promises and suspect our talks, even the enemies of the work got a very good chance to speak bad on us and you [the FMB]."[15]

Because religion was still a primary marker of social identity in the Middle East, conversion—especially conversion to a tiny minority sect—had profound social implications. Beyond religious conviction, it required a certain level of confidence in the missionary churches. Unsupported converts could easily become socially and even economically isolated. The reputation—the honor—of a church was thus important in winning and sustaining converts. When Hamlett made his flurry of promises and quickly departed, Baptist honor suffered, and the mission itself was threatened. Mosa understood this situation and worked quickly on the board to send another missionary to enlarge the work and "redeem our great Baptist name."[16] In April of the following year, Secretary Love wrote Mosa, "I do not doubt that you are embarrassed and discouraged in your work and I sympathize with you in this. The Foreign Mission Board in a like manner is embarrassed."[17]

Hamlett continued to harm the cause upon his return to the States, undertaking a justification tour of Texas churches in order to proclaim that mission work in Palestine was currently impossible.[18] He also published several frenzied articles in the *Baptist Standard* explaining away his failure. As Love expressed to Mosa, "These articles have added to our embarrassment and have caused many of our people to lose enthusiasm for the work in Palestine."[19] In February 1922, Hamlett noted that a state of war still existed between Britain and Turkey and claimed that recent protests in Egypt signaled trouble in Palestine: "The sons of Esau stand together, whether they are in Egypt, in Palestine, in Arabia, in trans-Jordania, in Syria, or in Mesopotamia. . . . Riots in Egypt mean a riotous frame of mind in Syria, or Palestine, or wherever that race lives in numbers."[20] He proceeded to describe the political deadlock in Palestine, claiming that "any new venture in that ravished land is not only insecure, but will also fail to obtain legalized protection to title to any property that might be purchased under the present hazard."[21] In addition to political instability and the tenuity of property rights, the obstinate mental attitudes of Jews and Arabs precluded "constructive mission work, as no such work can flourish among people whose minds are at war and whose bodies engage in daily riots somewhere in the country."[22]

Hamlett's flurry of writings and speeches slowed by spring 1922. His last major thrust was an apologia published in the March 2 *Baptist Standard* that cited a litany of authorities who apparently agreed with him that mission work was impossible: "our Consul advised me against undertaking what would transpire to be a very unwise thing, as well as an inevitable failure because of its impossibility. He knew. So did the British army officers know. So does anyone know who will go over there and study the situation intensely, instead of hurrying through the country with some tourist party."[23] The board and Mosa, it seems, did not "know." As soon as Hamlett had returned stateside in October 1921, they had begun planning to replace him.[24] In one of their first reports from Palestine, the new missionaries noted, "The people have been somewhat discouraged as the years have gone by without any enlargement of the work, especially after Dr. Hamlett returned to America." The small Baptist community had even "had to undergo quite a bit of ridicule" from other Christians in Nazareth.[25] Hamlett himself moved on. Sometime between late 1921 and late 1922, he joined the revived Ku Klux Klan, which had been recently introduced into Austin, left his Austin pastorate, and began working full-time for the so-called Invisible Empire as an itinerant promoter and organizer.[26] By December 1924, he had risen in the ranks to become editor of the Klan's official national periodical, the *Kourier Magazine*. This role was likely a better fit for him.

Establishment: 1923–1929

Appointed in 1922, Hamlett's replacements were not able to arrive until the following spring. The board chose two couples to serve as its next missionaries to Palestine: Fred and Ruth Pearson and James Washington (J. Wash) and Mattie Watts. Nearly thirty years old at the time of his appointment,

Fred Pearson had grown up on a farm in Moulton, Alabama, and attended Howard College in Birmingham, Alabama (later known as Samford University). After serving briefly as a chaplain in the army, he had moved on to SBTS in Louisville, where he earned a ThM in 1921. It was while working toward his ThD that Pearson, who had initially desired to be a missionary in China, answered the board's call to go to Palestine. His wife, Ruth Casey Pearson, had been born in Albertville, Alabama, and had also attended Howard College. After graduating in 1921, she worked briefly as a high school teacher before becoming engaged to Fred and agreeing to go to Palestine. Mattie Watts (born Mattie Leida Reid) had been born and raised in Spartanburg, South Carolina, and had attended Limestone College in Gaffney. After a brief tenure as a teacher, she had entered the Woman's Missionary Union Training School in Louisville, where she decided that she wanted to be a foreign missionary. In 1920, she married J. Wash Watts of Laurens, South Carolina. Like Fred Pearson, Watts had been raised on a farm and educated at Baptist schools. He had earned a degree from Furman University in Greenville, South Carolina, in 1913 before moving on to seminary in Louisville, where he earned his ThM. Like Pearson, he had originally hoped to be assigned to China but had been persuaded by the board's call for new missionaries to the Holy Land.[27] The two couples arrived on March 17, 1923.[28]

Their first step was to survey the field and offer recommendations to the board, which hoped to begin work in Jerusalem in accordance with E. C. Miller's wishes. Upon arriving in the holy city, though, J. Wash Watts and Fred Pearson encountered resistance from the established missions. "The belief that we are not needed seems to be unanimous," wrote Watts to J. F. Love.[29] The established local missionaries did not think that the Baptists should open work in Jerusalem unless they were planning a large operation: another boutique mission built "to satisfy a sentimental desire" would not be worthwhile.[30] After spending the summer surveying the area and consulting with Shukri Mosa, Watts and Pearson recommended to the board that they open work in Haifa the following year and try to develop a school. With the British interested in developing Haifa into a major regional port and oil depot, it seemed to be the city of the future.[31] Sentimental desires, though, were powerful forces. Secretary Love wrote to Watts that the board had to "look upon the Palestine work both from the viewpoint of the work itself on the field and the interest in the work at home. . . . Jerusalem is so fixed in the minds of Americans as the center and head of things Palestinian that it has a tremendous appeal for those who are asked to support a program for Palestine." The Haifa plan, he noted, "will not strongly appeal to the Board."[32] The missionaries' formal recommendation to the board straddled the fence, calling for aggressive work in the north, especially Haifa, aimed at Muslims and so-called nominal Christians, and a more cautious approach in Jerusalem aimed at Jews.[33] However, these plans were waylaid in 1923 when Ruth Pearson suffered a "complete nervous collapse" that required the Pearsons to return home and left the Wattses in charge.[34]

J. Wash Watts served as mission head until 1928. While the Haifa plan had to be abandoned, the Wattses did open a new work in Jerusalem, where J. Wash was able to organize a small congregation and secure property in the western part of the city, where new Jewish developments were concentrated. With gifts from supporters in the States, the mission constructed a house with a large meeting room there in 1927. That same year, of course, Mosa's Nazareth mission completed the Bottoms Memorial Baptist Church. Besides this expansion, Watts's tenure was characterized by the support and autonomy that he gave to the native workers. At a time when the FMB worried that Mosa was exceeding his subordinate position, and Secretary Ray was questioning Mosa's abilities as a leader, Watts lent his support to the Arab Baptist.[35] Watts frequently seconded Mosa's long-standing requests—for a church building, for a school, for an education for his son—and bought into Mosa's plan to use Nazareth as a base from which to reach out to smaller Galilean villages. When Mosa's nephew Louis Hanna arrived in the field, Watts gave him relatively free rein in working among Arabs in Jerusalem. He took a similarly light-handed approach in overseeing efforts among Jews. In summer 1923, soon before the Pearsons departed, Watts and Pearson had recruited a converted Jew named Chaim Volkovitch (later Negby) to work in Jerusalem. Watts allowed Volkovitch to function independently, an approach that sometimes left him vulnerable to the convert's exaggerations. By early 1924, Volkovitch claimed that he had interested two hundred young Jews in the work and that he might be able to win famed scholar Joseph Klausner to Christ.[36] In truth, Volkovitch had ten solid inquirers. Watts was hopeful that this ten might still be the vanguard of a Zionist Hebrew Christian movement "in which a Jew could be a nationalist and have religious freedom at the same time."[37] However, Volkovitch's efforts struggled after he was exposed among Jerusalem Jews as a missionary.[38]

Even if the Volkovitch experiment failed to fire a Hebrew Christian revolution, it spoke to the exciting possibilities that both Fred Pearson and J. Wash Watts saw in Palestine, particularly in Zionism. Pearson's initial 1923 report to the FMB quoted some nigh-millenarian remarks from British high commissioner for Palestine Herbert Samuel expressing hope that "some mysterious chemistry" between England, Palestine, and the Jewish people "will yet create a spiritual product of supreme value to mankind."[39] Pearson believed that Baptists might have a role in creating this "product." "Shall we strive . . . to introduce our element . . . Christianity as we understand it—into the High Commissioner's formula?" he asked the board. "Shall we give ourselves into His hands for bringing of His people into His will for them, the evolving of a 'spiritual product of supreme value to mankind'?"[40] Part of Pearson's enthusiasm was rooted in the missionaries' hope that the Zionist emphasis on national identity would allay Jewish resistance to conversion. Even before entering the field, Watts had argued in a 1922 article that religion, culture, and language no longer bound Jews together. Rather, the success of Zionism showed that Jews were increasingly bound by the concept of holy nationhood, wherein "even the Christian element may have its part."[41] Here, he was referring not to "those Christian Jews who have been assimilated by Gentile bodies" but rather to converted Jews who could "remain a part of the nation." Indeed, Watts believed that there were already significant numbers of secret Jewish believers willing to join the Jewish national movement "if the others will permit them." Anticipating his later hopes for Volkovitch, Watts asserted that such a Hebrew Christian vanguard could help bring "religious liberty"—most especially openness to Christianity—to a possible Jewish state.[42]

Watts was not only excited by the potential missionary implications of Zionism but animated by an Orientalist enthusiasm for its success in bringing a familiar vision of modernity to the land of the Bible. In a 1926 article, he described Zionist progress in developing the Jezreel Valley: "As I looked down upon [the valley], I observed that many places in it are today laying aside the drab garments they have worn through many centuries, great stretches of time that seem to have brought no change at all. And I remembered this question that comes to me rather often now, 'Will the Jews remain and succeed?' Then I found myself wishing that every questioner could look upon that scene with me."[43] Watts was impressed—even inspired—by the Yishuv. "In many places there are remarkable things to see," he wrote, "Jerusalem is spreading out over its surrounding hills. Tel Aviv is spoken of as the Los Angeles of the East."[44] Haifa was soon to become a great harbor. Rail lines were expanding. Swamps were being drained. Watts, though, went further than simply praising Zionist initiative, exclaiming: "How inextricably these scenes are intertwined in Israel's history!" He described a daydream in which great scenes of biblical history unfolded before him on the landscape. "And I dreamed of chapters in the history of Israel yet to be wrought amid these scenes."[45] For Watts, Zionism paired the familiarity of the biblical with the excitement of the modern—and the hope of the missionary.

Though Mattie Watts shared many of her husband's hopes for Zionism, she offered a different perspective on Palestine, one rooted in her office as a woman missionary. Baptists understood women missionaries to have a particular role concerned with women and children, an extension of domestic ideology into the mission field. Their actual work—and consequently, their writings on the mission—often evidenced the division of spheres between married men and women. Mattie's published articles focused on matters of family and children. To a much greater extent than her husband, she evinced a religious concern for the impact that the arrival of modernity might have on Palestine's Arab children. In a 1927 article, she criticized the mandatory government school system as being corrosive to Christian faith. For certain, she believed that the "children of the Bedouins—wild fierce and dirty" were "grossly ignorant" and in need of education, and that the British had "brought new life" through their government schools.[46] However, she worried that the secularity of those schools was causing the formerly ignorant children of the bedouin to question biblical truth. "A new era is beginning among these care-free, ignorant, and fanatical Arabs," she wrote. "Let us pray and work that their last state may not be worse than their first!"[47] Only a Christian modernity—perhaps a Baptist modernity—could give the Holy Land what it truly needed.

While the Wattses continued to write and speak on Palestine over the next several years, they returned to the United States in 1928.[48] The mission had never exactly flourished during J. Wash's tenure as superintendent, but the Wattses were nonetheless successful in putting it on stable footing and securing the FMB's investment in the region. In this success, they were certainly aided by a relative political calm that would be shattered shortly after their departure. The Wattses had bolstered the Mosas' work in Nazareth and the Galilee. They had put down Baptist stakes in Jerusalem. There is perhaps no better testament to the importance of their contribution than the work's very survival amid their 1928 departure and the unexpected death of Shukri Mosa soon thereafter. Though the Nazareth and Jerusalem stations struggled, they persisted. The board remained committed. From then on, it was clear that the Baptists would remain in the Holy Land.

Expansion: 1929–1941

In the years that followed the death of Mosa and the departure of the Wattses, the conflict between the Zionists and Arabs was becoming increasingly insoluble, increasingly violent, and increasingly difficult to work in.[49] The Wailing Wall riots of 1929 had brought unprecedented violence to the conflict, their destabilizing effects only compounded by the dithering of the mandatory government. Amid dramatic upticks in Jewish immigration brought on by growing persecution of Jews in Europe, Palestine's Arabs grew increasingly resistant to both British rule and Zionist expansion. Arabs initiated mass protests against British policies; the mandate police viciously broke them up with lethal force. Some turned to violent resistance, inspired by the message of Haifa imam Sheikh Izz ad-Din al-Qassam, who was killed in a shoot-out with police in 1935. Most consequentially, of course, Arabs' mounting frustrations culminated in a 1936 general strike that soon escalated into outright revolt loosely coordinated by the newly formed Arab Higher Committee, led by Grand Mufti Hajj Amin al-Husseini. After attempts at conciliation failed, the British crushed the revolt with force, placing the country under de facto martial law, enacting curfews and travel restrictions, outlawing the Arab Higher Committee and arresting or deporting its leaders (the grand mufti fled into exile), and eventually dispatching over twenty thousand troops to the country.[50] Peaking in 1938, the revolt only ended the following year, ultimately leaving much of Palestine, especially its Arab communities, in devastation and disarray.

Still, amid these events, the mission persisted and even grew, as a new crop of missionaries expanded into Haifa and reinforced the Nazareth and Jerusalem stations. One year before leaving the field, J. Wash Watts had hired a former Christian and Missionary Alliance worker named Elsie Clor to help oversee the Jerusalem mission. An experienced missionary, Clor had worked in Jewish missions and settlement houses in Chicago and Boston before relocating to Jerusalem with the alliance. By the time that Watts hired her in 1927, she had already spent five years running a girls' club in the city. She was aided by Eunice Fenderson, a nurse who helped her through a bout with influenza in 1929 before joining the mission as a volunteer in 1931. By 1933, the two had helped stabilize the small Baptist congregation (thirteen members), opened a Sunday school, and inaugurated the first Jerusalem Daily Vacation Bible School, which had about seventy students in attendance. Using contributions from the Lottie Moon Offering of the Woman's Missionary Union, Clor had overseen the purchase of a building for the new Good Will Center and the installation of a playground. Within the next two years, the Jerusalem station had a church building and was hosting Sabbath and Sunday schools, boys' and girls' clubs, women's meetings, mid-week services, Bible studies, English classes, and the growing Vacation Bible School (which by then had about 130 attendees).[51] In 1936, Clor reported that the station served about 250 people per week.[52] Though the mission did serve Arabs, Armenians, and more, its location in predominantly Jewish West Jerusalem, combined with Clor and Fenderson's special interest in Jews, resulted in a focus on the city's Jewish population.

Clor herself was a convert from Judaism who identified as a Hebrew

Christian, maintaining a Jewish ethnic or national identity within her adopted faith (this fact perhaps explains Watts's interest in her). She was actively involved in the Hebrew Christian Alliance of America (HCAA) and the International Hebrew Christian Alliance and believed Jews had a particular national role within Christianity. Clor was also a premillennial dispensationalist who believed that the return of Jews to Palestine and their eventual conversion were important precursors to Christ's second coming. Fenderson held similar beliefs, having been educated at Moody Bible Institute. Both missionaries understood Zionism and the mission within this premillennial context. In a 1934 circular letter, Clor noted that she had "received many letters this year asking whether we see any visible changes here in the Holy Land, especially in Jerusalem." "Yes!" she responded, noting, "The morning is beginning to dawn for 'bringing back the King,' and the deserts are beginning to 'blossom as the rose.'" These changes spoke to Christ's "soon appearing and confirm[ed] his blessed Word all the more."[53] Clor published similarly eschatological comments in *Home and Foreign Fields*.[54]

As the conflict between Jews and the British versus Arabs broke out into open warfare during the 1936–39 Arab revolt, Clor and Fenderson detected early tremors of the final clash between God and Satan. In a 1939 circular, the pair wrote, "It seems to us that the stage is gradually being set for the final conflict which is to take place in this land according to His Word." Clor and Fenderson viewed the local struggles of the mission as part of this conflict. "Not only in this outer conflict is Satan's power evident," they wrote, "but we are facing a very serious crisis right here in Jerusalem of the cunning attacks of the enemy." However, the two were not discouraged, instead proclaiming, "the King will soon appear."[55] While Clor and Fenderson's dispensationalist interpretations of the Bible drew their interest to Zionism's prophetic implications, they cannot be said to have supported the movement. Political questions were immaterial to the two, who believed that they were witnessing the world slip into an apocalyptic chaos that necessarily preceded Christ's return. Though both evinced a special concern for Jews and excitement at their return to Palestine, that concern and excitement almost wholly found expression in evangelism. Indeed, it was Jewish resistance to the mission that caused the two to lament "the cunning attacks of the enemy"—Satan.

Roswell and Doreen Hosford Owens arrived in 1929 to replace the Wattses, bouncing between Jerusalem and Nazareth before opening a new work in Haifa in 1932. They were joined by Kate Ellen Gruver later in the decade. Roswell, from Omaha, Georgia, had come slowly to missions, spending years as a pharmacist before earning a ThM from SBTS in 1927 and entering the field. Doreen, on the other hand, had been born to missionaries in Rosario, Argentina. The pair's first brief stop in Palestine had been Nazareth, where they had noticed the increasing migration of Arabs to the growing port city of Haifa and decided to follow the crowd (Louis and Velora Hanna took over the Nazareth station). For two years they held meetings "in any home that was opened to us"—typically single-room apartments on the outskirts of town where they "had flies and smells and illnesses to contend with." By summer 1934, the new station had grown enough to justify the purchase of a storefront chapel hall downtown that the missionaries called their "upper room."[56] Though the Haifa mission never grew to the size of the Nazareth or Jerusalem stations, the Owenses were successful in building a small congregation (twelve members by 1937) and training two young Arab pastors—Elias Saleeby and Augustine Shirrish—who joined the mission staff part-time.[57] Saleeby had come to Haifa from a new mission at Beirut. Shirrish, who was from a Melkite family, had been a longtime member of the Nazareth congregation before following the Owenses to Haifa, where he worked as a cobbler in addition to serving at the mission.[58]

Doreen had a larger voice as spokesperson for the field than did Roswell. Her two pedagogical children's novellas—*The Camel Bell* and *The Village Oven*—were published in 1937 as part of the FMB's graded mission study series (examined in chapter 6). Roswell contributed to the series as well, though only through a single chapter of the 1937 compilation *Questing in Galilee*. Beyond that, the Owenses contributed a mere handful of articles to Baptist periodicals. Because of their work, the writings primarily focused on Arabs. Doreen's novellas emphasized the power of the gospel to reshape Arab family life and overcome native superstition, especially the superstitions of local Christians. Both of her stories were based on the real-life family of Augustine Shirrish. Roswell's writings focused on the native Christians of Nazareth and Haifa. A 1932 article described the "open hostility" of the Greek Orthodox to Baptist efforts in Nazareth. Baptist inquirers were being threatened with disownment by their families. Orthodox hecklers were interrupting services. Some had even thrown stones at the mission's Arab workers. Owens's experiences paired well with his Protestant disdain for the "ignorant, corrupt, sensual" Greek Orthodox clergy, which he felt was "about as far from New Testament Christianity as any one could be."[59]

If the Baptist mission was proving divisive among Christians, Roswell Owens nonetheless believed that it could help bring Arabs, Jews, and the British together in peace. In 1932, he shared a photograph of two British soldiers posing with two Jewish converts, all of whom had been recently baptized at the Nazareth church. "The membership of the Nazareth Church until the coming of these recent converts was wholly Arabic," he noted, adding, "if we may judge from visible appearances, all were quite happy to welcome these of other races into their fellowship." The acceptance of Jews and Britons into the church was evidence that "Christ does break down partitions, override boundaries, and makes us see that down underneath the skin of all men are alike in so far as great eternal needs are concerned."[60] This theme was echoed in Doreen's *The Village Oven*, which depicted the gospel bringing together a Jewish boy and an Arab boy at Christmas. However, as the political situation in Palestine deteriorated during the Arab revolt, and the missionaries labored under the stresses of military curfews and frequent terror, Doreen came to question the hopes that she and her husband had earlier expressed. "Has the day of our opportunity passed us by?" she wondered as the death toll climbed in 1938. "To see the need and yet to feel one's weakness and inability to meet it adequately—it is just about enough to break one's heart."[61] Despite the near heartbreak, the Owenses remained in Haifa for three more years, only leaving when the outbreak of World War II forced the FMB to recall its workers.

H. Leo Eddleman arrived in the field in February 1936, his tenure roughly coinciding with the Arab revolt. A graduate of SBTS and the son of a Mississippi minister, Eddleman was only twenty-three when he joined the work at Jerusalem. One year into his appointment, he returned to the South to marry Sarah Fox, who had grown up in Arkansas and Kentucky before attending Meredith College in Raleigh, North Carolina, and the Woman's Missionary Union Training School. The two came to Palestine as a couple in late 1937. Leo was originally brought on to lead the Jerusalem mission and serve as the growing church's pastor; however the plan fell apart after repeated clashes with Clor.[62] While Eddleman agreed to serve as the Jerusalem pastor on Sundays, he refused to be stationed in the city, preferring instead to open work in Tel Aviv. Even as the Eddlemans made their home on the coast and excitedly proclaimed their status as the only Christian missionaries in an all-Jewish city, though, the station never succeeded. The main cause was simply bad timing. Soon after the Eddlemans moved to Tel Aviv, both the Owenses and Hannas went on furlough. Because of the recent expansion of the Nazareth work, Leo had to run the day school while also serving as the pastor of the Jerusalem church, all while weathering the effects of the Arab revolt. Hailed as the most linguistically gifted of the SBC's missionaries (he taught himself both Hebrew and Arabic during the tight curfew restrictions brought on by the revolt), Eddleman was never able to put down stakes in any one locale.

Still, Eddleman became an important voice for the mission and the region within the SBC, even after returning to the States. Like other Baptists, he drew Orientalist contrasts between Zionist modernity and Arab backwardness. He attributed the formerly poor state of Palestinian land to rapacious Turkish taxation and Arab laziness, while celebrating the Zionists for having "converted great stretches of arid lowlands into veritable gardens."[63] A premillennialist like his nemesis, Clor, Eddleman professed belief in the "Zionism of the Old Testament"—the expectation that Jews would "return to Palestine, some day be a nation again, and look upon him who they have rejected for 2,000 years."[64] He also admired the "progressiveness and tenacious spirit" of the Zionists, even claiming to take inspiration for his own work from their devotion and courage in the face of growing Arab violence. However, Eddleman's faith in Old Testament Zionism could only be reconciled with Zionism as it existed if Jews accepted Christ. He lamented of the halutzim, "these brave souls whose courage inspires us to deeper loyalty to our greater cause, are often without any correct ideas as to the place and purpose of Christ in history, to say nothing of their hearts."[65] While celebrating Zionist achievements, he nonetheless warned that the Bible "tells us that a great part of what is achieved in Palestine by the Jews before they accept Jesus Christ will be destroyed."[66]

Like Watts and Pearson before him, Eddleman had come to Palestine hopeful that the Zionist movement would open Jews up to evangelism, believing that "there is something strategic about approaching the Jew with the Gospel now."[67] His high hopes, though, soon turned to frustration, particularly because the Jews that he encountered in the Yishuv viewed Zionism and Christianity as utterly incompatible and understood Eddleman's evangelistic appeals as "an attack on their effort to establish their national home."[68] "They suspect us of wanting them to forsake their nation," he protested, "when we want them to become believers in Christ." Such Jews failed to realize that "a man can be Jewish by blood and Christian by faith."[69] Because of this failure, Eddleman believed that their attitude toward the gospel "was not that of a people willing to accept the truth when it is found."[70] Zionism, which Eddleman had hoped would provide an opening for the gospel, was instead proving itself to be a stumbling block.

Wars: 1941–1949

In summer 1941, as war spread throughout Europe and the Middle East, the Southern Baptist missionaries then remaining in Palestine—the Owenses and Gruver—were advised to leave.[71] By December, the three had returned stateside, joining Clor, Fenderson, the Hannas, and the Eddlemans, all of whom had returned earlier on furlough. Only Gruver and Fenderson later returned to the field. Clor, who had battled illness throughout her time in Palestine, died in 1944. The Hannas returned to Texas. While Eddleman remained an important spokesperson for the region over the next several decades, he never returned to Palestine as a missionary, instead continuing his education at SBTS before serving as president of New Orleans Baptist Theological Seminary and, later, Criswell Bible College in Dallas.

During World War II, Kate Gruver joined Eddleman as a spokesperson for the field in the Baptist press. Like Eddleman, Gruver believed that the Zionists' successes were the fulfillment of prophecy and celebrated their role in modernizing the region. She went beyond him, however, in tying the movement to the deepening Jewish refugee crisis. "Tortured, persecuted, deprived of home and life in other countries," Jews—as she wrote in 1940—were "finding new life, new incentive, new hope in the land of their fathers."[72] Even as Gruver saw hope in Zionism, though, she found a dark hopelessness in Judaism. In one article, she used her recollections of a blackout to segue into a discussion of the sorry state of religion in Palestine, asserting that Orthodox Jews had "shut from the eyes of their souls the Light of lights."[73] As dark as she found Jewish shades of error, Gruver found Islam darker still. The same article described a short-term mission school that the missionaries had conducted in Jaffa among Muslim girls. On the last day of the school, Gruver had watched the girls don the dresses and veils that they wore in public. The physical transformation, to her, had spiritual echoes: "Changed in an instant from laughing, lovable girls into dark, sinister-looking figures, they were going back into homes and surroundings dominated by sin and evil. Those black shrouded figures seemed so terribly symbolic of the blackout of hope and light within the Mohammedan religion—a religion whose evil and degrading teachings obliterate all faith in and desire for a purer, happier way of spiritual and temporal living, and which leads its manhood into vile and sinful lives, its womanhood into a bondage of servitude to man's lowest desires."[74] During her forced wartime furlough, Gruver sought to expand her knowledge of Islam by taking classes at Harvard, an experience that only increased her zeal for evangelism.[75]

While Gruver studied stateside, native workers and missionary allies attempted to fill the gaps left by the Baptist exodus. The FMB's 1942 annual report listed some of the accommodations.[76] A Russian Baptist refugee named Martin Doveley and a Jewish convert named Andrew Salyer tended to the Jerusalem church. Leola Davison, a non–Southern Baptist employee of the evangelical Nile Press, supervised the Good Will Center. The Nazareth work struggled as the interim pastor, Rev. Saleeby, was forced to return to his home in Beirut after contracting tuberculosis. These measures were stopgaps at best. Really, it was only the efforts of local Baptists that kept the Nazareth and Jerusalem stations alive as they withered during the war. The Haifa work effectively disappeared. In 1944, though, Gruver returned to the field. Over the next two years, six more missionaries joined her.

None would be more important than Robert L. Lindsey. Born in Norman, Oklahoma, Lindsey had spent parts of 1938 and 1939 as a student at Hebrew University in Jerusalem, where he learned modern Hebrew and worked for the Baptist mission. While in Jerusalem he had lived with a Hebrew Christian couple, through whom he "met face to face with that bitter problem of how to be a Christian in faith and a Jew in culture and nationality and yet be accepted by the Jewish community."[77] Lindsey had also spent some time at Kibbutz Dafna in the far north, where he had shared the gospel with a handful of kibbutzniks.[78] That same year he had returned to the States to continue his studies, knowing with clear conviction that he wanted to return. During the war, he studied at both Princeton and SBTS. In 1945, he returned to Jerusalem as an FMB missionary. He remained there for the next four decades.

Under Lindsey's leadership, the missionaries set about rebuilding Baptist life in Palestine. The Jerusalem church, which had atrophied during the war, was reorganized with Lindsey as its pastor. It had only nine members, but it soon grew.[79] The Nazareth station, which had likewise deteriorated, suffered an initial setback with the unexpected death of new missionary and pastor James Henry Hagood.[80] The American government's support for Zionism had also temporarily harmed the mission once "news of the President's denominational affiliations leaked out."[81] However, the mission nonetheless revived. Lindsey and local Baptist Jameel Hesson helped maintain the church, while Gruver and Hagood's widow, Julia, proceeded with plans to open the George W. Truett Home for Orphans. It took in six abandoned children in its first year. Elsewhere, Lindsey proved creative in expanding the mission's reach. In 1946, he loaned mission funds for the creation of what was intended to be a type of Baptist kibbutz at Petach Tikvah (it was later purchased by the mission itself). One of the repeated concerns of Baptist missionaries to Jews in the region had been that Jewish converts to Christianity were effectively frozen out of Jewish society and, thus, frozen out of the economy. The purpose of the cooperative was "to provide for Jews who accept Christ a home in which those concerned will learn to labor with their hands and support themselves while growing into a fellowship of believing Christians."[82] The following year, the Lindseys opened a youth hostel at the Jerusalem station. In concert with this reorganization, revival, and expansion, Lindsey called a conference of Near East missionaries, including representatives from Syria and Lebanon, to discuss moving the churches toward increased autonomy and decreased dependence on the FMB.[83] This call was part of a larger FMB effort to transition its more developed fields to native autonomy, wherein locals would take the lead in expanding and cultivating support for their churches.[84] In 1947, the churches at Nazareth, Jerusalem, Kfarmichky, and Beirut voted to form the Near East Baptist Convention.[85] Efforts at consolidating local control, though, soon took a backseat as war came once again to the Holy Land.[86]

On November 29, 1947, the United Nations voted to partition Palestine. Lindsey, located in predominantly Jewish West Jerusalem, watched as Jews poured into the streets to celebrate the vote with singing and dancing. He spotted amid the crowd a neighbor who had fled the Holocaust in coming to Palestine: "'Here,' [the neighbor] said, pouring a tiny glass of something stronger than missionaries are in the habit of drinking, 'Take this. It is healthy for today. *Ach, adon*, Lindsey, it is all because of the Americans. All because of your President. I really cannot believe it is true.'"[87] These exhilarating events were quickly followed by war. Having just united into the Near East Baptist Convention, the missionaries found themselves split by moving battle lines. They tried at first to weather the conflict. Lindsey opened the hostel to Jewish refugees from East Jerusalem, at one point housing twenty-six.[88] As fighting intensified, however, the missionaries began to evacuate. Lindsey became trapped outside the country after escorting a new worker to Cairo and was forced to wait out the war in the States.[89] A Jewish family, the Schreckingers, looked after the Lindseys' house, which was damaged by shelling, and the hostel, which continued to house about twenty Jewish refugees.[90] Of the missionaries, only Elisabeth Lee, a nurse who worked at the Truett home and the Scottish mission hospital in Nazareth, remained behind during the worst of the fighting. It was only a matter of months, however, before Gruver was able to return to Nazareth, accompanied by three new missionaries: Iola McClellan, Anna Cowan, and Mabel Summers. Before hostilities had ceased, they reopened the day school and established a kitchen for children, which served five hundred youths daily.[91] Once Israel and Transjordan reached an armistice, putting a de facto border through the middle of Jerusalem, Lindsey returned to reopen work in the city. All the established Baptist stations found themselves within the boundaries of the new Israel.[92] As Lindsey wrote in 1948, "We do not yet know fully what a Jewish State will mean to our work."[93]

The Meaning of Statehood: Two Missionary Perspectives

Even though he had left Palestine in 1939, Eddleman continued to speak for the field in the Baptist press, publishing several articles in the *Commis-*

sion throughout the 1940s that signaled an evolving perspective on the Holy Land. In winter 1941–42, he published a three-part series that reflected the emphases he had developed in the late 1930s, including his understanding of the Zionist movement as a fulfillment of biblical prophecy.[94] Though Eddleman never fully retreated from this prophetic perspective, his sense that the fulfillment of prophecy was ongoing or imminent waned. The politics of the Arab-Zionist conflict itself, which had gnawed at the margins of his earlier writings, chewed their way to the center. In a 1945 article, he sought to explain the conflict's origins and the reasons behind both Arab and Jewish violence, focusing on both parties' responses to the divergent promises made by Britain during and after World War I. Though Eddleman continued to contrast Zionist modernity with Arab primitiveness—noting half-admiringly that Arabs "sustain a culture some aspects of which revert to Abraham's day"—he did argue that Arabs were modernizing through the influence of the West.[95] In another contrast to his earlier writings, Eddleman deliberately sought to stake out a position as an impartial party to the political conflict. Citing his missionary experience in Tel Aviv, Nazareth, and Jerusalem, he noted, "we had the all-Jewish, the all-Arab, and the mixed environment in which to observe and study trends." "The result," he added, "is that we, as individuals, have absolutely no preference on the matter." Baptists, rather, had "something far greater than Pan-Arabism to offer the Arabs, and something far superior to a national homeland to offer the Jews."[96] He meant, of course, the gospel.

Eddleman's public drift toward political ambivalence masked a private drift toward a heated anti-Zionism. In December 1949—one and a half years after President Harry Truman recognized the newly formed State of Israel—he penned a letter to the president warning against supporting the Israelis. Citing his experiences in Palestine, Eddleman pointed out that the Zionists were predominantly Eastern European, with their "customs, politics, outlook, and other characteristics bear[ing] the spirit and imprint of Eastern Europe."[97] He added, in capitals, "In a crisis between Russia and the United States there is little, if any, doubt which direction their natural sympathies would fall." Further, American support for Israel was undermining the United States' standing among the Arab states. Ultimately, Eddleman found the Zionists to be untrustworthy allies who masked their true intentions to conquer larger swaths of Arab lands: "If there is one thing I feel certain about it is that the political ambitions of our Hebrew friends in the Near East envision more large areas of Arab territory under their dominion and that there is so much foolhardiness and fanaticism growing out of their combination of nationalism, racialism, and religion (such as Shintoism and Nazism) THAT THIS WILL BE A MAJOR SOURCE OF GRIEF AND BLOODSHED FOR DECADES TO COME."[98] The Israelis were treading the same destructive path that the Japanese and even the Nazis had recently trod. Unstated—but clear—is that Eddleman increasingly understood the new state as an enemy.

Despite this typographically loud letter, though, Eddleman largely kept quiet. His outright anti-Zionism does not seem to have made it into Baptist periodicals. Nonetheless, his case offers insights into how premillennialism, evangelism, and equal measures of Cold War realpolitik, prejudice, and paranoia could interact—even within a single mind—in shaping perspectives toward the Jewish state. Though Eddleman's journey was far from inevitable, each shuffling step betrayed a certain logic. As a young missionary in the late 1930s, Eddleman had been swept up in prophetic and evangelistic enthusiasm, believing that the Zionist movement might herald a new willingness among Jews to hear the gospel message, that Zionism and the Southern Baptist mission could be complementary forces reshaping Jewish existence and even the world. Eddleman was frustrated, then, when Jews rebuffed his message of salvation *in the name of* Zionism. Though he argued in 1938 that Zionism and Christianity were not in opposition, his experiences seem to have convinced him otherwise. By 1945, he was presenting the gospel as an alternative to Zionism, not as a complement. Between 1942 and 1945, too, he largely retreated from a prophetic understanding of events in Palestine. His second tenure at SBTS may have been responsible for this. Two leading anti-Zionists in the SBC, W. O. Carver and J. McKee Adams, were professors there at the time. Both understood the conflict on completely secular terms. Having grown to see Zionism as a rival to the gospel, and having come to see the conflict in an increasingly secular light, Eddleman wrote to Truman that Zionists were an enemy masquerading as a friend and that national interests must guide the United States' approach.

Lindsey's journey had much in common with Eddleman's, though he ended up in a vastly different place. The two had worked together briefly during Lindsey's first stay in Palestine and shared an evangelistic affinity for Jews. Both—at least at their first meeting—viewed the Zionist movement as somehow a fulfillment of biblical prophecy and as a personal inspiration. They also shared an academic interest and aptitude for foreign language. Eddleman and Lindsey had even studied at two of the same institutions—Hebrew University while in Palestine and, after returning stateside, SBTS. In a circular letter from his first time in Palestine, Lindsey recalled spending a few days with the Eddlemans in Nazareth. He and Leo had shared "some long talks" on the difficulty of reaching Arabs with the gospel. Clearly having imbibed some of Eddleman's explicitly Orientalist frustrations, Lindsey remarked to his readers, "One who does not know the Oriental mind cannot begin to realize what difficult ground it makes for gospel seed. These people have a vastly different background from the westerner."[99]

Lindsey, though, greeted such challenges with a smile. The type of frustrations that turned Eddleman against Zionism stirred Lindsey to creativity rather than resentment. As Eddleman had in the late 1930s, Lindsey hoped that Zionism's emphasis on Jewish nationhood would open Jews to Christ. "The forms of the old faith are not holding them," he wrote in 1944, "and with the Zionistic national definition of the Jews has come the real possibility that a strong Jewish loyalty to Christ may develop."[100] His hopes persisted, even intensified, as the establishment of a Jewish state became imminent. In 1948 he wrote, "many of us feel that with Jews being able at last to define themselves in national terms only, the religious connotation will be more and more dropped."[101] In Lindsey's eyes, statehood would reify Jewish nationhood and further displace religious definitions of Jewishness. Besides hoping that Zionism and the Baptist mission could be complementary, though, Lindsey actively worked to incorporate Zionist models into the Baptist mission. The most obvious example of this drive was the development of the Baptist Village at Petach Tikva, which Lindsey envisioned as a Baptist kibbutz (it later developed into more of a youth camp and retreat center). Lindsey's first stay in Palestine had left him truly inspired by the kibbutzniks. "These young people gripped my imagination," he wrote in the *Commission*. "Here was a modern group of people living with 'all things in common.'"[102] Lindsey's chosen quote from Acts 4:32 was no idle biblical reference but a deliberate allusion to the early Christian community. For Lindsey, something about the Zionist spirit clearly hailed back to the days of Pentecost, something he tried to harness in creating the Baptist Village.

Like Eddleman, Lindsey depicted Arabs as in the process of modernizing. To be sure, he felt that they lagged behind the Zionists. In 1944 he recalled an earlier drive through the Sharon Plain, where he "passed innumerable little Arab and Jewish villages and, like all Westerners, could not help contrasting the manifest poverty and squalor of the first with the cleanliness of the latter." Lindsey was careful to note, though, that there "are many different kinds of Jews and Arabs."[103] There were illiterate farmers who lived in villages "where life is probably not greatly different from life many hundreds of years ago," but there was also an educated urban elite. Thanks to British influence, the education system was advancing, and Western missionaries and the Zionists had improved the health system. The "fanaticism" that characterized Islam was likewise being ameliorated by the "increasing acceptance of Western ideals." Despite feeling that Arabs were somehow "behind," Lindsey nonetheless believed them to be "a highly intelligent people."[104]

Lindsey did not explicitly take sides on the political questions raised between 1947 and 1949 in the way that Eddleman did,[105] although he clearly identified with the Zionist movement's triumph. Besides holding a prophetic—if shifting—interpretation of Zionism's significance, Lindsey primarily worked among Jews and lived in the Jewish section of Jerusalem.[106] He was also personally inspired by the movement. When the results of the November 1947 partition vote reached West Jerusalem, Lindsey joined his Jewish neighbors to celebrate in the streets. In October 1949, months after the armistice agreements had been reached, he again seemed to take on the feelings of his West Jerusalem neighbors as he described the aftermath of the war: "Two things impress us about the people of Jerusalem as we see them today. One is the oft-repeated word 'miracle.' I have talked with no one who does not say that it is really a miracle that the Jews of Jerusalem were saved. We now know how little ammunition, guns and material were actually in the hands of Israelis. The great majority of people seem to believe deeply that only God saved them. . . . The other impressive thing is the spirit of the people. With victory has come a new stability, a new hope for the future. . . . The struggle has strengthened morale."[107] Lindsey tied this new sense of stability, hope, and confidence to the mission, arguing that it had already helped bring a greater tolerance for both missionaries and converts. "The attitude seems to be," he wrote two months later, "Look, we now have a country of our own. We Jews always have liked friends and wanted to extend hospitality and now we can do it." "I have seen no instance of maltreatment or disrespect of a Jewish Christian as yet," Lindsey added. "Today he is an Israeli whatever his faith."[108] At least, that was the hope of the missionary.[109]

Conclusion

Southern Baptist missionaries encountered Palestine as a mission field and wrote about it as a mission field. Even their loftiest impressions of the region were inextricable from the on-the-ground work of the mission. W. A. Hamlett's depictions of Palestine as a land of chaos and intractable conflict derived from his need to explain away his disastrous month as mission superintendent. Doreen Hosford Owens's novellas highlighting the transformative power of the gospel on Arab family life grew from her real experiences with the family of Augustine Shirrish. The hopes that Fred Pearson, J. Wash Watts, Robert L. Lindsey, and even H. Leo Eddleman expressed for Zionism proceeded from their recognition that the Zionist revolution in Jewish life might herald an unprecedented opportunity to reach Jews with the gospel. While the missionaries often provided wide pictures of the land, the peoples, and even the politics of Palestine, those images were captured through the sometimes-narrow lenses of their missionary priorities and experiences.

Even as they framed missionaries' understanding of the region, though, those priorities and experiences—and the impressions that they produced—were themselves framed by the same Orientalist mindset of Baptists in the States. In part, this commonality was simply a result of the missionaries sharing many of the same assumptions as other Southern Baptists writing about the region. This should not be surprising. Most missionaries came from the same background—white, Southern, educated, involved in denominational life, committed to evangelism—as, for instance, the Southern Baptist travelers examined in chapter 2. And, like the Arab Baptists examined in chapter 3, the missionaries had an incentive to speak and write about Palestine in terms that would appeal to the stateside Baptists who funded their work—to highlight both the seeming potential evoked by the Holy Land's transformation and the persisting need of Arabs and Jews for Christ. While the missionaries' engagement with local populations could serve to challenge Orientalist assumptions, in many ways their missionary task reinforced these views. That task was rooted, of course, in the presumption that locals needed what Southern Baptists could offer. To the missionaries, the Arabs needed Christ and needed modernity. The Jews, heralds of the modern in the Holy Land, needed Christ. Both, in that sense, needed the mission.

5
Jew

As noted in chapter 1, Southern Baptists had expressed periodic interest in evangelizing Jews since the very birth of the convention.[1] However, it was not until May 1921 that the Home Mission Board (HMB) hired its first missionary for the task. On the recommendation of the SBTS professor of missions W. O. Carver, the HMB chose as field secretary of its newly created Jewish Department "a most excellent and consecrated young man" named Jacob Gartenhaus.[2] Gartenhaus was an ideal hire. Himself a convert, the young missionary had been raised in a traditional Jewish home in Galicia and had immigrated to New York in 1913, where he was soon led to Christianity by his older brother, Zev, and by the missionaries of the Williamsburg Mission to the Jews. He had trained at three of the day's leading institutions of Jewish evangelism—the Williamsburg Mission in Brooklyn, the Chicago Hebrew Mission (CHM), and the Moody Bible Institute—and had connections to the HCAA, an organization of Jewish converts geared toward evangelism. While working for the CHM's Extension Service, Gartenhaus had completed his education at SBTS in Louisville, Kentucky. There, his ability to rally fellow seminarians around evangelizing Louisville's Jews had drawn the attention of Carver and the HMB.

Not only was Gartenhaus the Southern Baptist Convention's first missionary to the Jews, but for the next twenty-eight years he was effectively its only missionary to southern Jewry.[3] This position presented him with a unique challenge. The South's Jews, though somewhat numerous in cities like Louisville and Saint Louis, were dispersed across the region in far smaller concentrations than were found in the northern industrial centers. The methods that Gartenhaus had learned in the northern missions, which focused on developing neighborhood mission centers, were "neither practicable nor desirable" in the South.[4] Instead, Gartenhaus developed a congregational approach that sought to make local churches the locus of Jewish evangelism and make Baptist laypeople his field workers. For this project to work, he needed to convince local congregations that Jewish evangelism was necessary and effective, and to train them for the task. Gartenhaus's mission to the Jews thus became, in effect, a mission to Southern Baptists.

As the previous chapter has shown, missionaries often provided crucial channels through which Southern Baptists encountered other faiths and peoples. Gartenhaus's congregational approach to Jewish evangelism only intensified this aspect of his mission. Throughout a tenure that roughly coincided with the British mandate over Palestine, Gartenhaus became Southern Baptists' leading spokesperson on issues relating to Jews and Judaism, including Zionism and the Palestine question. Because of this role, he has garnered some scholarly attention as a representative of Southern Baptist attitudes toward Jews.[5] However, existing studies overlook the fact that, in practice and purpose, Gartenhaus was less a spokesman *for* Southern Baptists than a spokesman *to* them. More specifically, they overlook the extent to which Gartenhaus spent his twenty-eight years with the SBC working to spread a distinctly Hebrew Christian understanding of Jewishness throughout the South—a prophetic and national understanding that guided the convert missionary to become an ardent supporter of Zionism, even to the point of proclaiming, "To oppose it is to oppose God's plan."[6]

Gartenhaus's Background and Training

Both for Gartenhaus's singular role within the SBC and for his particular worldview, his approach to Zionism and Palestine would be intertwined with his personal background and identity to a much greater extent than for other figures in this study. Gartenhaus was a convert from Judaism who never left his Jewish identity behind; much of his life was devoted to wrestling with the question of what it meant to be both a Jew and a Christian. He had converted in 1916, shortly after immigrating to the United States, and soon dedicated himself to the evangelization of his people. He began his training at the Williamsburg Mission, which had helped guide him to conversion, but he quickly moved on to the CHM that same year. He worked with the CHM from 1916 until 1921, serving at its local mission centers while attending Moody Bible Institute and continuing as a member of the mission's Extension Service after leaving for Louisville in 1919.

These institutions were part of a growing movement among Protestant churches to evangelize Jews, a movement that was expanding and taking hold in the urban centers of the United States. While American Protestants had sought the conversion of Jews since the early republic, the number of mission societies exploded near the turn of the twentieth century.[7] Three circumstances fueled the explosion. The first was demographic. Between 1881 and 1924 nearly two and a half million Eastern European Jews, including Gartenhaus, migrated to the United States, most to escape increasing persecution and find economic opportunity. Almost overnight, densely packed Jewish neighborhoods had sprouted in northern cities like New York and Chicago. Neighborhood missions had followed. In 1887, pioneering Christian Zionist William Blackstone had helped found the CHM, which offered a variety of services to potential converts and needy immigrants in hopes of drawing them to the gospel.[8] During Gartenhaus's time at the Chicago mission, its three locations hosted an industrial school, boys' and girls' clubs, and sewing classes, among other activities. Convert Leopold Cohn, an immigrant from Hungary, founded the Williamsburg Mission (later the American Board of Missions to the Jews, then Chosen People Ministries) in 1894.[9] Begun as a storefront operation, by the 1910s it had grown into a community center much like the CHM. The mission included an auditorium, a medical clinic, and a reading room where it offered English lessons, citizenship classes, and evening education for working adults, all in attempt to increase Jewish exposure to the gospel.

The second circumstance encouraging the growth of missions was the spread of premillennial dispensationalism among American Protestants.[10] Dispensationalists believed that God had maintained a covenantal relationship with the Jewish people and understood the restoration of Jews to Palestine and the conversion of a Jewish remnant as key features of their eschatological schema, something that helped inspire Christian interest not only in Zionism but also in Jewish missions. Among the early American popularizers of the system was Blackstone, who had penned the first edition of his popular dispensationalist explainer *Jesus Is Coming* in 1878. All three institutions that were so crucial in shaping Gartenhaus's understanding of his new faith—the Williamsburg Mission, the CHM, and Moody Bible Institute—promoted dispensationalist interpretations of the Bible and Jewish history that would color Gartenhaus's thinking for decades.

The third circumstance was the development of an American Hebrew Christian movement.[11] Hebrew Christians were Jewish converts to Christianity who sought to maintain varying degrees of Jewish ethnic or national distinctiveness within their new faith. The movement had its origins in nineteenth-century Britain, where a string of fraternal convert and mission associations had maintained fitful existences since at least 1813. By 1903, Hebrew Christianity had spread to the American missions, resulting in the formation of the Hebrew Christian Alliance of America in 1915. While the HCAA did keep small numbers of missionaries on staff and publish periodicals, it primarily served as a meeting ground where converts worked to define the meaning of their corporate witness. Its members generally shared three main priorities—promoting Jewish evangelism, caring for converts within the church, and advocating on behalf of Jews—and tended to favor premillennial dispensationalism, which offered a biblical hermeneutic that affirmed their national distinctiveness. Gartenhaus likely became involved in the HCAA during his time with the CHM. There, he worked alongside several missionaries who became leaders in the movement, among them Jacob Peltz (later secretary of the HCAA), Elias Newman (later a member of the HCAA Executive Committee), and Aaron Kligerman (later president of the International Hebrew Christian Alliance).

Though brief, Gartenhaus's years in the northern missions and Moody Bible Institute were crucial in shaping both his identity as a convert and his approach as a missionary, training him in the techniques of Jewish evangelism, immersing him in its intellectual underpinnings, and binding him to the growing Hebrew Christian community. In the South, though, Gartenhaus would find that the circumstances shaping the movement to evangelize Jews in the North were essentially missing. Though he grew fond of noting that Saint Louis had twice as many Jews as Jerusalem, Saint Louis was the exception that proved the rule; there were far fewer Jews in the South and in far greater dispersion. The waves of Eastern European Jews that had come to the United States between 1881 and 1924 had remained predominantly concentrated in the North. The massive immigrant neighborhoods in which the Williamsburg Mission and the CHM operated simply had no southern analogue. Lacking such concentrated immigrant Jewish populations, the South lacked Jewish missions and, in turn, a Hebrew Christian community. Premillennial dispensationalism, which had gathered a respectable following in the North around the turn of the century, was not yet a widely held hermeneutical or eschatological system among Southern Baptists, particularly among the convention's leadership (see chapter 7). Gartenhaus was hired not because of a dispensationalist turn among Southern Baptist leaders.[12] Rather, his fortuitous appearance in Louisville had simply provided the HMB with an opportunity to act on Southern Baptists' long-standing but essentially passive interest in Jewish evangelism at a time of high enthusiasm for the expansion of mission work.

Gartenhaus's Mission

Over his twenty-eight years with the HMB, Gartenhaus brought the ideas and concerns guiding Jewish evangelism and Hebrew Christianity in the North to Southern Baptists. Before exploring these specific ideas and concerns, though, it is important to understand Gartenhaus's congregational approach, which sought in theory to make every local Baptist church a

Jewish mission center.[13] Developed in response to his southern circumstance, Gartenhaus's approach was unique among Hebrew Christian missionaries. He even presented a paper on the subject at the inaugural meeting of the International Hebrew Christian Alliance in 1925.[14] "Ours was a double task," he noted, "to win Israel for Christ and to awaken Christians to their responsibility."[15] In order to "awaken" Baptists, Gartenhaus had to convince local congregations of the need for Jewish evangelism and train them for it. Though based with the HMB in Atlanta, he spent the bulk of his time on the road giving guest sermons and clinics in churches or lecturing at associational meetings and conventions. He also composed scores of tracts, articles, and books aimed at Baptist audiences—and far fewer aimed at Jews.[16] The Southern Baptists' missionary to the Jews thus spent most of his time preaching to Baptists.

For almost three decades, Gartenhaus was a ubiquitous itinerant. In a 1966 article commemorating the anniversary of the missionary's conversion, Pastor Roy Mason claimed that Gartenhaus knew "more Baptist preachers and Baptist churches than anybody that I have ever met, for he has preached Christ and has pleaded for Jewish evangelism all over this nation."[17] Within seven years of his appointment, Gartenhaus had spoken to audiences in thirty-eight states, though mostly in the heart of SBC territory.[18] He kept an exhausting pace on his sermon tours, making multiple stops in multiple cities sometimes in the span of a single day. In 1925 he reported having given 203 sermons the previous year.[19] Ten years later, he reported giving 240.[20] On a 1938 trip to New Mexico under the sponsorship of the Woman's Missionary Union, he held nine clinics on Jewish evangelism in nine different cities across the state.[21] Gartenhaus also drummed up support for Jewish evangelism at statewide conferences and associational meetings throughout the South. In 1935, for example, he taught at six mission schools, spoke at thirty divisional and district meetings, and addressed three state conventions.[22] At one convention of the Florida Baptist Assembly, Gartenhaus served as a guest instructor for the assembly's mission study hour, giving a nine-day course titled "A Tale of Two Peoples—Gentile and Jew" to 162 attendees.[23]

Beginning in 1925, Gartenhaus also began implementing weekend mass meetings that were dubbed citywide or goodwill meetings, followed by a weeklong seminar on Jews and Jewish evangelism. As the names suggest, these meetings were typically hosted through the cooperation of several Baptist churches within a given city and were designed to cultivate positive relations between the community's Christians and Jews, all while preparing Baptist laypeople for evangelism. Though the weekday training sessions were held in churches, the mass meetings were often held in theaters or other large venues. As one South Carolina paper noted, "Few cities of the South have had auditoriums sufficiently large to accommodate the crowds which are attracted to these meetings."[24] The gatherings themselves were a mixture of entertainment, lecture, and dialogue in the form of question-and-answer sessions. Hebrew Christian violinist Alexander Kaminsky, who had served as a performer at the Russian imperial court, often received top billing in advertisements for the meetings. The bulk of the speakers were Gartenhaus's colleagues from the HCAA, convert missionaries like Aaron Kligerman, Henry Singer, and Elias Newman.[25] Most importantly, the mass meetings were followed by a week of evening training sessions and prayer meetings. Though the prayer services were open to the public, training sessions were reserved for Christian workers. Each night, Gartenhaus or his Hebrew Christian colleagues would speak on a different topic related to Jews, Judaism, or Jewish-Christian relations. Zionism was a favorite subject.[26]

Gartenhaus's efforts to cultivate interest in Jews and Jewish evangelism found their greatest reception among Southern Baptist women. Woman's Missionary Unions (WMUs), auxiliary societies devoted to supporting and promoting the SBC's missions, were especially important (see chapter 6). By the mid-1920s, the national WMU had begun supplementing Gartenhaus's literature budget.[27] In 1926, it provided a "self-denial offering" of $3,000 for his work, noting, "The hearts of the women have been moved, and their wills touched to action in the extension of their evangelistic efforts to the Jews, through . . . Jacob Gartenhaus."[28] Local WMUs were also crucial in supporting Gartenhaus's mission. They often sponsored his visits and helped fund and organize his citywide meetings.[29] By the mid-1930s, the missionary had begun actively cultivating Friends of Israel societies among local unions. In 1937, the national WMU reported that 383 local societies were involved in some way with Jewish work.[30]

Of course, the missionary Gartenhaus's primary goal was the conversion of Jews. While he sought to delegate personal evangelism to local churches and bodies like the WMU, Gartenhaus met with rabbis in various southern communities and visited Jewish homes. Several of his annual reports quantify his personal visits to Jews, which ranged in number from 750 to 1,500 depending on the year.[31] Despite his efforts, though, conversions were few and far between. In 1922 he reported three.[32] The following year, two.[33] In 1935 he reported ten, though the figure came by way of "indirect report."[34] For the most part Gartenhaus avoided quantifying conversions altogether, opting instead for anecdotes that tended toward the vague.[35] Unable to demonstrate hard progress, Gartenhaus sought to convey a sense of it, continuously asserting an ongoing sea change in Jewish attitudes toward

Christ. "There was a time when it was almost impossible to approach the Jews with the gospel," he reported in 1930, before adding that "vast changes have and are taking place."[36] He repeated similar lines year in and year out. If Gartenhaus was not successful in winning converts, though, his mission was by no means insignificant. Far more effective than his message to Jews was his message to Baptists.

Gartenhaus's Message

While the necessity of evangelizing Jews was at the heart of Gartenhaus's message, Zionism figured prominently in his work. His seminars included sessions on "Zionism or the Jew's Right to Palestine" and "Israel's Two-Fold Awakening."[37] His first full-length book with the SBC's Sunday School Board was *The Rebirth of a Nation*, a primer on Zionism. His public addresses and writings in SBC periodicals frequently engaged the topic. But while Gartenhaus often gave distinct focus to Zionism, his approach to the movement was inextricable from his broader approach to Jews and Judaism. After all, he was not simply interested in preaching support for the movement, but in conveying specific ideas about Jewish identity, history, and religion that were informed by his identity as a Hebrew Christian, his dispensationalist interpretation of the Bible, and his task as a missionary. Three interrelated elements of Gartenhaus's message had a particular bearing on his approach to Zionism: his understanding of Jewishness, his understanding of Judaism, and his understanding of the Jewish people's place in God's plan for history.

Gartenhaus presented Jews as a nation or a race, not simply a religious community.[38] This view evolved directly out of his Hebrew Christianity. Hebrew Christians, after all, did not see their conversion as immolating their Jewishness. The very name, Hebrew Christian, suggested as much. In the tract *Who Is He?*, Gartenhaus noted, "To many a Jew it would seem that we call him to become a Gentile. . . . We want nothing of the kind."[39] In another tract addressed to Jews, Gartenhaus referred to himself as "a member of your race, flesh of your flesh, blood of your blood."[40] Although such assertions served evangelistic ends, Hebrew Christians' claims to Jewishness were not solely a missionary tactic, as some scholars have argued.[41] They were, rather, both an expression of converts' self-identity and an attempt to answer the perennial question of what it meant to be a Jew.

That most Jews rejected his claim to Jewishness greatly rankled Gartenhaus. In 1932, he complained to the *American Israelite* that "a Jew may deny the God of Israel, disassociate himself entirely from his people, be an atheist, guilty of every imaginable crime and still be recognized among his people," while the convert to Christianity was considered "an enemy, a traitor, hated, shunned and abused."[42] Southern Baptists, for their part, largely accepted Gartenhaus's claim to Jewishness, with Baptist periodicals variously referring to him as a Christian Jew, a Christianized Austrian Jew, or a member of the chosen people concerned with the salvation of his "brethren according to the flesh" or "racial kinsmen."[43] In a 1931 editorial prompted by a discussion with Gartenhaus, F. M. McConnell of the Texas *Baptist Standard* argued that Jewish converts should retain their "national ties and ideals."[44] Helen Parker of Fort Lauderdale, Florida, expressed joy that converts like Gartenhaus "can always remain Jewish with their wonderful heritage, even after they become Christian."[45] Accepting Gartenhaus's Jewish identity, many Southern Baptists also believed that it granted him a special teaching authority. Ellis Fuller's foreword to Gartenhaus's *The Rebirth of a Nation*, for instance, declared the missionary to be "well prepared by birth, by training, and by Christian experience" to compose his work on Zionism.[46]

Even as Gartenhaus presented Jews as a distinct nation, frequently "away and aloof from the family of nations," and himself as a distinctly Jewish Christian, he argued that the Jewish people constituted an integral part of the South, the United States, and Western civilization.[47] He grew especially emphatic in this argument amid the escalating persecution of Jews in the 1930s and 1940s. In writings like *The Jew's Contribution to the South* and, most explicitly, *The Influence of the Jews upon Civilization*, Gartenhaus made his own entries in the genre of so-called contribution literature, designed to highlight the specific ways in which Jews (and Hebrew Christians) had contributed to the broader society and civilization as a whole.[48] Gartenhaus's depiction of those contributions evoked the concept of Judeo-Christian civilization (though he did not use the term) that would become so central to American self-definition in the wake of World War II and in the early years of the Cold War.[49] All the world, he insisted, "owes an everlasting debt of gratitude to this people for the Hebraic heritage."[50]

Gartenhaus tempered his celebration of the Hebraic heritage with harsh criticism of Judaism as a religion. Having grown up in a traditional Jewish home in Galicia, he was most aggressive in criticizing Orthodox Judaism and the rabbinate in particular. His 1934 *The Jew and Jesus* echoed centuries of anti-Jewish polemic in claiming that the rabbinate had "succeeded in blinding the eyes of a whole people" to Christ's true identity as the messiah.[51] Particularly irksome to Gartenhaus was the rabbinic emphasis on the Talmud; he was fond of claiming that "the Bible is a sealed book to Israel."[52] In *An Urgent Call on Behalf of the Jews of the South*, he claimed that Orthodox Jews thought of the Bible as "too holy to be handled and read by common people" and that the rabbis rightfully worried that reading it without guidance might "mislead [common people] to believe in Jesus." The "unbelieving Jew," on the other hand, "thinks of this book less than he thinks of a cheap novel."[53] Gartenhaus considered Reform Jews to be close to unbelievers, noting in *How to Win the Jews for Christ* that they have "practically no religion at all" and were primarily concerned with trying to "imitate [their Gentile] neighbors in speech, habits, and also in religious conduct."[54] Gartenhaus argued that Reform Judaism, beyond its spiritual shortcomings, failed to prevent anti-Semitism despite its assimilationism: "To the anti-Semites they were still despised Jews and had to be dealt with accordingly."[55]

Framing Gartenhaus's presentation of Jewishness and Judaism was his prophetic understanding of the Jews' role in history. "The Jew is the central figure of prophecy," he often asserted. "Without him it would be meaningless."[56] While Gartenhaus understood Jewishness in national or racial terms, he nonetheless held that Jews had a particular religious destiny. God had chosen the Jews and preserved them as a nation "for one purpose only—to proclaim Christ's name to the world."[57] In service of this national mission, God had inaugurated a covenantal relationship with the ancient Israelites. As a dispensationalist, Gartenhaus held that these ancient covenants still applied to contemporary Jews rather than to the church. Jews remained God's chosen people. Their promised land remained promised to them. Their national mission—"to proclaim Christ's name to the world"—remained their mission, even if they had hitherto failed in it.[58]

Gartenhaus preached that God remained constantly involved in Jewish history. His interpretation of that involvement, though, could be ambiguous. On the one hand, he frequently claimed that Jewish suffering was tragic and that God actively punished those who oppressed Jews. In the 1948 *What of the Jews?*, for example, he suggested that czarist Russia and Nazi Germany had brought on their own demise through their persecution of Jews. On the other hand, Gartenhaus also often depicted God as the author of Jewish suffering. Just following the aforementioned passage on czars and Nazis, Gartenhaus added, "Over and over again God has permitted Israel to suffer at the hands of her enemies, but His promise to Abraham remains intact."[59] At times, such assertions of God's role slipped into a functional view of Jewish suffering. In the 1930s, for example, Gartenhaus claimed that God was using Nazi Germany to weld the Jews into a nation.[60] The missionary never attempted to reconcile these seemingly contradictory views. If there is an explanation to be had, it likely lies in his dependence on the biblical model of national judgment and deliverance. Beyond that, depicting Jewish suffering as tragic and wrong allowed Gartenhaus to condemn persecution. Presenting Jewish suffering as necessary, on the other hand, allowed him to give meaning to that suffering.

Gartenhaus also urged that God was bringing history to its climax through the Jews. His dispensationalist reading of prophecy led him to anticipate a twofold national and religious awakening. This awakening, he believed and preached, was already happening in his day. "The eyes of the world today are focused upon the Jew," Gartenhaus claimed in an address that he gave repeatedly across the South in the 1920s. "Never were days so fraught with historical significance."[61] The Zionist movement—"one of the most remarkable of all fulfilled prophecies"—represented the prophesied national awakening. The Hebrew Christian movement—characterized as an "unparalleled spiritual revival"—represented the spiritual. In an article reflecting on the inaugural conference of the IHCA in 1925, Gartenhaus noted, "The student of Bible prophecies needs only to hear reports of the marvelous happenings in Palestine and of the inward awakening and acceptance of Christ in large numbers—then such prophecy at once becomes history."[62]

Gartenhaus's belief that God was guiding the Jews toward this twofold climax colored his approach to both the Holocaust and the Zionist movement. He was quite aware of increasing persecution of European Jews in the 1930s, having witnessed the early years of Hitler's reign firsthand as one of the SBC's delegates to the 1934 BWA meeting in Berlin. According to a letter from fellow convert and Southern Baptist Hyman Appelman (later a famed evangelist himself), the HMB had feared that Gartenhaus "might get in trouble, even physically, by raising some disputation concerning the Hitler-Jewish proposition."[63] Immediately after his return to Georgia, Gartenhaus began publicly speaking out against Nazism. In a 1934 address to the Central Baptist Church of Atlanta, he squarely asserted that "Jews are being killed every day in Germany." He also spoke of meeting in Europe several Baptist Hebrew Christians who "had been exiled from Germany not because they were Baptists but because Jewish blood coursed through their veins."[64] By taking an early stand against Hitler, Gartenhaus stood in stark contrast to Southern Baptists who were more sympathetic to the Nazi leader.[65] SBC president M. E. Dodd, who had also traveled to the BWA meeting in Berlin, praised the dictator and suggested that the rumors of Jewish persecution were misunderstood.[66] Ben Bridges, secretary-treasurer of the Arkansas Baptist State Convention, likewise argued in 1934 that Baptists "may wisely raise the question whether or not the Jew is really persecuted in Germany at all," while also offering that "Herr Hitler might be 99.44–100% right in his attitude toward the Jews in Germany."[67]

Gartenhaus continued to raise awareness as the crisis intensified. In a

1938 *Hebrew Christian Alliance Quarterly* article, he called attention to the growing Nazi persecutions and urged, "The plight of these hopeless millions is more than a Jewish problem."[68] That same year, he wrote to Una Roberts Lawrence, the HMB's mission study editor, "Our Baptist people have been lagging in their expressions of sympathy when other Christian bodies have publicly voiced theirs."[69] He also for the first time raised the issue of Nazi persecution in his annual report to the convention, declaring that Jews "are passing through one of the greatest tragedies in their history."[70] With the strikingly odd exception of the 1939 annual meeting, which was held only months after Kristallnacht, Gartenhaus continued to use his convention report to publicize the sufferings of Europe's Jews until the end of his SBC tenure. A 1940 Associated Press article on the HMB's annual meeting foregrounded Gartenhaus's efforts to raise awareness, noting especially his lament that "practically all doors are shut" to the growing numbers of Jewish refugees.[71] Concern over escalating anti-Semitism at home and abroad also led the missionary to publish the aforementioned *The Influence of the Jews upon Civilization* in 1943. As he wrote to Lawrence, "I know of nothing that will better check the wide-spread anti-semitism than the information contained in my book."[72] After the war, Gartenhaus worked to bring attention to the plight of the hundreds of thousands of displaced Jews who had fled or been pushed from Europe. In 1947, he again served as a delegate to the BWA, where he presented a resolution calling on Baptists to do "everything in their power to alleviate the sufferings of the Jews."[73] The resolution also called for continued evangelization.

Gartenhaus offered two seemingly contradictory explanations of the Holocaust that extended out of his ambiguous interpretations of Jewish history. On the one hand, he presented it as a product of human evil and "Satanic fury," something that Christians could and should take a stand against.[74] On the other, he presented it as God's doing. These attitudes can be seen side by side in the 1938 convention report. Gartenhaus devoted part of the report to reading and endorsing a manifesto signed by 170 Protestant pastors in the New York area who condemned anti-Semitism as a sin and pledged to strive "continuously for the realization of that brotherhood which humanity needs, democracy requires and Christianity demands."[75] In the same breath, though, he identified a teleological "ray of light" in the "dark sky." "Through all this suffering," he claimed, "the Lord is bringing his people closer to himself and they are beginning to wonder if after all their only hope does not lie in the Messiah, Jesus."[76] Shortly after Hitler's annexation of Austria, Gartenhaus contended to New Mexico Baptists that God was using Hitler as he had used the pharaoh before to weld the Jewish people into a nation and lead them to Palestine.[77] In 1944, in the depths of the war and amid growing knowledge of the Nazis' extermination campaign, Gartenhaus asked the convention, "In all their four thousand year history has God ever dealt with Israel as He is now dealing with them?"[78]

A similar mix of advocacy and prophetic speculation characterized Gartenhaus's approach to Zionism. In *The Rebirth of a Nation*, Gartenhaus offered an interpretation of both the prophetic and the practical implications of the movement. His second chapter, "God's Covenant with Israel," provided a dispensationalist reading of the Hebrew Bible, arguing that the biblical covenants between God and ancient Israel were still active and that Palestine rightfully belonged to the Jewish people.[79] Borrowing from the wording of the Balfour Declaration, Gartenhaus declared that the "covenant which God made with Abraham, which was renewed to Isaac, and again to Jacob, states definitely the geographical boundaries of this national home."[80] Gartenhaus also laid out his approach to prophecies concerning the restoration of the Jewish people to Palestine. He noted that there were generally three schools of interpretation: those that held that the restoration had occurred in the return from Babylon, those that spiritualized the promised restoration, and those that saw the restoration as an actual event to occur in the future.[81] In determining how best to interpret biblical prophecy, Gartenhaus urged, "The Scriptures are written in a plain and intelligible way and are to be applied to those to whom they were first addressed, where the obvious grammatical and literal meaning is capable of a plain and literal fulfillment and does not contradict other Scriptures."[82] He argued that reading the Bible in this way inevitably led to the belief that the restoration was yet to be fulfilled. Further, he claimed, "The prophecies concerning the return of Israel are being fulfilled before our very eyes."[83] The success of the Zionist movement was assured: "Zionism is going to win whether anybody likes it or not. . . . To oppose it is to oppose God's plan."[84]

Gartenhaus's interest in Zionism—and his presentation of it to Southern Baptists—involved more than just his interpretation of the Bible. As a convert, he was quite invested in many of the same ideological questions that animated different forms of Zionism. He himself had very specific ideas about Jewish identity and history, many of which—his emphasis on Jewish nationhood, his rejection of the rabbinate, and his belief that assimilation could never solve anti-Semitism—had analogues in mainstream Zionist thought. Gartenhaus also had a specific understanding of the movement itself that he presented to Southern Baptists: he saw Zionism as evolving out of two contexts. The first was Jews' centuries-long messianic hope for national restoration to Palestine, which Gartenhaus believed had bound the Jews as a nation throughout the centuries.[85] The second and more immediate was the failure of the Enlightenment and era of emancipation to solve the so-called Jewish problem. Within this latter context, Gartenhaus noted that European Jewish intellectuals like Theodor Herzl had come to understand that "the homelessness of the Jews was the cause for all their humiliation and suffering, and that only as they became politically a people with their own national home, would there be any home for them."[86] While Gartenhaus was aware of the different varieties of Zionism and presented them to his audiences, he himself favored mainstream, institutional political Zionism as embodied in the World Zionist Organization and Jewish Agency. In *The Rebirth of a Nation*, he included an extended quotation from Zionist statesman Chaim Weizmann explaining the aims of the movement as an effort to solve the Jewish problem: "The task of Zionism . . . is to create a home for the Jewish people in Palestine, to make it possible for large numbers of Jews to settle there and live under conditions in which they can produce a type of life corresponding to the character and ideals of the Jewish people."[87] Though Gartenhaus was certain that Zionism was not *the* answer to the Jewish problem—Christ, of course, was his answer—he presented the movement to Baptists as *an* answer.

Echoing—and perhaps informing—Baptist missionaries in Palestine, Gartenhaus expressed hope that the Zionist emphasis on nationhood might prepare the way for greater openness to Christ. More than Baptist missionaries Fred Pearson or J. Wash Watts, though, Gartenhaus tied this hope to Zionist ideological concepts, especially the idea of the New Jew. Every form of Zionist ideology in some way emphasized the negation of the Diaspora—the shedding of the mentalities and habits of life as a scattered minority—and the creation of a New Jew in the land of Israel. In a way, every type of Zionism had a type of New Jew.[88] Gartenhaus's Christian Zionism was no different. He noted that while Jews were coming to Palestine from all over, "after a few years they all become types of the New Jew."[89] These Jews were "not the slaves to tradition that their fathers were"; they "think freely in matters of religion and thank God for it." They were captive neither to the rabbis "with their perplexing sophistry and maze of ridiculous and impossible law and rituals" nor to the "cruel and bloodthirsty world." Gartenhaus saw this negation of the conditions of Diaspora, both internally and externally, as an opportunity for the Christian message: "They are being emptied of all mixed and man-made religions, in order to be more prepared to receive the full blessing of the faith in him, the Unchangeable."[90] After becoming New Jews, Gartenhaus believed, they would surely become Hebrew Christians.

Like other Baptists, Gartenhaus praised Zionism for bringing modernity to a blighted region. He repeatedly drew Orientalist contrasts between the innovation of the Zionist settlers and the perceived backwardness of the former Ottoman government and native Arabs. "It is difficult to believe that Palestine ever was a country 'flowing with milk and honey,'" he noted, "so disastrous to the fertility and welfare of the land has been the blighting hand of the Turk."[91] The Arab farmer "always took what he could from the soil, returning nothing to it."[92] The Zionist settlers, on the other hand, were using modern agronomy to make "two blades of grass grow where only one grew before."[93] Gartenhaus noted, too, the disparity in health and sanitation works—and the broad benefits that Jewish advancement was bringing: "Arab villages know as little of sanitation, hygiene, or health as they knew before the World War. But the Jews have begun to care for their health, and already they have achieved wonders."[94] The missionary filled *The Rebirth of a Nation* with statistics documenting the transformation that the Zionists had wrought, a product of both the Jewish national genius and the hand of God.[95]

Gartenhaus revisited the movement in detail in a chapter of his 1948 mission study manual *What of the Jews?* Looking back, he considered the movement a great success on Zionist terms, noting that "More than a half million victims of prejudice and intolerance have been enabled, without infringing on the rights of any other people or religious group, to remake their lives in dignity and self-reliance on their ancestral soil."[96] Not only had Zionism proven successful for Jews, but he claimed in Orientalist terms that it had become "a boon to the Arabs," who received "more employment, better sanitation and health, and more education, without which they would have remained in the uncivilized state in which they had lived for centuries."[97] Still, Gartenhaus recognized a growing crisis in the wake of the British white paper of 1939, which had enacted severe immigration restrictions on Jews (the manuscript for *What of the Jews?* must have been submitted in early 1947; it shows no knowledge of the United Nations' partition plan or Great Britain's impending withdrawal). He criticized the white paper on Zionist terms, arguing that it meant "the complete reversal of British policy toward the Jew in Palestine." Tying the issue of Jewish immigration to the Holocaust, Gartenhaus argued, "Unless THE WHITE PAPER is abolished, there is no hope left for the stricken and homeless Jews who may survive the greatest persecution in their history, and new rivers of Jewish blood may flow in Europe." He called on Jews and "their friends in the United States and in the rest of the world" to bring pressure "to keep the doors of Palestine open."[98] Gartenhaus paired this largely secular appraisal with a confirmation of the prophetic implications of the movement, concluding, "The Jew will have Palestine with or without the help of Britain or any other nation on the earth!"[99] By the time that *What of the Jews?* was published, Gartenhaus's prophecy had been confirmed. The State of Israel already existed.

Conclusion

Gartenhaus's tenure with the SBC ended shortly after the establishment of Israel. In his autobiography, written decades after the end of his tenure with the HMB, the missionary implied that his departure from denominational mission work in 1949 had been tied to his agitation over the lack of a strong Baptist stance on the Holocaust. He also suggested that his denominational superiors had long been antagonistic to his work and had "tried on several occasions to do away with the Department of Jewish Evangelism."[100] In truth, the HMB had increased its support of Gartenhaus's mission in the years leading up to his dismissal, attempting to enlarge the work through the hiring of a secretary and an additional field worker. Gartenhaus was fired in March 1949 not due to a change in the HMB's priorities but due to allegations of misconduct made by a newly hired field worker, Lucille McKinney.[101] It was the second time that Gartenhaus had faced such accusations.[102] Though McKinney retracted her allegations four years later, Gartenhaus was never brought back to the HMB.[103] He moved on quickly, serving as president of the HCAA until 1951 (he had begun in 1948, before his firing) and founding the International Board of Jewish Missions in Atlanta in 1949, which still operates to this day, though its headquarters were moved to Chattanooga in 1971.

For many Baptists in the crucial decades of the 1930s and 1940s, Gartenhaus was not just a missionary, nor even just a spokesman, but an embodiment of the boundary between their faith and Judaism.[104] As one colleague described him, the missionary represented both "the cultured Jew and the consecrated Christian."[105] Decades before Southern Baptists engaged in interfaith dialogue with Jewish leaders, Gartenhaus, in a sense, served as Baptists' representative of the Jewish perspective. He used that position to argue forcefully for Zionism at a time when it was far from a settled issue among Southern Baptists or even among southern Jews. In Gartenhaus's home base of Atlanta, for example, Jewish leaders were quite divided over the movement. Harry Epstein, rabbi of the Orthodox Ahavath Achim Synagogue, supported the movement, while David Marx, rabbi of the Reform Temple, helped found the anti-Zionist American Council for Judaism.[106] In that light, it is especially significant that the Jewish perspective that Southern Baptists were most consistently exposed to offered unquestioning support for Zionism. For nearly three decades, the Baptists' Jew traveled unceasingly throughout the South, teaching Southern Baptists that Jews were a holy nation, that this nation was an integral part of Baptists' own civilization, and that Zionism was bringing that civilization to Palestine—teaching, too, that God was behind it all, leading the Jewish people homeward and, ultimately, to Christ.

6
Auxiliaries

If the Southern Baptist Convention's missionaries provided crucial channels through which Southern Baptists encountered Palestine, it might be said that the Woman's Missionary Union was their corps of engineers. Founded as an auxiliary to the missionary efforts of the SBC in 1888, the national WMU and its thousands of affiliate societies were crucial in supporting domestic and foreign missionary efforts through fundraising and mission education.[1] Building on efforts that had originated in local societies, the convention-wide WMU had begun vigorously promoting systematic mission study in 1907. By 1918, 2,900 societies in fifteen states were conducting mission study courses using materials provided by the Home and Foreign Mission Boards (HMB and FMB, respectively).[2] Soon thereafter, the WMU began organizing graded courses for mission study students of different ages. The national WMU set the curricula, offering plans of study, lessons, book suggestions, and book reviews in its official journal, *Royal Service*. The WMU thus came to be among the most important pedagogical institutions in the SBC, providing hundreds of thousands of Baptists with trusted depictions of the world around them.

The structure of *Royal Service* reflected this pedagogical emphasis. Each issue featured program materials that provided the content for lessons. In issues that concerned specific mission fields, the program materials typically gave background information on the field—its history, its geography, its people, and so on—and described Southern Baptist work in it. The accompanying Program Plan specifically described how local WMU leaders should teach the material, suggesting skits and posters that would reinforce the message. Each issue also contained sections on how to implement these materials in group meetings like the Business Women's Circles (BWCs), as well as relevant book reviews and Bible studies. The lessons published in *Royal Service* were taught in thousands of affiliate societies across the South. The convention-wide WMU even enforced engagement with the magazine and other SBC publications. One of the criteria required of a local society to obtain an A-1 rating from the WMU was that it have "two denominational periodicals in at least one-half of the homes represented in the society."[3] In 1922, the WMU reported 573 A-1 societies. Almost seven thousand societies met four of the ten criteria.[4]

Royal Service was thus a crucial vehicle through which thousands of Southern Baptists encountered mission fields around the world, including Palestine. Thirteen issues of the magazine featured material related to the region during the Mandate era. In A-1 WMU societies (and probably in hundreds that did not merit the highest ranking), this focus in the magazine meant thirteen months of programming related to the Holy Land. These mission study materials are worth examining in two regards. The first is perhaps obvious: they represent a massive WMU effort to educate Southern Baptists (especially Southern Baptist women) on Palestine. The second is less so. *Royal Service*'s program editors not only presented Palestine to their readership, they also interpreted mission study materials produced by Southern Baptist missionaries. In this sense, the magazine's program materials give insights into how the editors interpreted and reconciled the diverse perspectives offered by Baptist missionaries, including a graded series of mission study books on Palestine that the FMB produced in 1936–37. By World War II, the magazine's program editors were presenting the region in a way that aggregated Orientalist distinctions between Jews and Arabs, prophetic interpretations of Zionist success, and expressions of political sympathy for Palestine's Arabs, all tied together by a message of missionary hope.

Palestine in *Royal Service* before the Graded Mission Study Series

Prior to the publication of the FMB's graded mission studies series in 1936–37, five *Royal Service* issues contained program materials dealing specifically with Palestine as a mission field. Two program editors were responsible for content during this time. Elizabeth Brower (Eliza, or often "Mrs. W. R.") Nimmo was program editor for the two issues published in the 1920s. By then, Nimmo had spent decades working on mission study literature, having served as either chairman or secretary of the WMU's literature department from 1892 to 1921.[5] Myrtle Robinson ("Mrs. C. D.") Creasman served as program editor from 1931 until 1948. A Tennessean for most of her life, Creasman had graduated from Virginia Intermont College in Bristol in 1907 and attended the Chicago Conservatory of Music in 1910. She had served as president of the Tennessee WMU in the 1920s and would go on to serve as vice president of the convention-wide WMU in the 1940s.[6]

Because the raison d'être of the WMU was to promote and support the

SBC's missions, the magazine's program materials tended to be structured around a sort of missionary formula: demonstrate the need of the mission field, describe ongoing efforts to meet that need, and give reasons for hope for the future. The concept of missionary need circumscribed every discussion of particular peoples or regions. Before the readers of *Royal Service* knew anything specific about Palestine, they understood that the region and the peoples therein were not whole without the gospel. They also understood that whatever problems the region and its peoples had could be solved or at least ameliorated by acceptance of that gospel, regardless of whether those problems were explicitly religious in nature.

Nearly every discussion of Palestine began with an exaltation of its status as the Holy Land, a place of past and future glory. It was the land "where earth's history centers and toward which prophecy points as the place of the fulfillment of God's plan for the world." The fulfillment of that plan was growing nearer, evidenced by the revitalization of the region. The Holy Land was, for the first time in centuries, in Christian hands. Jews were returning to the land in great numbers. The country was being developed. "Today the eyes of the world are on this land," Creasman wrote, "eagerly watching the events that are transpiring there, reading again the prophecies that must yet be fulfilled within her borders, wondering what new purpose God is working out on that favored spot of the globe."[7] If others wondered at God's purpose in Palestine, Creasman was certain that it involved the restoration of true biblical—or evangelical—Christianity to the land. "Palestine shall be redeemed," she wrote. "The Banner of the Cross shall wave in triumph over the Land of the Lord."[8]

The people also required redemption. In 1927, Nimmo described Jewish women as "Sarahs who are blind to the Messiah of Calvary" and Arab women as "Hagars who have never been told of Him."[9] Nimmo conflated Arabs and Muslims. She made no mention of Arab Christians in describing the Nazareth mission, despite the fact that they were its primary targets. Creasman was more attentive to the presence of Arab Christians in Palestine, considering them unsaved, nominal Christians. In a 1933 issue, she quoted missionary Doreen Hosford Owens in describing local Christian leaders as being "as fanatical as the Jew or Moslem and just about as ignorant as can be."[10] "In Jerusalem, and in all Judea today," Creasman added, "Jews and Arabs are alike sinful and needy—without the Word—waiting!" Echoing Baptist travelers, Creasman believed that the population of Palestine was "for the most part grossly ignorant, intolerant, superstitious, fanatical, poor, sinful and seemingly satisfied."[11] It was a population that desperately needed the civilizing influence of the gospel.

While Nimmo and Creasman highlighted the spiritual needs of Jews and Arabs alike, they evinced a special interest in Palestine's Jews. Both editors believed that Jews remained central to God's plan for history. In this, they were reinforced by Jacob Gartenhaus, whose materials were frequently used and cited in *Royal Service*. Nimmo understood the Zionist movement as "a literal fulfillment of prophecy" and lamented "that but a small part of these Zionists" realized as much. "Even the most worldly wise of the Jews," she argued, "who are desiring a national home for their people . . . are unconscious that this inborn hope is of God and that He it is who hath stirred their spirits in this enterprise." She urged her readers to remember that, despite the movement's seeming worldliness, "it is of the Lord."[12] Creasman believed much the same, arguing that prophecy pointed to the redemption of the land and to the restoration of the Jewish people to a glorious national life. In terms of the former, Creasman repeatedly highlighted Zionist development as the fulfillment of specific biblical promises. In terms of the latter, she argued that Jewish national restoration was not leading to "the Jewish nation that the Zionists dream of," but to a "Jewish Christian nation with Jesus Himself ruling on the throne of His father David."[13] Even if the Zionists' own dreams would not be fulfilled, Creasman believed that the movement was a necessary part of God's plan that Christians should support. "Christians," she wrote, "who love the Jews and who realize the great debt which they owe to this unfortunate race, rejoice in this movement toward the re-establishment of Jewish national life in this land which rightfully belongs to the house of Israel."[14] Most important to Creasman, though, was the restoration of true Christianity in Palestine: Baptists could "hasten" the "glorious consummation" of Palestine's redemption by supporting the FMB's work in the region. Whether or not Baptists met the call, Creasman was certain that true Christianity would eventually triumph in Palestine: "The Bible promises it: therefore, it will surely happen."[15]

The Graded Mission Study Series

In 1936 and 1937, the WMU's mission study materials were boosted by the FMB's publication of a series of mission study books on Palestine. It was one among six such series published by the board, which was seeking to educate the Baptist population on its various missions and mission fields. Each series focused on a particular field (Europe, China, Africa, South America, or Palestine) and was graded for different age groups (Sunbeams and Primaries, Juniors, Intermediates, Young People, or Adults).[16] The FMB published the series to be used in mission study courses put on by WMUs and church mission schools throughout the South. Several contained built-in lesson plans. The series marked the SBC's single largest denominational effort to educate the Baptist public on Palestine during the Mandate era.

With one crucial exception, all the Palestine works were written by current or former missionaries. While stationed at Haifa, Doreen Hosford Owens wrote two narrative works, *The Camel Bell* and *The Village Oven*, intended for Primaries and Juniors.[17] Both were short and filled with illustrations; *The Village Oven* included a lesson plan. Former missionary Mattie Watts collaborated with Velora Hanna (then at Nazareth), Roswell Owens (Haifa), and Everett Gill (the FMB's secretary for Europe, who had been part of the 1920 mission survey) in producing *Questing in Galilee*, a series of brief instructional biographies aimed at Intermediates and Young People.[18] Watts also penned *Palestinian Tapestries* for Young People and Adults.[19] The lone nonmissionary among the authors was J. McKee Adams, a Bible scholar and SBTS professor who had visited Palestine on several occasions and occasionally published articles on the topic.[20] His *The Heart of the Levant* was the longest (still a mere 163 pages) and most academic of the series, although it maintained an emphasis on readability and included a small number of photographs. These were primers, not weighty reads.

Series authors voiced many themes that would be familiar to readers of *Royal Service*. As the Holy Land, Palestine demanded special missionary attention. Adams wrote, "We owe it to Palestine to give back all that we have received and to give it with a sense of privilege."[21] Like Nimmo and Creasman, series authors celebrated the revival of the land. They also shared with the program editors of *Royal Service* a belief that the region remained part of God's plan for the future. "In times past God has manifested himself in marvelous ways in Jerusalem," wrote Watts. "In times to come, according to His promises, He will do so again."[22] A repeated goal of the authors of the series was to "develop an abiding interest in and a friendly feeling toward the peoples who live today in 'the Land of Our Lord.'"[23] These peoples included both Jews and Arabs. As with *Royal Service*, the series sought to cultivate this interest and friendly feeling so that they might be expressed through support for evangelism. Because of this objective, the authors' portraits of foreign peoples were designed to highlight their potential as converts. This objective called for a mixture of identification (emphasizing commonalities between Arabs or Jews and Baptists in the South) and differentiation (emphasizing the need for Arabs and Jews to turn to Christ).

Both Owens and Watts emphasized to their Southern Baptist readers that Arabs, too, were white. "The Arab people are white people," assured Owens in *The Camel Bell*. "When they are not sunburned, their skin is quite white."[24] Owens worked primarily among Arabs in Nazareth and Haifa and was particularly interested in getting Baptist children to identify with their Arab counterparts. The lesson plans in *The Village Oven* were designed to teach students "that the boys and girls are warm-hearted, like to play and are eager for adventure just as the boys and girls of America are," with the goal for the teacher being to lead the class "into a feeling of comradeship and friendly fellowship with the boys and girls of Nazareth."[25] Both of Owens's books featured narratives told from the perspective of Arab children. Owens even drew parallels between her recurring character Assad (based on the son of Augustine Shirrish, a trainee of the mission) and Jesus: "even though Jesus was a Jew and [Assad] was an Arab, they both knew what it meant to be boys in Palestine."[26]

The extent of Baptist identification with Arabs was limited by their potential as converts and Baptists' Orientalist understandings of Arab life and culture. Spiritual and cultural needs were frequently intertwined. Like other Baptists, the series authors saw Catholic and Orthodox Arabs as nominal Christians, depicting them as overly ritualistic, superstitious, and idolatrous with regard to sacred places and relics.[27] In *The Camel Bell*, protagonist Assad laments that "the people here in Nazareth surely forgot the things Jesus told them day by day in his carpenter's shop."[28] Series authors likewise echoed other Baptists in depicting Muslims as idolatrous, fanatical, and specifically and actively inimical to Christianity. The lone footnote in *The Camel Bell* incorrectly defined a "Mo-ham-me-dan" as "a person who, instead of believing in Jesus, prays to a man named Mo-ham-med who died hundreds of years ago."[29] Mattie Watts noted that two-thirds of Palestine's population were "Mohammedans, defying the most sacred principles of Christ."[30] Even so, her husband, J. Wash Watts, noted in *Palestinian Tapestries* that "One cannot go into these mosques, note their beauty, their quiet, their meditative atmosphere, and not realize that there is in the hearts of this people something fine to which we may appeal."[31]

Series authors also emphasized the superstition of both Christian and Muslim Arabs. Of particular interest was the evil eye, which frequently served as a representative superstition. Belief that envious or hateful glances had actual destructive power was relatively widespread among Arab Christians (as well as among Muslims and Middle Eastern Jews).[32] Baptist authors, particularly the missionaries, frequently positioned evangelical Christianity against the ritualistic measures that locals took against the eye. In *The Camel Bell*, the mother of a sick child believes that the eye caused her son's illness. She refuses to take him to a missionary doctor, instead dangling blue beads on his forehead. The child's sister reports, "Our grandmother taught us that these evil-eye beads will keep away the evil spells of those evil, blue eyes of the foreigners."[33] Here, Owens deliberately contrasted local ritual practice with evangelical Christianity, intertwined with modern medicine through the missionary doctor. Mattie Watts's descriptions of Arab culture in *Palestinian Tapestries* likewise emphasized the eye, noting that Arab parents often adorned their children with charms to combat its pernicious effects. Tying superstition to the perceived "filth" of Arab children—and thus spiritual deficiency to a lack of modern hygiene—Watts added, "To look admiringly at a child is a form of the 'Evil Eye,' and to prevent this from happening many lovely children are dressed in the oldest, the dirtiest, the most ragged clothes, and are allowed to run about filthy and unkempt."[34]

Baptists were particularly critical of Arab family life and gender roles. The overarching critique was that Arab men were excessively harsh to both women and children. Both of Owens's novellas for children contrasted a harsh "traditional" family with a loving convert family (as noted, the convert family was based on the real-life family of trainee Shirrish). In *The Village Oven*, Assad "noticed that his own father was more thoughtful and kind than the father of his little playmates next door."[35] In *The Camel Bell*, a girl from an Arab Christian family longs for the love and kindness that she sees in Assad's family life and begins to wonder whether the missionaries have a role in it: "As Ameeni stood watching her friends go down the trail, she wondered what made them so different from her family. A strange longing came into her heart. She wanted to learn the secret of their kind words and ways. They always seemed so happy together. . . . Ameeni wondered if their friendship with those blue-eyed foreigners, and their going down to the church had anything to do with that family's being so kind and different. She wished that her own family were like them."[36] Jameeli, Ameeni's brother, is also struck by the family's loving ways. He is puzzled when Assad's mother holds her son's hand and when she refers to her daughter as "dear." "That was something which Arabs never did," Owens noted through Jameeli.[37] Velora Hanna's biography of Munira Mosa in *Questing in Galilee* likewise emphasized that Munira's Protestant parents celebrated her birth, "contrary to the custom in the Holy Land, for people rejoice when sons are born, but rarely when a daughter is born."[38] Such passages evinced the missionaries' particular concern for the treatment of women in Palestinian Arab society. Hanna's biography of Mosa noted that Munira's "heart ached at the poverty, the ignorance, the neglected babyhood, and the abused womanhood surrounding her."[39] The cure for these entangled ills was conversion. Only Christ could make Arab men into loving husbands, and Arab women into sturdy wives and daughters.

Series authors described Jews as a wayward chosen people, defined by paths alternate to Christ. They cast Jewish religious or political movements as either intentional deviations from Christian truth or vain distractions from it. Still, like other Baptists, they found much to admire in the Zionists. Both Watts and Adams lauded Zionists' hard work and devotion in bringing modernity to Palestine—a contrast to their depictions of Arabs. "Space does not permit us," Watts noted, "to tell of the wonders that have been wrought in making this desolate land to 'blossom as the rose.'"[40] The Zionists were "stalwart, educated young people" who were ready to work in fulfilling their dream—"to drain swamps, to break rocks, to build highways, to earn a livelihood from this land, so long neglected."[41] Though Adams viewed the Zionist movement as politically problematic, he praised it for much the same reason as Watts. In addition to restoring the land and building up the country's industry, the Zionists had revived the Hebrew language and reawakened Jewish life and thought.[42] Adams particularly admired "the spirit of sacrifice, the heroic devotion to a most difficult undertaking, and the unfailing consecration of young and old to the reclaimed homeland of a wandering and dispersed people."[43] While both Watts and Adams praised the movement, they likewise made it clear that Zionism was no substitute for what Jews truly needed—Christ.[44]

The FMB published its graded mission series on Palestine just as revolt was breaking out among Palestinian Arabs against both Zionist settlement and British rule. The series also came as the British were releasing the report of the Peel Commission, which called for partition of the land.[45] While these developments did not make it into the series, the shape and stakes of the conflict were already clear. The authors did not avoid it. Even Owens, writing for children, wove the tensions between Arab and Jew into the plot of *The Village Oven*. The lesson plan included in the book called for teachers to impart "an unprejudiced idea of the friction between Mohammedans and Arabs, and Arabs and Jews in Palestine."[46] Watts opened *Palestinian Tapestries* by declaring, "A million children of Ishmael and of Esau are expressing in no uncertain terms their resentment at the presence of more than 400,000 sons of Jacob in Palestine."[47] *Questing in Galilee* proclaimed the comprehension of "the reasons for the prejudice and hatred existing between the Moslems, the Jews, and the nominal 'Christians' of the Catholic churches" to be an educational goal.[48] Adams devoted the entire second half of *The Heart of the Levant* to the conflict. On this topic, the series authors offered noticeably different takes.

Watts viewed the return of Jews to Palestine in prophetic terms, though she did not see the Zionist movement itself as divinely ordained: "Would that we might say of [the Zionists] that they are seeking God's will and reading His Book! But Zionism is a political, and not a religious movement. Nationalism, and not a spirit of consecration to a God-given task, leads them on."[49] Even so, the movement could serve God's purposes. The return of Jews to Palestine would set the stage for an ultimate missionary effort to bring Jews to Christ.[50] While belief that God may be behind the return of Jews to Palestine did not necessarily spell support for the creation of a Jewish state, it did mean—within the political context of the late 1930s—support for the Zionists against the Arabs (who sought to stop Jewish immigration) and the British (who as of 1939 sought to restrict it).

Adams, on the other hand, argued that in "any question regarding the future of Syria-Palestine, by every canon of justice and fair-play, the Arab is the man of first importance."[51] In *The Heart of the Levant*, Adams reiterated points that he had earlier made in travel writings (examined in chapter 2): that maximalist Zionist interpretations of the Balfour Declaration were the source of Arab-Jewish hostilities, and that Palestine's Arabs justifiably feared dispossession.[52] However, Adams also went beyond his earlier writings in arguing that Arabs were seeking not just to avoid dispossession but also to realize a dream of their own—the creation of a pan-Arab state. This quest was "the subject matter of old men's dreams and the visions of youth, the one aspect of Arab life and thought which claims support from all factions, sects and classes, and which transcends even religious differences between Moslem and Christian, uniting both in a powerful surge of nationalistic fervor—the rebirth of an Arab State!"[53] Arabs throughout the Levant were organizing around this dream, developing political societies, and working through colleges and universities. They were crafting a "new nationalism which intends to achieve the full expression of Arab independence, namely, the creation of a national independent government within the framework of a recognized and respected constitution."[54] For Adams, the only solution that could bring "even a semblance of peace" to Palestine would be the "explicit denial of and cessation from any political schemes of Zionism which seek ultimately a *Jewish state in Palestine* and the consequent *dispossession of the Arab*."[55] The easiest step in this direction was one that he had long sought: the removal of the word *national* from the Balfour formula. In calling for this change, Adams placed himself close to the British policy adopted in the later 1939 white paper, which effectively abandoned the promises of the Balfour Declaration by limiting Jewish immigration and land purchases.

Even as series authors disagreed on the Palestine question, all shared the conviction that Christ offered the only true way to settle the conflict. In Owens's *The Village Oven*, this truth was demonstrated through the relationship between Assad, a faithful Arab Baptist, and Jacob Levi, an unconverted Jew, in Haifa. The two meet when Assad finds Jacob injured in the street after being hit by a car. Assad takes Jacob to the hospital, repeatedly returning in the following days to check on his health. At first, Jacob is skeptical of Assad's intentions: "He had never felt like saying 'thank you' to an Arab before, and that same ugly feeling made him keep silent now." Jacob "had always hated the Arabs and had thought that all the Arabs hated him because he was a Jew."[56] However, Assad's gospel-inspired example wears him down. The novel ends with Jacob attending the mission's Christmas service with Assad, the birth of Christ bringing Arab and Jew together. Everett Gill, who penned the last chapter of *Questing in Galilee* for Intermediates, closed his chapter by proclaiming that only Christ's love "could bring peace and harmony to these peoples who must live side by side in the land of their heritage."[57] Adams echoed this sentiment for adult audiences, urging that conflict would continue "until Christ is brought again into the midst of their relations."[58] No Baptists—especially devoted members of the WMU—would have argued against this point.

Palestine in *Royal Service* after the Graded Mission Study Series

The publication of the graded mission study series brought a number of new resources to the WMU and Creasman, who remained *Royal Service*'s program editor through the end of the Mandate era. Eight *Royal Service* issues relevant to the region were published during that time. Three trends stand out in their program materials. First, Creasman's prophetic interpretations of the Jewish people's place in the world and the modernization of Palestine remained consistent with earlier program materials. Indeed, they were bolstered by new material from Gartenhaus, who published *The Rebirth of a Nation* at the same time as the FMB's series (there is probably no better evidence of Gartenhaus's continued influence than a 1947 group activity plan for Business Women's Circles that called for a group member to impersonate the missionary).[59] Second, Creasman provided increasing focus on ongoing events and political concerns, specifically regarding the Nazi persecutions in Europe, the refugee crisis, and the Palestine question itself. Third—and most striking—Creasman's writings reflected a growing sensitivity to Arab perspectives in the Arab-Zionist conflict, a sensitivity that was undoubtedly inspired by Adams's *The Heart of the Levant*.

Under Creasman, *Royal Service* continued to promote a prophetic understanding of the Zionist movement. More and more, though, the editor drew connections between the return of Jews to Palestine and the increasing persecutions in Europe. In 1937, she surveyed the tragic history of Jewish persecution while emphasizing the "need to realize that there is, in our own enlightened day, Jewish persecution almost as bad as that of any age."[60] Echoing Gartenhaus, Creasman tied this suffering to prophecy, exclaiming "How terrible are these Jewish persecutions of centuries' duration! How wonderfully do they fulfill the prophecy of the Jews' own Sacred Book!"[61] After the war, Creasman described millions of Jews "suffering beyond human endurance," turning "with longing hearts toward Palestine as a hoped-for refuge."[62] Always accompanying humanitarian and prophetic interest, though, was a sometimes callous missionary mindset. Creasman remarked that Jews' wartime sufferings were "making them realize that there is something wrong with their race and, seeking a solution to the problem, they are more willing to study the claims of Christianity than they have been in the past."[63] Gartenhaus had said much of the same.

As Creasman more overtly connected the situation in Europe to Palestine, she increasingly focused on the conflict that was wracking the latter. She organized the October 1938 program materials on the Near East around the subjects of Progress and Problems, twin themes that permeated her writings on the region for the next decade.[64] Throughout that time, Creasman continued to associate the progress of the region with Zionism.[65] However, it was not until a 1947 issue on "Jews and Arabians" that she explicitly compared Jews and Arabs in terms of progress. Creasman offered a mixed picture of Arabs that was clearly influenced by Baptist missionaries. On the one hand, she described Arabs as "naturally active, intelligent and courteous" and "noted for their hospitality."[66] On the other, she emphasized that most Arabs "are Mohammedans and heirs to the evils which go along with that false religion." "The women are degraded," she asserted, "and the people for the most part are ignorant and poverty-stricken."[67] Echoing portions of Gartenhaus's *The Rebirth of a Nation*, Creasman argued that part of the ongoing conflict was rooted in Arabs' envy of Zionist progress as the former sought to modernize, even though the "example and competition of Jewish colonies" were helping them achieve their goals.[68]

The problems identified in Creasman's 1938 program materials included the increasingly violent conflict between Jews and Arabs—and demonstrated the clear influence of Adams. After rehearsing her material on Zionism, Creasman noted that "there are other people who claim Palestine as their home" and "resent the Jews coming in as if the land belonged to them." Many Arabs had sold their land to Jews "before they realized what was happening" and now found themselves "in danger of being thrust out of what they consider their national home." Following Adams's emphasis on pan-Arabism from *The Heart of the Levant*, Creasman wrote that Arabs dreamed of "bringing together all the Arabians of the Near East" in a great Arab state. "So there they are," she wrote, "Jew and Arab, each with claims to the land dating back for many centuries and each with a dream of a national home on this sacred territory." These dual claims were the crux of the conflict, which Britain hoped to settle by dividing the land. Creasman was not optimistic about partition; Jews and Arabs alike wanted all of Palestine, so the plan was unlikely to succeed.[69]

After that 1938 issue, Creasman continued to foreground the conflict in her program materials. Even the 1940 issue titled "To the Jew First," which was focused specifically on Jewish evangelism, included a description of the Arab perspective in its program materials on Palestine—a sharp divergence from the pre-1937 issues. After noting that "we find ourselves wishing that Palestine could once more belong exclusively to the Jews," she wrote, "we must remember that the Arabs have lived in the land for many centuries and consider it their national home." Britain had made promises to Arabs and Jews alike.[70] Beyond pointing to those promises, Creasman wrote in 1944 that World War I had unleashed a new "spirit of nationalism," a "new enthusiasm for democracy," and an "atmosphere of progress" in the region. Through their unfulfilled promises, though, the Great Powers had failed to capitalize on these developments after the war. Creasman hoped that similar mistakes would not be repeated after the Second World War.[71]

Whatever Palestine's political fate would be, for Creasman and the WMU—as for the authors of the graded mission study series—Christ remained Palestine's only hope. "When the Jews receive their rejected Messiah, when the Arabs realize that full salvation can be found in the cross of Christ," Creasman wrote in 1938, "then will Jesus come again to Palestine bringing peace and good will to the peoples of this land."[72] She repeated much the same wish in every article or lesson dealing with the region. In one issue, *Royal Service* even suggested visualizations. In Mrs. Charles Mullins's 1944 instructions for the BWCs, she advised leaders to make a display featuring a map of Palestine that was torn and stretched, "as if it were being pulled apart." "At the left of the map paste a picture of a Jewish scroll," she suggested, "at the right a Mohammedan mosque, beneath a swastika, above a cross."[73] The display was to read "Who will win Palestine?" The expectation and hope, clearly, was that the cross would triumph.

Conclusion

As mentioned, part of the value in viewing the program materials in *Royal Service* lay in seeing how program editors Elizabeth Brower Nimmo and, especially, Myrtle Robinson Creasman interpreted the sometimes divergent materials produced by other Baptists. How, for example, did Creasman integrate new material like the graded mission study series into her programming on Palestine? How did she reconcile seemingly contradictory perspectives, such as those of Jacob Gartenhaus and J. McKee Adams? Examining the *Royal Service* program materials shows that Creasman's tendency was to aggregate different perspectives rather than to weigh them against each other. Like most Baptists of the era, she drew Orientalist distinctions between Zionists and Arabs. Echoing Gartenhaus, she interpreted Zionist material progress and the return of Jews to the Holy Land as a fulfillment of biblical prophecy that demanded the support of Christians. Echoing Adams, however, she understood Arab nationalism as a just and worthy cause. Other Southern Baptists, including the many readers of *Royal Service*, likely did the same.

In the end, these seeming contradictions were probably not so important or even so apparent to most Baptists. After all, *Royal Service*'s program materials were more than just an agglomeration of the sometimes-divergent perspectives of Baptist missionaries. Nimmo and Creasman synthesized those perspectives around the magazine's goal of promoting Baptist missions in a way that resolved those contradictions or—perhaps more accurately—subsumed them to the ultimate priority of the WMU. In the pages of *Royal Service*, Zionist progress was a fulfillment of prophecy, but it was one that pointed toward the Jewish people's ultimate need for salvation. Arab national hopes were legitimate, but they spoke only to the greater hope to be found in Christ. The national conflict dividing the Holy Land was inflamed by real ambitions and grievances, but those ambitions and grievances revealed only the underlying need of both peoples for the Prince of Peace. As Creasman wrote in 1938—the year in which the Arab revolt was reaching its greatest intensity—"if all groups could learn of Jesus and let Him rule in their hearts, all national differences could be adjusted. His Golden Rule of love could solve every problem."[74] In supporting Southern Baptist missions, readers of *Royal Service* knew that they could do their part in solving those problems, too.

7
Premillennialists

From the late 1960s and into the twenty-first century, the most fervent evangelical supporters of Israel have been premillennialists, who believe that the Jewish state is in varying ways part of God's plan for history. In that same span, a majority of Southern Baptists have come to consider themselves premillennialists. Examining the decades leading up to the establishment of Israel, however, shows that neither of these developments was inevitable. Although premillennialists were scattered through the Baptist membership, premillennialism—especially in its dispensational form—was marginal and frequently controversial in the SBC, its popularity alternately boosted and constrained by its associations with the fundamentalist movement, led in the South by the divisive J. Frank Norris. In 1920, the editor of the Oklahoma *Baptist Messenger* could even call it "unBaptistic."[1] Still, premillennialism was spreading, becoming more "Baptistic" by the year. Its spread, though, did not on its own translate to growing support for Zionism. Many of the growing numbers of Baptist premillennialists remained uncertain whether God's word pointed the way to a secular Jewish nationalism. Some were quite certain that it did not. But premillennialist supporters of Zionism within and without the SBC—including, most effectively, Norris—were making the case that the movement was indeed part of God's plan and that Christian believers should get behind it.

Premillennialism within and without the SBC

As noted in chapter 1, a handful of Southern Baptist leaders had touted variations on premillennial eschatology and biblical interpretation since the nineteenth century. With the qualified exception of J. R. Graves, promoters of premillennialism like Len Broughton and M. E. Dodd tended to have connections to the protofundamentalist movement that was coalescing in the urban North. They paired those connections comfortably enough with their commitment to the SBC. Once the fundamentalist-modernist controversy began splitting the Northern Baptist Convention (NBC) after World War I, however, premillennialism came to be mired in controversy.

The northern split had been long in coming. Northern Baptist fundamentalists had grown increasingly concerned over the spread of theological modernism throughout Baptist institutions. Moderate fundamentalists like Curtis Lee Laws, editor of the *Watchman-Examiner*, wanted the NBC to adopt a confessional statement affirming the fundamentals of Christian orthodoxy and so secure the denomination against modernist drift. More radical fundamentalists like William Bell Riley, founder of the World Christian Fundamentals Association, wanted to go further, insisting that premillennialism was a fundamental of orthodox Christian faith and seeking to purge church institutions of modernists altogether. When fundamentalists failed to secure control of the NBC at the 1922 annual meeting, radicals like Riley called on their supporters to separate from the NBC and focus on building interdenominational fundamentalist alliances and institutions.

Southern Baptists watched the northern split with interest. Editorials on the controversy and its implications for the South proliferated in the denominational press.[2] Largely united against religious modernism, Southern Baptist leaders were more ambivalent toward the fundamentalists themselves. In response to the northern controversy and an upsurge in fundamentalist activity in Texas, L. R. Scarborough (by then, president of Southwestern Baptist Theological Seminary, SWBTS) penned a 1922 editorial in the *Baptist Standard* explaining his own mixed feelings. On the one hand, Scarborough noted that Southern Baptists largely shared moderate fundamentalists' emphasis on the supernatural and opposition to certain forms of ecumenism (cooperation among different church bodies). "Southern Baptists in the main . . . have sympathized with the main motive of Northern fundamentalism," he noted. On the other hand, Scarborough decried both the interdenominationalism and antidenominationalism of the radical fundamentalists, who tended to be "squarely and with deep-seated purpose against all our denominational movements."[3]

For Scarborough, the worst aspects of fundamentalism had a name: Norrisism. By the time that Scarborough penned his editorial in 1922, J. Frank Norris of the First Baptist Church, Fort Worth, was becoming the face of fundamentalism in the South.[4] He was also becoming an absolute menace to denominational leaders like Scarborough and George Truett. Though theologically and socially conservative, Scarborough and Truett were committed to what Bill J. Leonard has called the Grand Compromise—the acceptance of relative ideological diversity within the SBC in the name of building the denomination and carrying out its missionary imperative.[5] Norris's career was characterized by attempts to destroy this unspoken agreement. Tied to Riley's radical wing of northern fundamentalism, Norris believed that Southern Baptist institutions were becoming infected with modernism and should be purged or abandoned. Indeed, Scarborough's 1922 article critiquing fundamentalism had been prompted by a Norris fusillade aimed at Baylor University (Norris smelled Darwinism on the faculty).

Wrapped up in this controversy was premillennialism.[6] Though the moderate fundamentalists had premillennialists in their ranks, the radicals were dominated by them. By the early 1920s the radicals had come to insist that premillennialism was as fundamental and nonnegotiable a Christian doctrine as the virgin birth or substitutionary atonement (the doctrine that Christ's death had atoned for humanity's sins). As Norris waged his many wars against the convention, he repeatedly sought to use adherence to premillennialism to organize Baptist churches along fundamentalist lines. In 1922, he began promoting Riley's premillennialist Baptist Bible Union, which appeared to confirm the suspicions of SBC denominationalists that Norris wanted to use premillennialism to peel away Southern Baptist churches, congregants, and funds in order to create a new denomination.[7]

Norris's continued agitation against established Baptist institutions and promotion of the Baptist Bible Union quickly erupted into open conflict with the Baptist General Convention of Texas. In 1923, the convention refused to seat delegates from his First Baptist Church of Fort Worth, effectively pushing Norris out of institutional Southern Baptist life. He was not gone, though. Even as Norris increasingly aligned himself with organized fundamentalism and began splitting time between Fort Worth and Detroit, his presence continued to be felt within the SBC by supporters and detractors alike.[8] Norris's periodicals and books continued to exert an influence on Southern Baptists, especially within Texas and Oklahoma. In 1933, he again tried to draw Southern Baptist premillennialists into his orbit by forming the Premillennial Baptist Missionary Fellowship (later the World Baptist Missionary Fellowship). He also repeatedly showed up to agitate at conventions and organized sympathetic delegates to push his agenda. An anecdote from W. A. Criswell, Truett's successor at the First Baptist Church of Dallas and a leader in the SBC's conservative resurgence in the 1970s, is revealing of Norris's continued impact among Southern Baptists. Having grown up in a Baptist household in Oklahoma and Texas, Criswell recalled that his mother had been wholly devoted to the denomination and Truett, while his father had loved Norris.[9]

In addition to Norris, a growing cohort of independent Baptist evangelists were sympathetic to fundamentalism and partial to premillennial dispensationalism. Perhaps the most important of these evangelists was

John R. Rice, an ally of Norris's who had left the SBC in 1927. Rice built his own fundamentalist network organized around his newspaper, the *Sword of the Lord*, which he began publishing in 1934. Though he relocated to Wheaton, Illinois, in 1940, Rice remained influential in the South until his return in the 1960s.[10] Mordecai Ham was another independent premillennialist and fundamentalist evangelist with Southern Baptist ties; Ham would become most famous for leading Billy Graham to Christ at a 1934 revival.[11] Hyman Appelman, a Hebrew Christian and professional evangelist, drifted in and out of affiliation with the SBC while leading revivals across the country and touting premillennialism.[12] There were countless others.

While Norris was successful in creating a fundamentalist fiefdom in Fort Worth, he and his allies were never completely successful in using premillennialism as a dividing wedge against the SBC.[13] Southern Baptist leaders effectively pushed back by invoking the Grand Compromise, arguing that the question of millennialism was too disputable to be made a fundamental of the faith.[14] As eminent Southern Baptist theologian E. Y. Mullins noted amid the Baptist Bible Union controversy, "Our work is too important, our unity is too pronounced, our vision is too clear for us to be swept away from our moorings by prophets of the unknown future on a matter which the Scriptures leave unrevealed."[15] Although SBC leaders sought to avoid making millennialism a divisive question, growing numbers of premillennialists were emerging in denominational life.[16] Most premillennialists were presumably happy to, in Mullins's words, "repudiate any effort to make this issue a divisive one."[17] Among the more prominent premillennialists was the aforementioned M. E. Dodd, who paired his premillennialism with a wholehearted devotion to building up SBC institutions. Dodd helped devise the Cooperative Program in 1925, which integrated the fundraising mechanisms of local churches, state conventions, and the SBC, and he even served as SBC president from 1934 to 1935. In 1945, the predominantly amillennialist Southern Baptist Theological Seminary hired historical premillennialist Dale Moody to its faculty, where he served for decades. A number of figures already examined in this study espoused premillennialism while working in SBC institutions, including Len Broughton, W. A. Hamlett, Myrtle Robinson Creasman, H. Leo Eddleman, and Jacob Gartenhaus. The convention's Broadman Press published Gartenhaus's 1936 *The Rebirth of a Nation*, which offered an appraisal of the Zionist movement significantly colored by a premillennial dispensationalist hermeneutic, and the journal *Royal Service* comfortably dabbled in it. Though such direct support for premillennialism was relatively rare, most Southern Baptist bookstores carried premillennial texts, which were advertised and reviewed in denominational publications.[18] State editors, no matter their own stances on the millennium, were usually willing to give premillennialists space to defend their viewpoints.

Because premillennialism was marginal within the SBC, it is hard to measure just how widespread it was. Often, the presence or absence of premillennial materials in denominational periodicals was more indicative of levels of controversy than of adherence. Regardless of the actual number of premillennialists, more and more Southern Baptists encountered premillennialism through Bible colleges and prophecy conferences, as well as through widely circulating dispensationalist texts like the *Scofield Reference Bible*, which included dispensationalist commentary in its notes. One of the best sources for documenting the spread of premillennialism is perhaps its chief opponent within the SBC in the 1930s and 1940s, longstanding SBTS professor of missions W .O. Carver.[19] In 1940, Carver lamented "that the dispensational millennialism has gotten such an extensive hold on our Southern Baptist pastors."[20] He was particularly irritated that the Sunday School Board was inadvertently encouraging its spread by offering the Scofield Bible. That same year, Carver published articles in *Review & Expositor* and *Western Recorder* attacking premillennialism (or Pentecostal millennialism, as he sometimes referred to it) as "one of the serious menaces to the progress of New Testament Christianity just now."[21] Angry rejoinders poured in. A few months later, Carver remarked, "nothing I have ever written has in so short a time brought expressions from so many of my brethren."[22] In 1946, Southern Baptist premillennialists who remained devoted to the denomination began organizing into premillennial fellowships. Some Baptist leaders like Lee Roberson remained involved with the SBC while building independent Baptist institutions that preached premillennialism.[23] By 1953, most states in Southern Baptist territory had premillennial fellowships, and membership in the convention-wide Southern Baptist Premillennial Fellowship had topped ten thousand.[24] The actual number of Southern Baptist premillennialists was certainly much larger.

Premillennialists and Palestine

For the same reason that it is difficult to gauge how widespread premillennialism was in the SBC, it is difficult to trace Baptist premillennialists' approaches to the Palestine question in the Mandate era. Though many Southern Baptist supporters of the Zionist movement have been and are inspired by premillennial thought, such connections should not be assumed in the absence of positive evidence. W. A. Hamlett, the FMB's first superintendent of the Near East Mission, was a prominent premillennialist who did not initially see God's hand in Zionism. "When [the Jews] turn to God and God's Christ," he wrote in a 1913 travelogue, "then God will turn to them and give them their land and their Temple."[25] In a move that was demonstrative of the plasticity of premillennial geopolitics, Hamlett resurfaced in the late 1940s, claiming that the newly established Israel had a biblical right to its territory.[26] Dodd went in the opposite direction. In the 1917 *Jesus Is Coming to Earth Again*, Dodd had described meeting a religious Zionist who expressed hope "that Jehovah will manifest Himself to us again as He did in the ancient times" should the movement succeed.[27] Writing during World War I, Dodd noted, "It looks in these days as if this hope of Israel is to be speedily realized. While students of prophecy must not themselves attempt to turn prophets, yet it seems clear that of all the results which may be anticipated from the present war, the one most certain will be the extermination of the Turks from Europe and the freedom of Palestine from his terrible tyranny."[28] However, the Louisiana pastor made no mention of prophecy in his 1935 travelogue, *Girdling the Globe for God*, which included a chapter on "Jerusalem, Jesus, and the Jews."[29] Dodd had not abandoned premillennialism. He would continue to interpret the Bible in a premillennial manner into the 1940s.[30] He had simply abandoned—or perhaps come to avoid—using it to explain events in Palestine.

Others within the SBC wondered with passive curiosity whether the Zionist movement did represent the foretold ingathering of the Jewish exiles. Many in this camp maintained concerns about Zionist irreligion and antagonism to Christianity. Even among premillennial dispensationalists, who maintained the continued covenantal status of the Jewish people, it was not clear whether Jewish title to the promised land was contingent on conversion. Of course, some people did explicitly see God's designs in the Zionist movement. Famed antievolutionist T. T. Martin wrote in the *Western Recorder* in 1917 that Luke 21:24 indicated that the British were certain to hand over Palestine to the Zionists.[31] A few years later, he mixed anti-Semitic stereotypes, interpretations of biblical prophecy, and Orientalist excitement at Zionist material progress when he stated, "Remember that the Jews have over half the money of the world in their possession; that September, 1920, England signed the papers making Palestine a Jewish country, that they are going back there now, by the multiplied thousands; that they have money by the millions to back up their making Palestine the garden spot of the world; that they are working on vast irrigation and electrical projects."[32] These happenings, Martin was certain, fulfilled the predictions of Ezekiel 38. During World War I, W. E. Tynes wrote in the *Baptist Courier*, "The Lord is Providentially stirring [Jews] in preparation for a great world movement—their conversion and restoration."[33] Missionary convert Jacob Gartenhaus went even further in *The Rebirth of a Nation*: "To oppose [Zionism] is to oppose God's plan."[34]

The independent Baptist pastors and evangelists associated with the fundamentalist movement were no more unified on the issue. Norris—the most influential—was exceptional in his clear, consistent, and outspoken support of Zionism throughout the Mandate era. Though he came to his original interest in Zionism through his dispensationalist interpretation of the Bible, the Fort Worth controversialist was distinguished by his aggressive synthesis of premillennialism and Orientalism. Whereas many Baptists and fundamentalists were suspicious that Zionism might somehow be part of God's plan, Norris argued with certainty that God had promised Palestine to the Jews, that Zionism was a fulfillment of prophecy, and that Christians were duty bound to support the movement. Whereas almost all Baptists drew Orientalist distinctions between Jews and Arabs in Palestine, Norris argued with venom that these distinctions pointed to a clash of civilizations that the Jews would inevitably win. Norris was exceptional both in the amount of writings he left on Zionism and his political support for the movement in the late 1940s (see chapter 8).

While Norris convinced many of the need to support Zionism, he could not convince everyone. Though John R. Rice had been a follower of Norris (the two fell out in the late 1930s), he eventually came to dismiss the idea that Zionism was in any way a fulfillment of prophecy. In the 1940 *World-Wide War and the Bible*, which weighed current events against Rice's interpretation of prophecy, the evangelist did argue for God's hand in the movement, claiming, "The modern Zionist movement and the world persecution which has put hundreds of thousands of Jews back in Palestine has made it so we must expect Jesus to come soon."[35] Rice believed that the full ingathering of Jews to Palestine would occur after a treaty with the Antichrist, whom he expected to emerge from Italy. Based on this interpretation, Rice anticipated that Palestine would likely come under an Italian mandate at some point, noting, "we may certainly expect to see British influence in Palestine and Egypt to decrease and that of Italy to increase."[36] In the 1941 *Jewish Persecution and Bible Prophecies*, Rice argued that the prophecies of Jewish restoration did not refer to the Zionist movement, but that a small number of Jews needed to be in Palestine to make the prophesied treaty with the Antichrist.[37] Zionism, in other words, had only a bit part in the coming eschatological drama. By the 1945 *The Coming Kingdom of Christ*, which offered the evangelist's particular understanding of the dispensationalist eschatological timeline, Rice had come to completely dismiss the idea that Zionism was a fulfillment of prophecy. Rice argued that the biblical land covenant between God and Abraham was both everlasting and unfulfilled, that Jews would someday come into eternal possession of the land. However, he was also clear that "unbelieving Jews" were "not really Abraham's seed."[38] "Romans 4:13 shows," he argued, "that only converted

Jews, those who like Abraham believed in God, shall inherit the Abrahamic promises."[39] As for Zionism, Rice argued that the movement had no connection whatsoever to the prophesied ingathering of the Jews: "The Zionist movement is a movement sponsored by unconverted Jews with a laudable purpose of restoring some Jews to their own land, Palestine. Those who are successful, prosperous and happy in other nations around the world remain where they are. Those who are unhappy, and long to go back to Palestine are encouraged to go. The movement rests on the will of men, not the will of God. The Zionist movement is not a fulfillment of the prophecies about Israel being restored. Preachers who think so are mistaken."[40] Rice believed that only God could gather the Jews back to Palestine. Citing Isaiah 11:10–12, he claimed that the ingathering of Israel would occur in a single day—the same day as Christ's return to earth at the end of the Great Tribulation—at which point, all surviving Jews would be saved and Christ would inaugurate his millennial kingdom.[41]

Countering Premillennialism and Christian Zionism

Premillennialism and support for Zionism were not necessarily intertwined (though they easily could be), either for premillennialists themselves or in the eyes of observers and opponents. W. O. Carver, professor of missions at SBTS, was perhaps the leading opponent of premillennial dispensationalism within the convention. He was also a strong opponent of Zionism. Though it is tempting to view Carver's opposition to both as connected, Carver himself may not have connected the two views. His two 1940 pieces attacking premillennialism—published in *Review & Expositor* and *Pastor's Periscope*—argued that premillennial dispensationalists overemphasized eschatological doctrine at the expense of Christ's ethical teachings.[42] Carver also felt that premillennialists' belief that "prophecy is pre-written history" involved "a basally erroneous conception of prophecy" that contributed "directly to turning people away from the serious business of preaching the gospel of the kingdom of God in the living generation."[43] His critique took up neither the covenantal status of the Jews nor the significance of the Zionist movement. Likewise, Carver's political critiques of Zionism (examined in chapter 9) did not consider Christian support for the movement.

However, Carver's SBTS colleague H. Cornell Goerner did draw explicit connections between premillennialists and those he derided as "Christian Zionists" in the *Review & Expositor* (edited by Carver), the SBC's main theological journal. Goerner noted that the changes wrought in Palestine by the Zionist movement had stirred "a strong recurrence of interest in biblical prophecy, especially as it lends itself to an explanation of the events transpiring in Palestine, an interpretation of those events, and a prediction of the future outcome."[44] Goerner described the situation: "The untrained Bible student, his interest in the subject once aroused, stands well in the way of being swept off his feet by the flood of literature, nearly all along the same line, which offers to him a ready-made interpretation of the Scriptures. It is declared that the present return of the Jews to Palestine is a fulfillment of specific Biblical prophecies; that the Scriptures clearly foretell the complete re-establishment of the Jewish nation as a geographical, political, and cultural entity; and that certain other events, apocalyptic in nature and intimately related to the restoration of the Jewish nation, are definitely prefigured."[45] Goerner posed two questions in challenging this method of biblical interpretation. First, "are those specific passages which seem capable of being interpreted as predictions of current events rightly regarded as such, or does the belief rest upon a misinterpretation?" Second, "are there other scripture passages which contradict this idea and force us to place a different interpretation upon the passages in question?"[46] With these two questions, Goerner argued that prophetic passages in Scripture should be interpreted according to their immediate context and according to the larger themes of the Bible as a whole. In his eyes, Christian Zionists failed on both counts. In terms of immediate contexts, Goerner argued that most prophetic passages referring to the restoration of the people of Israel to their land were fulfilled in the ancient Judeans' sixth-century return from Babylonian captivity. In terms of larger biblical themes, Goerner offered the classic supersessionist argument that the Jews' covenantal relationship with God had been invalidated and transferred to the church.

Though Goerner did assert "that the Bible does contain prophecies of the restoration of Israel," he was clear this event was a "spiritual restoration, namely, the salvation of the Jews through faith in the Messiah, Jesus Christ."[47] Acknowledging some secular reasons to support Zionism, Goerner asserted that pursuit of spiritual restoration should nonetheless define Christians' approach to Jews and Zionism: "Here then is the Zionistic hope that should stir the hearts of Christians! They may indeed be interested, for humanitarian reasons, in the establishment of a colony of refuge for Jews made homeless by persecution. They may even hope that the wandering Jew may find a permanent haven of rest in a national home. But, as Christians, their religious hope will be for the coming of the Jews personally to Christ! And rather than being thrilled over the colonization of some hundreds of thousands in ancient Palestine, they will be stirred and challenged by the realization that Jews by the million in nearly every land on earth are today approachable, interested, and unprejudiced in their attitude toward Jesus and Christianity to a degree never before known in history."[48] Goerner felt that Christians—*as* Christians—should restrict their religious hopes to the conversion of Jews rather than to their national restoration. However, Goerner was unable to bury his own theological perspective in forming his approach to Zionism. "The Zionistic Jew of to-day," he averred, "is making the same mistake that cursed his forefathers."[49] In other words, Zionism was not simply another nationalist movement but rather a continuation of the Jewish repudiation of Christ.

Conclusion: The Premillennial Tangle

The efforts of fundamentalists like Norris to make premillennialism a test of orthodoxy failed to split the SBC in any significant way. Indeed, this failure probably aided premillennialism's spread within the convention; for the moment, the Grand Compromise was grand enough. Even as premillennial interpretations of the Bible remained controversial and contested, more and more Baptists within and without the convention adopted them. Those within it often remained comfortably committed to denominational institutions and initiatives. Premillennialists could be found in the Home Mission Board and Foreign Mission Board, in the Woman's Missionary Union (WMU), in the pages of Baptist periodicals, in some of the most important Southern Baptist pulpits, and by mid-century, even in the faculty directory of the SBTS, the home of premillennialism's greatest opponents in the SBC. For sure, premillennialism was something for Baptists to debate. For convention loyalists, though, the right to have that argument was more a test of Baptist orthodoxy than was premillennialism itself.

Because so many prominent Christian supporters of Zionism and Israel have been premillennial dispensationalists, it can be tempting to assume that the spread of premillennialism meant the spread of support for the creation of a Jewish state. Yet, while many vocal Baptist supporters of Zionism in the Mandate era were inspired by premillennialism—and while critics like H. Cornell Goerner identified connections between it and Christian Zionism—premillennialists could be quite ambivalent toward Zionism, even as they remained interested in events on the ground in Palestine. It took those motivated advocates of Zionism to make the case, to argue that premillennial interpretations of the Bible indeed pointed to support for this specific movement. It took supporters like Myrtle Robinson Creasman and Jacob Gartenhaus inside the convention—and crusaders like J. Frank Norris, the subject of the next chapter, at its edges.

8
Fundamentalist

Among Baptists—even among fundamentalists—J. Frank Norris came to be distinguished by his firm support of Zionism. As Norris had grown closer to William Bell Riley and the northern fundamentalists during the 1910s, he had come to favor a premillennial dispensationalist interpretation of Scripture, which became a defining feature of his ministry.[1] Indicative of this predilection is that the pastor chose to build the inaugural 1917 issue of his periodical, the *Searchlight* (later the *Fundamentalist*), around an article titled "Jesus Is Coming," which laid out the basic dispensational eschatological scheme, describing how the Rapture (the "taking up" of Christian believers) would precede the unfolding of a seven-year tribulation in which Jews would be "gathered back to Jerusalem" and "pass through the fire of a great trial" before recognizing the returning Christ as their messiah and serving as the "very Central Glory" of his millennial kingdom.[2] For Norris, these events were not distant; World War I and the rise of Zionism pointed to their imminence. Like other premillennialists, he found his prophetic imagination fired by the Balfour Declaration and the British conquest of Jerusalem in December 1917. He even renamed First Baptist's young men's Sunday school class "the Allenbys" in honor of victorious British general Edmund Allenby.[3] One week after the signing of the Treaty of Versailles in 1919, Norris took to the pulpit to argue that the cause of the war had been "that Palestine should be restored to the Jew," proclaiming that Jews had a "divine title" to the land "given direct from heaven to Abraham and reaffirmed to succeeding generations."[4] For Norris, the Zionist movement was clearly "a fulfillment of prophecy" that "should be encouraged and supported by the whole Christian world."[5]

While the Bible provided the basis for Norris's interest in Zionism, what distinguished his support for the movement was an inflamed Orientalism that framed the Zionist-Arab conflict in terms of civilizational clash. In some ways, this framing was unremarkable: many Baptists at this time drew similar contrasts between the two peoples. Norris, though, took what were for many Baptists vague impressions and reshaped them into clear implications. The Zionists were Western, the Arabs Eastern. The Zionists were progressive, the Arabs backward. The Zionists represented civilization, the Arabs its enemies. The Zionists would triumph, the Arabs fail—an inevitability that Norris believed was written into the characters of the two peoples as much as it was written into the pages of the Bible. In many ways, Norris's depictions of Palestine anticipated the "marriage of religion and geopolitics" that Stephen Spector has found in contemporary American Christian Zionism.[6] Indeed, that marriage could very well be called the Norris synthesis. For no other evangelical or fundamentalist supporter of Zionism in the Mandate era so clearly synthesized a biblical interest in Zionist success with an argument that—through common values and common enemies—God-fearing Americans and Zionists were linked together.

Travel and the Norris Synthesis

While a number of factors contributed to the development of Norris's synthesis, undoubtedly the most important was his frequent travel to the Holy Land. Norris traveled to the region five times between 1920 and 1950. The bulk of his writings on Palestine in the *Searchlight* and the *Fundamentalist* appeared according to the rhythms of these trips. Besides providing the pastor with both the occasion to write on the subject and the authority of the eyewitness perspective (authority that Norris was keen to claim), these trips confirmed and vivified Norris's interpretations of prophecy while providing him with the postcard impressions that he used to draw contrasts between Arab and Jew.

Norris's initial 1920 journey to Palestine stirred in him an emotional attachment to Zionism that he would never shake. He reported to readers of the *Searchlight* that his ship from Italy to Alexandria was filled with hundreds of Jews heading toward Palestine, a scene that clearly moved the pastor: "They are so anxious to get back to Palestine that they crowded the ship without a place to sleep. They stay on the deck night and day and sleep on the bare floor. They are very poorly dressed. But they are all happy. They sing the songs of Zion. Every ship going in this direction is crowded with Jews."[7] Norris would return to these images year after year in describing his impressions of Zionism, as the prophecies of Ezekiel and Zechariah conjured these memories. After visiting Egypt, Norris arrived in Palestine in time to witness the transition from military to civilian administration. He was delighted that the British had appointed Herbert Samuel, a Jew, as the first high commissioner of Palestine. "For the first time in nearly three thousand years," he exclaimed, "all Palestine has been under the dominion of one Jewish ruler!"[8] Norris believed that the British could claim the promise of Genesis 12:3, that God would bless those that bless Abraham and curse those that curse him. "In light of prophecy, in meaning to the present world crisis, and above all, in its deep significance to the future of all the world," as Norris wrote, the Balfour Declaration stood "alongside that of Cyrus of Babylon, if not above it."[9]

On the ground in Palestine, Norris already found the unfolding conflict between Arabs and Jews to be a clash of civilizations. Acknowledging that both Zionists and Arabs had legitimate political claims, he argued that the conflict would boil down to survival of the fittest—clearly, the Zionists. To Norris, this outcome was inevitable, just like the "American Indian giving way to the white man." The Zionists embodied civilization and industry. The Arabs embodied backwardness and indolence: "The Jew is industrious, the Arab lazy; the Jew is progressive, the Arab is only half civilized. I know there are those who undertake to prove that the 'Natives' have a high state of civilization, even if not after the western ideals. I crossed Palestine in a Ford car in four different directions, visiting all the places of interest and I found only ignorance, poverty, disease and superstition among the natives."[10] Of course, other Baptist travelers had said much the same, albeit without Norris's force and without his bald certainty that these contrasts pointed to Zionist victory in the conflict. Norris claimed that "only a casual glance at the new and modern Jewish village will convince any man what is going to happen. . . . The irrigated land with acres of orange groves, olive trees, almonds, figs and mulberry for silk worms tell it all."[11] He described seeing two different work gangs during his trip—one Arab, one Jewish—and witnessing as the Arab crew walked off the job at 10 a.m., while the Jewish crew worked deep into the evening. Norris quipped, "A man doesn't need divine inspiration to know what the main result will be in a few years."[12] He coupled this impression of Arab indolence with a fear of Islamic fanaticism informed by hotel gossip. During his travels, he "learned" that "Mohammedans have special revelations and visions in which they are told to kill the Christians and the white race." Norris claimed that many Muslims believed that killing Christians was a benevolent act, as it provided them with a path to Heaven. Evoking a long-standing Western Christian trope that Islam is spread by the sword while Christianity is spread by persuasion, he asserted, "They go about their bloody work killing the Christian with the same passion that we as Christians go about to win the souls of our lost friends."[13]

Norris's return from Palestine was a major occasion at First Baptist and in the pages of the *Searchlight*. The pastor invited members of the Orthodox Ahavath Sholom congregation to sing the Zionist anthem "Hatikvah" at a presentation of his slides and films, an event advertised as "Unprecedented since Abraham's Time!"[14] When the Jewish singers were unable to perform due to a scheduling conflict, Norris invited A. W. McKee, described as a "noted tenor," to sing "The Holy City."[15] Norris himself was invited to speak on "Palestine Restored to the Jews" at a meeting of the Fort Worth Zionist District held at Ahavath Sholom's Hebrew Institute, an occasion likewise hyperbolized by the *Searchlight* as "the most unheard of thing of all time."[16] The *Searchlight* continued to publish Norris's trip reflections into December, when he concluded his series of articles by laying out how Jerusalem "has a large place in the prophecy concerning the last days."[17]

Norris returned to Palestine in 1937 and 1939, amid the Arab revolt and the intensifying persecution of Jews in Europe. His 1937 trip came only months after the publication of the Peel Commission's report recommending the partition of the country. Perhaps surprisingly, given his sympathies for Zionism, Norris was frank in asserting that Arabs had legitimate political complaints over the partition plan, that they were caught in "the most pathetic as well as the most impossible situation."[18] Norris included in his write-up extended excerpts from Jamal al-Husseini, nephew of Grand Mufti Hajj Amin al-Husseini, laying out the Arab case against partition. Following al-Husseini's lead, Norris noted that there was a meaningful difference between saying that "Palestine shall be the national home for the Jews" and saying that "the Jew shall have a national home in Palestine": "There is a difference in the two statements just like if a man comes to my house and I will say to him, 'I am going to give you a home in my place,' and then later he understands that to mean that my home will be taken over by him." Besides calling attention to this distinction, Norris noted that the partition plan would give "the heart and meat of the watermelon to the Jews and the rind to the Arabs."[19] He asked his American readers whether they would be willing to "slice off California for the Japanese," noting, "That is exactly the proposition from the Arab point of view."[20]

Despite his growing understanding of the Arab claims, however, Norris maintained that "over against these and all other claims is the fact that God Almighty gave the title to Palestine to the Jews. Who then can contest it? It would be to fight against God."[21] His impressions of Arab society and culture remained likewise unchanged. Norris repeatedly stated that the Jews would triumph in Palestine because they were the fitter people. He also went beyond simply claiming that Arabs lacked the advancement of the Zionists, arguing that Arabs were the perennial opponents of civilization and progress.[22] "The Arab never builds," Norris asserted, "he destroys." Arabs had destroyed the Great Library of Alexandria, the "greatest of all temples" at Baalbek, and the land of Palestine. "They allowed the fertile soil to wash away," he wrote. "They permit these fine lands to grow sterile." Therefore, he argued, "They have forfeited all title to this fair land of promise. They killed the land and did not till it."[23]

Norris argued, conversely, that the Jewish people had an intrinsic connection to the land that allowed it to flourish. He asserted that modern archaeology was revealing that the centuries after the Israelite conquest had been "a period of remarkable development," that the united monarchy of David and Solomon had achieved a "high level of political military and economic organization," and that the reign of the Hasmoneans had yielded "a period of even greater prosperity than the preceding one."[24] When Jews controlled the land, it thrived. It was beginning to thrive again. This renewal, Norris believed, was to the Arabs' benefit, a claim that contradicted his assertions that Jews and Arabs were engaged in a zero-sum battle for survival. Jewish hospitals were open to Arabs. Jewish medicine was lengthening Arab life spans. Jewish business was making Arabs wealthy. Jews were helping maintain Arab schools and raising the standard of living for both populations. If only Jews and Arabs "were left alone and if it were not for outside agitation," he claimed, "they would get along together."[25]

Increasingly, Norris drew geopolitical connections between the Palestine question and the rise of fascism in Europe. He had paid close attention to the plight of European Jewry since 1933, when he had delivered a sermon on the persecution of Jews in Germany and prophesied the destruction of any nation that mistreated God's chosen people.[26] Norris's trips, paired with his interpretation of the Bible, led him to understand the Palestine question as crucial to the resolution of the Jewish question in Europe.[27] They also led him to believe that the same persecutory impulses that were guiding fascists in Europe were inspiring the Arab revolt. "Mussolini is on the radio and his voice covers the whole of three continents," he wrote. "He is inflaming the whole Arab world." Citing his experiences on the ground, Norris claimed that "every Arab that I have talked to is for Mussolini and Hitler because of the Jewish question."[28] He even asserted that Hitler was "a Sunday School teacher compared to the Arab in hating the Jew."[29] Norris's 1939 trip came shortly after Britain's white paper limiting Jewish immigration to Palestine. He directly tied Britain's reversal to the political crisis in Europe, arguing that it was the result of "threats from Hitler and Mussolini." He also highlighted the pitiful attempts of European Jewish refugees to reach Palestine, only to have their ships confiscated by the British. "I . . . saw six hundred half starved, half dead human beings in a stockade at Haifa who had been taken from off the ships," he wrote. "All continental Europe is aflame against the Jews . . . AND NOW THEY ARE FORBIDDEN TO ENTER THEIR OWN LAND!" Norris wondered whether events pointed to "the time of Jacob's trouble" prophesied by Jeremiah.[30]

While Norris had been an outspoken supporter of Zionism for decades and had built relationships with local Jews in Fort Worth, it was not until the late 1940s that he began interacting with pro-Zionist organizations and became active in calling for the US government to support the Zionists. As usual, travel provided the occasion for this turn. As the United Nations took control of the Palestine question in 1947 (and as the United States was increasingly involved in the issue), Norris planned another trip to the region. Ahead of this trip, he contacted Jewish organizations, Zionist or otherwise, to ask to be introduced to Zionist leaders in Palestine. A vain and boastful man, Norris gloried in rubbing elbows with influential people—then reporting on it in the *Fundamentalist*.[31] He was therefore disturbed when his efforts to gain contacts in the Yishuv were initially rebuffed. In reply to Norris's queries, Ben Goldman of the Anti-Defamation League (ADL) noted that the organization did not have contact with Zionist leadership, however Norris's associations with renowned anti-Semite Gerald Smith would have made the organization "most troubled about furnishing you with a letter of introduction" had contacts existed.[32] While Goldman's letter did not discourage Norris from further attempts to gain access to the Zionist leadership, it did affect his strategy: from that point forward the pastor was keen to make American Jewish organizations like the ADL and the American Zionist Emergency Council (AZEC) aware of his own *anti*-anti-Semitic activities and active support of Zionism.

To demonstrate his pro-Zionist bona fides, Norris became more activist in his approach to the intensifying conflict in Palestine. During his 1947 trip, he mailed and published a letter to President Truman calling on the US government to support the Jewish bid for statehood. "In that whole controversy the big issue is who owns the land, who has the title to the land?" he wrote. "If that question is settled there is no other question." Norris argued that the land belonged to the Jews by right of divine title and international law. Their right of title derived from Genesis 17, which specifically stated "that the title to Palestine is given not to Ishmael, the ancestor of the Arabs, but to Isaac and his seed forever."[33] In terms of international law (a "second and very important authority in addition to Scriptural authority"), the British mandate for Palestine committed the British to the creation of a Jewish national home in Palestine. Both the League of Nations and the US Congress had confirmed this commitment. Norris argued that the 1939 white paper was therefore a violation of the mandate and illegal under international law. "Illegal" Jewish immigration to Palestine, on the other hand, was perfectly legal. Further, Norris emphasized that Jews had "invested six hundred and fifty million dollars in Palestine, built cities, public works" on the basis of "the mandate given to Great Britain over Palestine, and confirmed by the United States Government and confirmed by the League of Nations." Norris declared that "the curse of God Almighty" was "on every hand that violates this most solemn agreement—the mandate three times over confirmed."[34] For Norris, international law gave definition to the prophetic.

Besides making a positive case for the Zionists, Norris argued that Arab leaders were geopolitical enemies of the United States who had aligned with both Nazi Germany and the USSR. Doffing his earlier sympathy for the Palestinian Arabs' political claims, he described them as mere "usurpers" and "robbers of property that belongs to the Jews."[35] Norris reminded the president that Hajj Amin al-Husseini, the leader of the Palestinian national movement, had been an ally of Hitler's, noting that it should "cause us to stop and think that the Arab leaders from the Grand Mufti on down were allies of Hitler, and it ill becomes them to come now into court with their hands dripping with the blood of the Jews—six million of them murdered by Hitler."[36] Just as he had attributed the Arab revolt of the 1930s to fascist agitation, he blamed current Arab resistance to Zionism on the Soviet Union. Having "interviewed many Arab leaders," Norris found "that the whole crowd are for Stalin, just like they formerly were for Hitler."[37] As for the United States, its responsibility was to "keep its promise and take a firm stand for law and order in that land that has given the world its Bible and Saviour."[38] Norris was delighted to receive a personal—if somewhat dismissive—reply from the president thanking him for the "expression" of his views.[39]

After the United Nations voted in favor of partition (which Norris described as "the most far-reaching action . . . since the birth of Christ"), Norris came to distantly cooperate with the American Christian Palestine Committee (ACPC), the most important American Christian pro-Zionist organization of the Mandate era.[40] The ACPC both lobbied the US government in support of Zionist policies and recruited American Christians to the cause, closely coordinating its efforts with AZEC, which helped fund the ACPC.[41] As scholars of the ACPC have shown, it primarily focused its efforts on recruiting mainline and liberal Protestant support for Zionism. It was less interested in fundamentalists like Norris, in part for the same reasons that the ADL had been reluctant to cooperate with him. Tellingly, Norris only came into contact with the ACPC through his own outreach to Jewish groups—it was AZEC that put him in touch with the organization and informed him of a statement that it was preparing to issue in continued support of partition.[42] In February, Norris published the statement in the *Fundamentalist*.[43] Pleased that Norris had done so, AZEC officials invited him to visit their offices in New York prior to his next trip to Palestine and promised possible contacts with the Yishuv leadership.[44] While Norris did not become deeply involved with the ACPC, his exposure to its propaganda did help give political definition to his support for Zionism. Norris followed up the ACPC's February statement, for instance, with a telegram to President Truman echoing the committee's lines that the "only safe course" for the United States to pursue in Palestine was to "back up partition plan which was fostered by this government and do so immediately" with the "necessary armed forces to put down disorder." The Haganah (the main Zionist militia) "should be furnished all necessary arms immediately," otherwise "we will be guilty of too little and too late."[45] In advocating for direct American military aid for the Zionists—in giving a very specific, direct, and practical way in which Christians and the United States could support the creation of the Jewish state—Norris went beyond what almost any Baptist, within or without the convention, was willing to contemplate.

Conclusion

As noted in the introduction, Norris brought his activist approach to the SBC Annual Meeting in Memphis, Tennessee, in 1948. Boxed out of actual convention proceedings, he set up a counterconvention at the Peabody Hotel that included a May 17 address about the Palestine question, just days after the declaration of the State of Israel and President Truman's near-immediate recognition. When the day arrived, Norris called on the president to raise the arms embargo against the Zionists, while calling on the SBC to send Truman a telegram of congratulations for recognizing Israel. A Norris ally proposed a motion to do the latter at the convention, which was overwhelmingly voted down. Baptist critics of the motion presented their "no" votes as a rebuke of the president for "playing politics with the Jewish vote."[46] As Terry Lindley has argued, though, a major factor in the motion's overwhelming defeat was likely its association with Norris. A convention that had voted against seating the fundamentalist was not likely to adopt a motion that he had publicly endorsed.[47] For at least some Southern Baptists, it seems, support for Zionism had come to be too inextricably tangled with the Baptist controversialist.

Even as Southern Baptist leaders rejected Norris's initiative, though, his synthesis remained a compelling case for Zionism and Israel, speaking as it did in the two languages that Baptists shared when discussing the Holy Land: the language of the Bible, given urgency by Norris's premillennialism, and the language of Orientalism, given force by his claims of civilizational clash. Of course, others examined in this study had in varying ways paired premillennial interest in Zionism with Orientalist understandings of Palestine. However, none so thoroughly intertwined them or drew out their implications, and none so clearly tied their understandings of Zionism and the Palestine question to specific policy goals or acted, in however limited a fashion, to achieve them. For Norris, Christians had a duty to both God and civilization to support Zionism against the enemies that the United States and the Zionists shared. In articulating his support for Zionism in this manner, in seeking to coordinate with Jewish organizations, and in actively supporting specific pro-Zionist policies, Norris in many ways heralded the kind of evangelical Christian Zionism that would come to prominence and influence decades later.

9
Commentators

Though J. Frank Norris came to be quite political in his support for Zionism, most of the Baptists of the era (and those here studied) did not directly engage the Palestine question as a political question. This chapter, however, focuses precisely on politics, looking at how Baptist editorialists across the South approached the political questions raised during British rule over Palestine. Every state Baptist periodical had an editorial section, though the extent to which Palestine appeared in Baptist editorials varied from editor to editor. Under J. S. Farmer, for example, North Carolina's *Biblical Recorder* featured several editorials on the topic during the years of the Arab revolt. However, L. L. Carpenter, who edited the *Recorder* during the decisive years of 1947 to 1949, published no editorials on Palestine or the newly created Israel. Some convention-wide periodicals featured commentary. W. O. Carver, the longtime professor of missions at SBTS, published a news commentary column in both *Pastor's Periscope*, a review journal for Southern Baptist pastors, and the *Commission*, the periodical of the FMB. The *Commission* also featured commentary from FMB leaders. The *Review & Expositor*, the leading Southern Baptist theological journal (edited by Carver from 1919 to 1942), infrequently featured commentary essays on news items; its January 1930 issue contained two articles on Palestine. Unsurprisingly, the Palestine question tended to stir the Baptist commentariat when major events broke into the American news cycle; editorials peaked during World War I, the Wailing Wall riots, the Arab revolt and Jewish refugee crisis, and the events surrounding the creation of Israel in 1948. Unsurprisingly, too, Southern Baptist editorialists offered no unified voice on the Palestine question. Few even agreed on the parameters of the question itself.

A Question of Life after the "Unspeakable Turk"

It was, of course, the British conquest of Palestine during World War I that first raised significant public discussions in the United States over the political fate of the Holy Land. In general, Americans were united in celebrating the end of Ottoman rule but divided over what should come next. At particular issue in that divide was the Balfour Declaration, which for the first time prompted public debate over Zionism, hitherto largely "an in-house affair" among American Jews.[1] As noted in chapter 3, Americans with established connections to the Arabic-speaking world, especially those affiliated with Presbyterian and Congregationalist missions, opposed the declaration and the Zionist movement as inimical to the interests and desires of Palestine's native inhabitants. Jewish supporters of Zionism, of course, celebrated Balfour, arguing that the Jewish national home would provide a needed haven for oppressed Jews and serve as a boon to Palestine's native inhabitants.

Not all American Jews, however, were happy with Britain's commitment. Though the American Zionist movement had gained in numbers and prestige under the wartime leadership of Louis Brandeis, many Jews worried that support for the movement might call into question Jewish loyalty to the United States. American Zionists countered by articulating a distinctly American approach to Zionism that deemphasized its ideological elements, prioritizing instead the matters of fraternal aid to suffering Jews and practical support for the upbuilding of the Yishuv. American Zionist leaders also contended that Zionism and Americanism were not just compatible, but complementary—an argument encapsulated by Brandeis when he quipped, "To be good Americans we must be better Jews, and to be better Jews, we must become Zionists."[2] That American Jews were concerned about the implications of Zionism for questions of national loyalty was not without reason, though. In the xenophobic post–World War I climate, much of the broader public debate over Balfour and Zionism indeed centered on those implications.[3]

Southern Baptist commentators did not join that particular debate. Of much greater interest was the end of what Baptists had long considered to be the backward and despotic rule of the Ottomans. This interest was not out of concern for Palestine's inhabitants—they figured little into Baptist editorials on the region—but of hope for the prospect of Protestant influence in the land and, for some, the prospect of Jewish restoration. Especially hopeful as British forces neared Jerusalem was editor A. J. Holt of the *Florida Baptist Witness*. Holt had traveled to the region in the 1890s and written of its missionary potential for the *Foreign Mission Journal* (examined in chapter 1). With British forces advancing on Jerusalem, he wrote with prophetic suggestion, "It will be a notable event when [Jerusalem] is taken possession of by the Gentiles. Then it is frequently predicted that as a result of the war, it will pass once again into the hands of the children of Jacob."[4] After the city fell on December 11, Holt celebrated the British victory as a triumph of Christianity over Islam and reveled in the fall of an Ottoman regime that had laid the land low. "Palestine under the Turks was a desolation," he wrote, noting that he had been "an eye witness to Turkish atrocities and cruelty."[5] Remarking on the difficulties under which Christians—especially Christian missionaries—had lived within the Ottoman world, he exulted that the "shackles of religious despotism" had fallen away. Looking toward the future, Holt declared that it would be a "splendid thing for Palestine to be turned over to the Jews, with certain restrictions." Of particular concern to Holt was that "Jerusalem is not a manufacturing city. Neither is it a commercial city." Holt was certain that Palestine could be developed agriculturally but questioned the ability of Jews to do it, since they were "almost everywhere commercial people." Still, he remained hopeful that the land would flourish under "a benevolent government, protected always by Christian nations."[6] A godly modernity was surely in the offing.

No other state Baptist periodical here examined was as engaged with the Ottoman theater of the Great War as was the *Florida Baptist Witness*. For the most part, only brief, scattered references to Palestine made their way into other state papers. These references tended to follow Holt in celebrating the defeat of the Ottoman Empire and expressed curiosity, if not excitement, for the prospect of a Jewish Palestine. The week after Jerusalem fell to the British, Livingston Johnson of the *Biblical Recorder* published a brief note in its Current Topics column, celebrating "that the 'unspeakable Turk' has been driven out" of Jerusalem. The column noted, too, that a Zionist activist (in Johnson's terms, a "very able Hebrew") had recently delivered a lecture in Raleigh, North Carolina, calling for the creation of a Jewish democracy in Palestine that would become "the hyphen nation between the East and the West, friendly to both and serving as a connecting link between the two." While Johnson was as yet unsure of the speaker's proposal, he firmly declared it to be "a matter for great rejoicing that the land in which our Lord spent His earthly life has been wrested from the hands of the most cruel and barbarous people on the face of the earth, and let us hope and pray that never again will it fall into their possession."[7] That same week, John William Porter of the *Western Recorder*, who understood the war as having prophetic significance, published an editorial celebrating the British victory while warning that events suggested that "the battle of Armageddon is near at hand."[8] After the 1918 armistice, E. C. Routh of the *Baptist Standard* attempted to make broader sense of the conflict, remarking that the conclusion of the war would mean "age-long wrongs will be corrected." Among the possible corrections was that "Jews after two millenniums, may have a country of their own." Routh made no mention of

Arabs—or, explicitly, of the Middle East—though he did celebrate that Turkey "will no longer be tolerated" in Europe.[9] Baptist editorialists betrayed no suspicion that the inhabitants of Palestine might not welcome the changes that British rule would bring.

A Question of Causes: The Wailing Wall Riots

The riots of 1929 renewed the American public debate over the Palestine question.[10] Initially, the attacks against Jews stirred broad public sympathy for the Yishuv. However, public opinion soon turned against the Zionists, as increasing numbers of commentators came to be convinced that the riots had been motivated by legitimate Arab grievances. As Naomi Wiener Cohen has argued, in the months following the riots "a composite and highly unflattering picture of Zionism emerged from the nation's leading journals" that characterized the movement as an undemocratic imposition on Palestine's native inhabitants, one that was dependent on the military force of imperial Britain and the wealth of American Jews and disruptive to the social and economic harmony of the Holy Land.[11] While this picture was not universally accepted, it was widespread (including in the Protestant press) and promoted by journalists and scholars with ties to the region. Especially disconcerting to American Zionists was that the violence of 1929 did not just open a debate over the riots themselves; it reopened debate over Zionism and the Balfour Declaration. Finding themselves on the defensive, they eschewed talk of Jewish statehood while arguing for the necessity of a Jewish homeland, the right of Jews to Palestine, the accomplishments of the Yishuv, and the capacity of Palestine's land and economy to sustain a growing Jewish community.[12]

This time, those debates penetrated the Southern Baptist press. As noted in chapter 2, biblical scholar J. McKee Adams, writing in a 1929 travelogue, called on the British to withdraw the Balfour Declaration. Soon thereafter, editor W. O. Carver of the *Review & Expositor*, Southern Baptists' leading theological journal, invited two contributors to write on the Palestine question for the journal's January 1930 issue. The first article, titled "Palestine—A Problem," was penned by Dr. Ryland Knight of Delmar Baptist Church in Saint Louis. A graduate of SBTS and Richmond College, Knight had served in Baptist pulpits in Kentucky, Virginia, Tennessee, and Missouri, as well as on a variety of denominational boards.[13] His goal in the article was to provide historical context for both the Zionist movement and Arab responses to it in light of the riots. Knight was careful not to take sides and shrugged off any discussion of a possible solution. He described the origins of Zionism and the movement's internal diversity, and he noted that a "cohesive force" bound the disparate strands of the movement together: "the cohesive force in Zionism is the conviction that the Jew is in danger of being absorbed by the nations among whom he is scattered, and that the Jewish hope for the future lies in the establishment of at least a center of Jewish life and thought to which, as to a shrine, the affections and aspirations of Jews everywhere may turn."[14] Knight's appraisal of the movement was clearly influenced by the father of cultural Zionism, Ahad Ha'am, whom he quoted in the piece. Cultural Zionists sought the creation of a Jewish cultural center in Palestine that did not necessarily require a state. Knight did not explicitly address the matter of Jewish statehood, but he lamented that "the zeal which makes Zionism possible makes almost inevitable the outbursts of a few individual Jews who hope to find in Zionism not only a restoration of the Jews to Palestine, but an intolerant usurpation of all rights in Palestine to the displacement of all other people."[15] He cited the noted Northern Baptist Harry Emerson Fosdick in condemning this aggressive form of political Zionism. Though Knight did not specifically stump for the binational or federated approach to Palestine that Fosdick favored, his political sympathy for the movement clearly stopped short of independent Jewish statehood.

Still, Knight believed that there was "much to commend the Zionist movement." He celebrated its achievements in Orientalist terms, noting, "In the communities established under its auspices irrigation, modern agricultural methods, sanitation, hygiene, education, conspire to contrast the Zionist settlement with the nearby Arab communities."[16] Like many Baptist travelers to the region, Knight drew contrasts between the "narrow and dirty" streets and "unsightly" buildings of the predominantly Arab Jaffa and their counterparts in the Jewish Tel Aviv, which he described as resembling a "newly built American city."[17] Such contrasts, he noted, were evident throughout the region. However, unlike many Baptists (most especially J. Frank Norris), Knight did not attribute these divergent impressions to matters of national or racial character, noting instead that they were in part related to disparities in access to capital.

Knight treated the Arab cause with great sympathy, although with less detail than he used in his description of the Zionists. He laid out the long history of Arab inhabitance of the land, starting with the Islamic conquest of the seventh century, and he noted the sacrality of Jerusalem in Islam. He also laid out the contradictory promises made by the British during the war, describing the "present situation in Palestine" as "another miserable hangover from the world war."[18] Like many other Baptist observers, Knight presented the Arab cause as a justifiable reaction to British policy and Zionist encroachment rather than as a movement of its own: "the Arab feels that possession is nine points of the law and for a thousand years Jerusalem and Palestine have been his. His religious interest in Jerusalem is as great as the Jews. He does not propose to be dispossessed. And he is suspicious of Christendom." Knight never articulated any specific Arab goal beyond avoiding dispossession. Sidestepping any offer of a possible solution to the Palestine question, he was only able to conclude that it was "an intricate problem" that would tax all the "tact and patience" of the British.[19] Despite his sympathy for the Arabs, it should be noted, Knight would later join the American Palestine Committee (APC), a pro-Zionist precursor of the ACPC. At the time of Knight's joining in 1941, however, the aims of the group were limited to calling on the British to implement the promises of the Balfour Declaration, again short of a call for statehood.[20]

The second *Review & Expositor* article from January 1930 was a guest column of sorts penned by Rabbi Joseph Rauch of Temple Adath Israel in Louisville. The Reform rabbi's educational path had been unique, but it had uniquely suited him to write in the journal; he had the rare distinction of having studied at both Hebrew Union College and SBTS, and as rabbi of Louisville's Reform congregation, he had maintained good relations with the seminary and its faculty.[21] Though Rauch would come to be considered an anti-Zionist (he was later involved in the creation of the anti-Zionist American Council for Judaism), his article "Contemporary Palestine" offered a basic American Zionist approach to the Palestine question—which in 1930 meant that it stopped short of calling for statehood.[22] The article called on the British to continue to allow Jewish migration and purchase of land with an eye toward building a Jewish national home, as promised in the Balfour Declaration. The small number of Jews already in Palestine had worked wonders, doing "more in a generation agriculturally, economically and culturally than the Arabs had done in five centuries."[23] Rauch argued that the Zionists did not seek to displace anyone, nor had they met any authentic resistance from the Arabs. "From all available reports," he claimed, "the Arab masses were perfectly satisfied with the Jewish efforts in Palestine. They benefited in every way from the improvements that were made by the Jewish settlers." Of course, organized resistance to Zionist land purchases and immigration predated the Balfour Declaration. However, Rauch attributed what resistance there was—including the shocking violence of the Wailing Wall riots—to the incitement of the "Arab chieftains" and "the religious and secular aristocrats" who "looked with hostility on the Jewish arrivals, their programs and their success." He dismissed Arab resistance to Zionism on explicitly Orientalist terms that spoke well to Baptist assumptions about the region, claiming, "These oriental overlords feared the occidental enlightenment which Zionism was introducing in the land."[24]

Rauch believed that there could be peace with the Arabs if the British committed themselves to enforcing the mandate. In allowing "effendi bolshevism" to rile the masses, the mandate government had "made itself culpable of the Jewish tragedy in Palestine." As a first step toward authentic peace in the region, the British government had to "preserve law and order" and enforce the terms of the mandate.[25] "The League of Nations has granted permission to the Zionists to come and settle in Palestine and build there a national home for themselves where they can develop their own culture," he wrote. "This promise must be kept inviolate." Beyond that, the Zionists had a "historic and moral right" to revive their homeland, a right that "should not be denied them." "The normal status between Arabs and Jews is friendliness," Rauch concluded, "and this can be restored if England and the League of Nations will see fit to bring it about."[26]

One reader of the two articles, J. S. Farmer of the *Biblical Recorder*, found that they had much in common, noting, "It is interesting to see how nearly these two writers agree on many important points."[27] On the matter of Zionism itself, there indeed was some overlap between Knight and Rauch. Though Knight did not overtly endorse the cultural Zionism that he described, he favorably contrasted it with the positions of more aggressively political Zionists. Rauch, for his part, was explicit in his endorsement of specific Zionist goals—namely continued migration and land purchase—although he did not call for statehood. Both Knight and Rauch viewed the movement as the main vehicle of modernity in the region, drawing Orientalist distinctions between Jews and Arabs. As the discussion shifted to the underlying causes of conflict, though, clear differences emerged. Knight blamed overreaching Zionists and Britain's contradictory wartime policies for spurring the conflict. He viewed general Arab resistance to Zionism as reasonable. Rauch, on the other hand, blamed the conflict on rabble-rousing effendis cynically trying to preserve their own power, and he viewed authentic Arab resistance to Zionism as nonexistent. These meaningful differences seem to have escaped the notice of Farmer, who aggregated the two essays' contents rather than playing them against each other.

A Question of Refugees and Rights

Nazi Germany's escalating persecution of Jews and the outbreak of the Arab revolt again brought Americans to engage the Palestine question between 1936 and 1939. As the deteriorating situation in Germany contributed to a growing Jewish refugee crisis, American Jewish leaders and their non-Jewish allies worked to secure US government cooperation in facilitating the immigration of German and—after 1938—Austrian Jewish refugees, albeit within the bounds of the restrictive quota system established in 1924. For the most part, American Jewish leaders feared that a direct campaign against the quota system at a time of economic uncertainty and high anti-immigrant sentiment would stimulate an already growing domestic anti-Semitism.[28] Indeed, while the American public was generally horrified at Germany's treatment of Jews, particularly after Kristallnacht, this horror did not translate into support for the lifting of the quotas. It was amid this background that American Zionists and Christian organizations like the Pro-Palestine Federation presented Palestine as a solution, calling on the British to keep the gates of Palestine open and arguing that the crisis confirmed the need for a Jewish national home in Palestine to serve as a safe haven for persecuted Jews.[29] Their calls came, of course, as the large influx of European Jews into Palestine was helping to stir Arabs to revolt. As had the 1929 riots, the revolt reopened debate over Zionism, the Balfour Declaration, and the Palestine question. While supporters of Zionism sought to connect that debate to the urgent refugee crisis, allies of the Arabs argued that the Palestine question and the Jewish question in Europe should be considered separately.

Most Southern Baptist editorialists identified the connections between the two questions but insisted that the resolution of the Palestine question should not be determined by the plight of Jews in Europe. The Arab revolt led the previously ambivalent J. S. Farmer to take a stand against continuing Zionist immigration to Palestine. Though he blamed the conflict between Jews and Arabs on the "two incompatible promises" made by the British during World War I, he was certain that the "promise to the Arabs was really the only one that the British had a right to make, since the Arabs were the inhabitants of the country and they had a right to stay there."[30] Farmer was less inspired by Zionist achievement than were many of his fellow Baptists. Though he blamed the British for the conflict, he also attributed the modernization of the region to them: for Farmer, it was the British who were making the land blossom "like a rose."[31] He viewed the Zionists less as modernizers than as well-funded land grabbers who had "known how to get much of the best land from the poor Arab farmers, and are in consequence hated by the Arabs worse than ever."[32]

Though Farmer repeatedly voiced concern with the persecution of Jews in Europe and the developing refugee crisis, he did not view Jewish immigration to Palestine as a moral solution to the problem.[33] "[What] is it but hollow mockery for one to be outraged at the driving of Jews from their homes in Germany and Italy and at the same time to strive to find homes for them by taking their lands away from the Arabs of Palestine," he wrote in 1938.[34] Farmer reported with approval that he had heard rumors that the British government and wealthy American Jews were trying to secure "some African colony, perhaps one of the former German colonies" to "provide a refuge for the harassed Jews of Germany."[35] In 1939, he published part of a letter from J. H. Rushbrooke of the FMB, calling on Americans to help secure exit permits for German Jews.[36] After hearing of the MS *St. Louis*, a ship filled with Jewish refugees that had been turned away from both Havana and American ports, Farmer wrote, "as much as we dislike undesirable immigrants, we think it would be well for our Government to find some place for these refugees rather than let them despair and perish. That, it seems to us, would be the Christian thing to do."[37] Farmer was not clear whether that place could be in the United States. He was clear, though, that it was not in Palestine. "Removing a people by colonization is a method which cannot be defended," he had written the previous year. "In all this our sympathies are with the Arabs, who have occupied the country for more than a thousand years and certainly have as much right to it as the Irish have to Ireland."[38]

Such sentiments were echoed by W. O. Carver in the *Pastor's Periscope*. Carver insisted that continued Jewish immigration to Palestine was no solution to "the problem of the Jew." The "insoluble Palestine situation" was not even "a very large part of the Jewish problem."[39] "It involves at present only a half million Jews. The problem has to do with at least ten million Jews. And the problem becomes increasingly acute and difficult in almost all countries."[40] Carver called for an international conference to attempt to deal with the worldwide Jewish problem. He insisted, too, that Jews recognize that they themselves were part of the problem (a point that unsurprisingly raised the ire of Rabbi Joseph Rauch).[41] While admitting that Christians had committed "gross and shameful" injustices to Jews over the centuries, Carver claimed that "the Jews themselves must share largely in the responsibility for the unending Jewish problem" and complained that Jewish leaders "do not admit that they rightly constitute a problem within any nation." Carver did not take up Zionists' arguments that Zionism *was* an attempt by Jews to solve "their own problem" themselves. He believed that the British should scrap their wartime promises to Jews and Arabs alike and "work out the nearest approximation to a just, rational program for Palestine and inaugurate it as a fixed policy."[42] The following year, he voiced his approval of Britain's 1939 white paper, which limited Jewish immigration and land purchases (and effectively walked back the Balfour Declaration): "the decision reached does seem essentially to conserve basal ethical issues with reference to human rights. To demand on the grounds of sentiment and of Jewish need that the British shall pursue a course involving the removal from Palestine of three times as many Arabs and others as the present Jewish population, is to ignore reason and right in the interest of sentiment and an actual need." Carver went on to reiterate his call for the "enlightened governments of the world" to "unite in seeking a humane and righteous solution of the problem of the Jews." Despite having been reproached by Rauch for his earlier article, Carver reiterated his call for Jews themselves to "face frankly the question of their own position among the peoples of the world through the long centuries of their existence." Unfortunately, "too many Jews are apt to seek preferential consideration based on a more or less conscious and definite claim of superiority and of Divine purpose."[43]

Charles Leek, who published a weekly news commentary column called Watching the World in the *Alabama Baptist*, also blamed Europe's Jews for their persecution.[44] Leek had earlier expressed sympathy for Nazism after attending the 1934 BWA meeting in Berlin, but he changed his tune as Hitler's campaign against Germany's Jews intensified.[45] However, despite feeling "sorry for the Jews" in 1938, he argued that "one cannot [help but] feel that they are largely responsible for their plight."[46] That same year, he criticized Jewish comedian and radio personality Eddie Cantor for condemning Henry Ford's acceptance of a medal from the Nazi regime, claiming that it was "a sad mistake" for Jews to "causticly criticise every pro-Naziism [*sic*]." Leek urged that Jews should rather "have as their single aim the winning of the friendship of the races. Until they do this they are to continue in a pathetic plight."[47] Writing of the MS *St. Louis*'s failure to find a home for its Jewish refugee passengers, Leek claimed, "The sons of Abraham have lived too aloof to be loved."[48]

If Leek's appraisal of the Jewish question was similar to Carver's, his approach to the Palestine question lacked Carver's clear stance. Though Palestine appeared with relative frequency in his column, it primarily served to hold water for shallow witticisms. Writing of the Peel Commission's partition plan, Leek quipped, "Assuming the role of a Solomon in trying to decide the question regarding the ownership of this Palestinian baby, John Bull lifted his political sword to divide this 'child,' . . . only to learn that both 'parents' claim it with such fervor as to make Solomon's situation appear as just mere baby play in comparison."[49] A 1938 column commented on a report that more American Jews had left Palestine in the previous year than had immigrated there. Contrasting the low number of American immigrants with the high amount of American investment in the Yishuv, Leek joked, "The American dollars are remaining in Palestine."[50] Behind such sneers, though, lay some Orientalist admiration for the achievements of the Zionists. A 1937 article praised the women's organization Hadassah for bringing "modern American medical science and sanitation to the superstitious and epidemic-ridden lands of the Near East."[51] In 1938, Leek commented on a report published by the United Palestine Appeal that highlighted the increased Jewish population, agricultural output, factory construction, and investment in Palestine. He concluded the brief note, though, with a characteristic quip: "It's fine to think that 71 per cent of the persecuted Jewish emigrants from Europe since 1931 have found a new home in Palestine, but it is disappointing that Palestine, in view of these things, cannot be preserved in its original state as an International park."[52] In this column alone did Leek draw connections between the persecution of Jews in Europe and the development of the Yishuv.

Though W. O. Carver had published several of his anti-Zionist commentaries in the *Commission*, the editor of the FMB periodical (and executive secretary of the FMB), Charles Maddry—along with his wife, Emma—was avowedly favorable to the movement. Both Maddrys had visited the Baptist missions in Palestine on a 1940 trip, where Emma was struck by the number of Jews "who have fled from the persecutions in Europe to build anew their homes in Zion."[53] Though Emma ascribed no prophetic significance to Jewish settlement in her brief travelogue, Charles later painted the movement with prophetic strokes in his recurring column World Trends. In April 1941, he drew connections between prophecy and the rehabilitation of the land in a column occasioned by a report that the Jewish Agency's plan to commercialize the minerals of the Dead Sea was ahead of schedule. Maddry believed that the Dead Sea was a "storehouse of Almighty God," built in anticipation of "the day when He would need it for the rebuilding of a home for His Chosen People." Elsewhere in the column, Maddry also described the sufferings of the Jews in Europe, offering a prayer that petitioned God to "Shorten the time of their agony, if it can come within the purpose of Thy holy will."[54] Maddry, though, made no explicit connections between these two topics, the suffering of Jews in Europe and the rehabilitation of Palestine. During World War II, Maddry did draw a connection between Palestine and Europe—albeit in a different manner, noting that Jews were volunteering in far greater numbers than Arabs to fight for the Allies. Despite his clear inclination toward the Jewish cause, Maddry nonetheless expressed hope that the Palestine "problem" could be settled "to the mutual advantage of Arabs and Jews."[55]

A Question of American Interests

The United States' greater involvement in the Middle East after World War II brought a renewed interest in the Palestine question. During the war, the combination of the unfolding Holocaust and Britain's 1939 white paper had convinced American Zionists that only Jewish sovereignty could guarantee a home for Jews fleeing persecution. In 1942, they endorsed the

Biltmore Program, which for the first time explicitly called for the conversion of Palestine into a Jewish commonwealth.[56] Besides causing a shift in the policy of American Zionists, growing awareness of the Holocaust also brought large numbers of previously resistant American Jews to support the creation of a Jewish state. One signal of this shift was that the 1943 American Jewish Conference, which included delegations from both Zionist and non-Zionist Jewish organizations, itself endorsed the Biltmore Program, the first time that a representative American Jewish body had endorsed the aim of a Jewish state in Palestine.[57] Greater numbers of Christians (predominantly mainline and liberal Protestants) also joined the cause, coordinating with American Zionists through groups like the APC and the Christian Council on Palestine.[58] By 1944, both the Republican and Democratic Parties had endorsed the creation of a Jewish state in their party platforms, a recognition of the shift in both Jewish and non-Jewish public opinion. After the war, the Truman administration began directly intervening in the Palestine question (Truman's approach will be examined in the next chapter), eventually throwing its support behind the United Nations' partition plan and the creation of a Jewish state in part of Palestine. The Zionists had argued for such a plan since 1946, believing it to be their best bet in quickly achieving an independent Jewish state. Critics of the plan, the most prominent of whom would organize into the Committee for Justice and Peace in the Holy Land in 1948, decried partition as a usurpation of the Arab majority's will, warning that its imposition would threaten the region's stability and that American support for it would harm national interests in the Middle East.

Southern Baptist commentators were not so concerned with the merits of partition or the claims of Arabs and Jews. Of much greater interest was how the situation in Palestine might affect the emerging American-led world order or the United States itself. L. L. Gwaltney, editor of the *Alabama Baptist*, kept a particularly close eye on events.[59] The Alabamian stood out among state Baptist editors in his persistent political editorializing and was never hesitant to comment on domestic or world affairs, whether or not they pertained to matters of religion. Gwaltney had originally been enthusiastic for Zionism. In his 1947 book *The World's Greatest Decade*, he noted that the events of World War I had led him to hope "that the Scripture was being fulfilled concerning the turn of the Jews to their fatherland." However, he had become "terribly disillusioned" when American Jews did not give up "their businesses, palatial homes, automobiles and servants to return to their native land and once again become shepherds of sheep and vine dressers."[60]

Gwaltney was never shy about dabbling in anti-Semitism. In 1948 he invoked the "blood curse" of Matthew 27 in pondering—in specific light of the Holocaust—whether there was "a connection between the persecution of the Jews and the responsibility for the 'blood' which the Jews willfully invoked upon themselves."[61] The Bible likewise colored Gwaltney's view of Arabs. Two weeks after the United Nations voted in favor of partition in Palestine, he argued that the ongoing strife in the region was a continuation of the strife between Sarah and Hagar in the biblical house of Abraham. The Bible prophesied that the hand of Hagar's son, Ishmael, who is understood as the father of the Arab peoples, "would be turned against every man and every man's hand against him." This biblical strife, Gwaltney urged, accounted for the current troubles in Palestine. "Since United Nations has voted for a partition of Palestine," he wrote, "the row which began in Abraham's home has been greatly intensified."[62] Two months later, Gwaltney suggested to his readers, "if one will study that prophecy [concerning Ishmael] in regard to what is now going on in Palestine he will never again doubt the prophets were divinely inspired."[63]

Gwaltney's overriding concern, however, was how the strife in Palestine fit into the development of the postwar order and the unfolding Cold War. A dedicated Democrat and internationalist, the editor was a supporter of Roosevelt and Truman's push for the creation of international institutions that could secure a liberal postwar order. Of particular concern to Gwaltney was the success of the United Nations. In *The World's Greatest Decade*, he declared, "It is my hope that United Nations will hold the world in peace until there evolves from it a world state under law."[64] It was this hope that would predominate in shaping Gwaltney's approach to the Arab-Zionist conflict. More than anything, he simply wanted a result that would bolster the stature of the United Nations. To that end, he supported partition. In February 1948, he called for the United Nations to provide "a military force sufficiently strong" to enforce it. At stake was the legitimacy of the organization. Gwaltney warned that "unless force is used, if it is necessary, then the representatives of the peaceful nations at Lake Success had just as well fold up the organization and go home."[65] When it became clear the United Nations would not use force to ensure partition, he worried that the "United Nations must back track" on the issue, something that would "further weaken the prestige of that organization."[66] Amid the war between Israel and the Arab states, Gwaltney was heartened by the ceasefire reached by UN negotiator Folke Bernadotte in June, less for the prospect of peace itself than the possibility that a truce would bolster the United Nations' world standing.[67] When it shortly failed, Gwaltney concluded that the organization "simply must be superceded by a world state" with power to enforce its decisions.[68]

Other Baptists focused more narrowly on what the Palestine question meant for American interests. Several editorialists agreed with Gwaltney that an outside military force would be necessary in Palestine, but they worried that the United States might have to fund or provide it. Even before the United Nations called for partition, Carver argued that any effort to create a Jewish state could only succeed "by physical force and military domination." Americans were not helping solve the Palestine question "by their sentimental espousal of the claims of the Jews."[69] In early 1948, Finley Tinnin of the *Baptist Message* repeatedly warned of the bloodshed that would occur if the British left Palestine without there being an adequate military force in place to secure the region. "Who will supply the necessary military force to police the country?" he asked, noting that the United Nations did not have an army. Tinnin worried that even if the United Nations abandoned partition for a possible trusteeship, it would require "a full-size military occupation" bolstered by American troops and money.[70] Charles Wells of the *Baptist Student* was more concerned that American involvement in the Palestine question was inviting special interests to dictate American foreign policy. In 1947, he declared, "The question of Palestine is not about Jews getting in or out—the question is OIL." American politicians "with an eye to Jewish votes" were calling for Jewish entry into Palestine, but reversing themselves at the insistence of oil interests.[71] After the declaration of the State of Israel in May and Truman's subsequent recognition, Wells declared that military policy and politics "have gotten criss-crossed." Politics, namely the pursuit of the "large Jewish vote," had guided Truman to support the establishment of Israel over the protests of the "great American oil companies," the "bosom buddies . . . of our armed forces," who had "gotten the country deeply embedded in the Near East Arabian world where we have staged the biggest oil grab in history."[72] Wells himself offered no suggestions of what the United States' Palestine policy should be. He was certain, though, that President Truman would have his hands full.

Conclusion

While Southern Baptist commentary on the Palestine question was characterized by variety, some patterns are apparent. If there existed anything that could be called an anti-Zionist bloc within the SBC, it resided at SBTS.[73] W. O. Carver's editorials against Zionism echoed critiques made by seminary colleagues J. McKee Adams and H. Cornell Goerner (examined in earlier chapters). As professors at the Southern Baptists' leading seminary and as active denominationalists, the three had widespread influence in the SBC. Their opinions were valued by denominational peers and former students, which were many. Every male foreign missionary to Palestine during the Mandate era, for example, had a degree from SBTS. Two of those foreign missionaries who had studied at SBTS with Carver and Adams, H. Leo Eddleman and Robert L. Lindsey, had been premillennialists, believing that the Zionist movement was somehow fulfilling biblical prophecy. Both, possibly under the influence of the SBTS faculty, later changed their minds.

Broadly, Southern Baptists who took a more secular approach to the Palestine question inclined toward the Arab perspective. This alignment did not necessarily mean identifying with any particular Arab political movement—be it pan-Arabism or Palestinian nationalism—but rather expressing a sense that Arab resistance to Zionism was reasonable and that Zionism was not a responsible solution to the problem of anti-Semitism. They also often proved more willing to indulge in anti-Semitic suggestions, hinting that the Jewish people were responsible for their own persecution, as seen in the cases of Carver and Charles Leek. Even so, these critics of Zionism sometimes expressed admiration for it, believing that the movement was bringing a needed modernity to the Holy Land. This Orientalist appreciation, though, obviously did not translate to support for Zionist political goals—especially statehood. In such qualified admiration, they echoed liberal Protestant commentators from outside the convention like Harry Emerson Fosdick, who supported the creation of a Jewish cultural center in Palestine but opposed the creation of a Jewish state.[74]

Overall, however, Southern Baptist political commentators engaged the Palestine question in diverse ways, not only in terms of possible solutions, but in terms of the shape of the question itself. For some, it was a question of God's dealings with the Jewish people. For others, it was a question of self-determination, of humanitarian interest, or of international rights. For L. L. Gwaltney, it was a question of a postwar liberal world order. For Finley Tinnin, it was a question of potential American entanglement. And for Charles Wells, it was just another question to be cynically exploited by special interests, all of whom were tugging at the sleeves of the next chapter's subject, the president of the United States.

10
Cyrus

Whatever their perspectives on Palestine, Southern Baptists knew that the perspective of their coreligionist President Harry S. Truman simply counted for more.[1] Some even tried to use their denominational connections to the president to shape his policy. Jacob Gartenhaus sent Truman a copy of his 1936 *The Rebirth of a Nation* and reiterated its message during a 1947 visit of SBC missionaries to the White House.[2] J. Frank Norris wrote to Truman in support of Zionism that same year. Shortly after the establishment of Israel, H. Leo Eddleman warned the president against supporting the new Jewish state and haltingly offered to discuss the matter at the White House, noting "Your pastor, Dr. Pruden, and I have appeared on Convention programs together."[3] Truman did not take Eddleman up on the offer. Nor did the petitions of Gartenhaus or Norris influence the president's policy, despite their hopes and claims. Nevertheless, the appeals of Gartenhaus, Norris, and Eddleman do raise a worthwhile question: Was there, as these men's entreaties would suggest, something in Harry Truman's Southern Baptist faith that they could appeal to in making their different cases for the fate of the Holy Land?

As president, Truman made a number of decisions that contributed to the establishment of Israel in 1948.[4] UN secretary general Trygve Lie even went so far as to say, "if there had been no Harry Truman there would be no Israel today."[5] Especially important were the President's support for the 1947 UN partition plan, which provided the legal basis for the establishment of Israel, and his near-immediate recognition of Israel at the expiration of the British mandate on May 14, 1948, after months of warfare in Palestine had thrown the viability of partition into doubt. The question of what led Truman to take these steps has been debated for decades. Especially lauded—or lamented—has been that, in taking them, the president defied the wishes of the State Department's professional diplomats as well as that of his own secretary of state, the eminent general George C. Marshall, who feared that support for Zionism would send the Arab world and its vast oil reserves into the arms of the USSR.[6] Some scholars, in what historian Michael Cohen terms the White House school, argue that Truman's humanitarian concern for Jewish survivors of the Holocaust led him to support the creation of Israel in the face of cynical State Department opposition.[7] Others, in what Cohen terms the State Department school, argue that the president acted out of narrow political concern for Jewish votes in New York at the expense of the national interest (many Southern Baptists, including Charles Wells of the *Baptist Student*, argued the same).[8] Since the 1980s, however, scholars have increasingly suggested what Gartenhaus, Norris, and Eddleman implied in their hopeful pleas—that Truman's Southern Baptist faith played a crucial role in his Palestine policy.[9]

For the most part, scholars addressing the role of religion in Truman's decision-making have tended to fall in line with the White House school, seeking to explain the president's actions apart from naked political self-interest.[10] In his 2015 survey of the religious lives of presidents, for example, Gary Smith directly challenges the State Department school, writing that Truman refused to take "the politically expedient route" and was instead "guided by his Christian faith and humanitarian instincts" in making his decision to recognize Israel.[11] Some scholars in this line have even directly claimed that Truman believed that the creation of Israel was a fulfilment of biblical promises. Michael Benson has described Truman as "a student of and believer in the Bible and the Old Testament promises to the Jewish people."[12] Smith, who draws heavily on Benson, has argued the same. Though it is not a central argument in their work, Allis Radosh and Ronald Radosh's *A Safe Haven* claims that biblical prophecy lent Truman "a stamp of approval from a higher authority to the decision to recognize Israel."[13] Paul C. Merkley, focusing more on how Truman understood his own role, has argued that Truman modeled his approach on the biblical example of Cyrus the Great, the Persian ruler who allowed the exiled Judeans to return to Jerusalem.[14] Others have repeated these scholars' claims.[15]

Truman, however, lacked any sense of trajectory when it came to his Palestine policy. Though he ended up providing crucial support in the creation of Israel, he was in many ways dragged there by events and competing interests, rather than driven there by his own concerns. The president did not believe that the establishment of Israel was an inevitable fulfillment of biblical promises, nor did his reading of Cyrus guide his policy choices. As will be seen in this chapter, those claims depend on questionable evidence and fail to explain the policy vacillations that preceded Truman's support for the creation of a Jewish state. At the same time, Truman's Baptist faith should not be discounted in attempting to understand his various Palestine policies. While it was not a driver of his policies, Truman's faith did prepare him in many ways to be amenable to the arguments of Zionists and their supporters, who appealed to Truman's sense of moral duty in calling for him to help suffering Jews in Europe, to his sense of history in articulating Jewish claims to Palestine, and to Orientalist assumptions that he shared with other Baptists in arguing that Jews would make better use of the land than would Arabs. That there were clear political advantages in following these arguments toward supporting the creation of Israel only deepened their resonance.

Truman's Baptist Faith

Writing in the *Christian Century* shortly after Truman's death in 1972, political scientist Merlin Gustafson eulogized the former president as "a sincerely religious man—in fact, one of our more 'religious' presidents."[16] For his entire adult life, Truman had associated himself with Baptist Christianity. His parents, John and Martha, had attended the Blue Ridge Baptist Church, located next to Martha's family's farm in Grandview, Missouri. In 1890, however, the family relocated to Independence and began attending the First Presbyterian Church, where young Harry regularly attended Sunday school. In 1903, when Harry was eighteen, the family moved again—this time to Kansas City, Missouri, where he was baptized into the Benton Boulevard Baptist Church. After moving to Grandview to work the family farm in 1906, he transferred his membership to Grandview Baptist Church, where it remained for the rest of his life.

Truman was not a typical Southern Baptist. Indeed, there was much in Truman's approach to religion that the pastors, missionaries, and denominational workers in the rest of this study would have objected to. He drank. He played poker. He cussed and danced. Yet Truman proudly identified as a Baptist and was sincerely devoted to an independent faith built around three intertwined emphases: morality, democracy, and ecumenism. Morality was most central. Truman believed that the primary function of religion was to create moral individuals and build a moral world. He expressed this attitude most succinctly in a 1911 letter to his future wife, Bess, proclaiming, "I am by religion like everything else. I think there is more in acting than in talking."[17] For Truman, what counted was how religion made individuals act in the world. He claimed to have prayed every day since high school that God would help him "to be, to think, to act what is right, because it is right."[18] In many ways, his approach to Christianity echoed one of his presidential predecessors and personal heroes, Thomas Jefferson. According to Richard Lawrence Miller, Truman enjoyed Jefferson's *The Life and Morals of Jesus of Nazareth*, which famously excised supernatural passages from the Gospels in order to emphasize Jesus's moral teachings. In

1952, he even declared Jefferson to be "the greatest ethical teacher of our time."[19] Truman's favorite passage from the Bible was the Sermon on the Mount, which he understood as the cornerstone of Jesus's ethical teachings and which he believed offered a clear guide for private life and public policy.[20] In a 1951 speech, he proclaimed, "The essential mission of the church is to teach the moral law."[21]

Though Truman was invested in the social and even global implications of religious faith, his understanding of religion was essentially democratic and individualistic. He detested religious formalism and was utterly uninterested in doctrine. For Truman, religion was a matter of the individual's relationship with God and the way in which that relationship made the individual act. "I've always believed that religion is something to live by and not to talk about," he wrote in 1945. "I'm a Baptist because I think that sect gives the common man the shortest and most direct approach to God."[22] Between those two lines lay an unelaborated but evident connection between Truman's emphasis on morality and his embrace of religious democracy. This connection was clearer in a 1952 jab against religious formalism: "Forms and ceremonies impress a lot of people, but I've never thought that The Almighty would be impressed by anything but the heart and soul of the individual." Of course, for Truman, the quality of an individual's heart and soul would be weighed by how they acted—not their adherence to doctrine or participation in "forms and ceremonies." "That's why I'm a Baptist," he continued, "whose church authority starts from the bottom—not the top."[23]

Truman's emphasis on moral action and his democratic approach to religion underlay a type of folk ecumenism that he expressed throughout his adult life. What mattered to Truman was not the type of religion, but its effect on how individuals lived. In 1918, he wrote to Bess from France that "all churches, even the Roman Catholic can do a man a lot of good."[24] In a 1936 letter concerning their daughter's enrollment in Sunday school, he said much the same: "If a child is instilled with good morals and taught the value of the precepts laid down in Exodus 20 and Matthew 5, 6, and 7. . . . It makes no difference what brand is on the Sunday school."[25] Once president, Truman grew increasingly concerned with religious unity and began actively promoting religion—broadly construed—as a necessary moral force in meeting the challenges of the postwar world.[26] In his 1946 speech to the Federal Council of Churches, Truman called for a revival of religion to summon the spiritual and moral forces necessary for the survival of the "civilized world" in the atomic age: "The Protestant Church, the Catholic Church, and the Jewish Synagogue—bound together in the American unity of brotherhood—must provide the shock forces to accomplish this moral and spiritual awakening."[27] Increasingly throughout Truman's administration, this interfaith vision came to be tethered to his Cold War concerns. In 1947, he worked with Myron Taylor, his on-again, off-again representative to the pope, in attempting to unify world religious leaders against Communism. Truman characterized Taylor's efforts as a push to "get the morals of the world on our side."[28] Even as Truman failed to create an international, interfaith movement against Communism, his openness to other faiths apparently only grew. In a note found in his desk after his death, he had written, "Jews, Mohammedans, Buddhists and Confucians worship the same God as the Christians say they do."[29]

Several historians, in describing the president's religious outlook, have seized onto Gustafson's quip that Truman had "an almost fundamentalist reverence for the Bible."[30] Indeed, Truman loved the Bible and read and quoted it frequently. He claimed to have read it through multiple times as a youth in Independence.[31] He also cited his involvement with Freemasonry, an involvement that began in 1909, as crucial in deepening his familiarity with and love for the Scriptures.[32] As president, Truman frequently peppered his speeches with biblical passages and, as noted, claimed that he derived his political philosophy from the Sermon on the Mount. However, if Truman had a fundamentalist reverence for the good book, he did not have a fundamentalist interpretation of it. Far from it. Truman viewed the Bible as a source of moral and spiritual guidance, of wisdom and beautiful literature, and of history. He found the Hebrew prophets inspiring because they "were the protagonists of the common man."[33] He adored Psalms 96 and 137 (the Zionists' favorite) because they were "just like poetry." He loved the Ten Commandments both for their moral content and "sonorous language," and the Sermon on the Mount, "the greatest of all things in the Bible," because it provided "the real way of life."[34] As Gustafson himself noted, "there is little evidence that he had any academic interest in complex theological issues."[35] Truman remained unconcerned with doctrine—the "talking" that he frequently disparaged in his comments on religion—throughout his life.

Prophecy and Cyrus

There was nothing evident in Truman's general approach to religion or in his interpretation of the Bible that would suggest a predisposition toward the Zionist cause. The things that made him similar to other Southern Baptists—his affection for the Bible, his democratic faith—did not suggest it. Nor did the things that set him apart—his interpretation of the Bible or his folk ecumenism. These things may have colored his interpretation of the Palestine question, but they did not provide him with an inherent inclination to support the Zionists. However, some scholars have argued that Truman believed either that the creation of Israel was a fulfilment of biblical promises to the Jewish people or that he was destined to recreate the example of Cyrus the Great. While these claims stand in contrast to Truman's general approach to the Bible, it is entirely possible that Truman could have held contradictory views. He would not have been the first Baptist to do so. However, the evidence that scholars have marshaled for these claims is questionable at best.

In his 1997 *Harry S. Truman and the Founding of Israel*, Michael Benson argues that one of Truman's five motivations for supporting partition and the recognition of Israel was that Truman "was a student of and believer in the Bible and the Old Testament promises to the Jewish people."[36] Allis Radosh and Ronald Radosh's 2009 *A Safe Haven* and Gary Smith's 2015 *Religion in the Oval Office* essentially repeat the same case. All depend heavily on the account of Clark Clifford, Truman's counsel and his primary advisor on Palestine in 1948. Though Clifford was certainly privy to Truman's thoughts on Palestine in the late 1940s, his specific recollections that Truman cited biblical prophecy in support of the Zionist cause were not made until decades after the fact and were mobilized to combat accusations that political considerations had guided the administration's Palestine policy.[37] For example, as Benson cites, Clifford commented at a 1984 congressional celebration of Truman that the president believed that "the Old Testament had made a commitment to these people that some day they would come into their right and some day they would have a homeland of their own," and Clifford later noted in his 1991 memoir, *Counsel to the President*, that Truman was fond of quoting Deuteronomy 1:8 in support of the Zionist cause.[38] However, in a 1977 article, Clifford had made the more moderate claim that as "a student of the Bible," Truman "believed in the historic justification for a Jewish homeland."[39] A belief in historic justification, which implies a recognition of the millennia-long Jewish connection to the land, is something quite different from a belief in divine promises.[40] Smith and Radosh and Radosh have made the same case as Benson, based on Clifford's recollections as well as those of Alfred Lilienthal, who served as a lawyer for the State Department and, later, for the anti-Zionist American Council for Judaism.[41] Lilienthal's recollection that Truman quoted Deuteronomy 1:8 in support of Zionism, however, did not come until 1999.[42] In his earlier, more detailed works on the subject—the 1953 *What Price Israel*, the 1957 *There Goes the Middle East*, and the 1978 *The Zionist Connection*—Lilienthal made no claims that Truman's actions were influenced by a prophetic interpretation of the Bible, despite offering extended explorations of Truman's motivations and, in *The Zionist Connection*, devoting an entire chapter to criticizing Christian support for Israel.[43] Lilienthal, it seems, was himself dependent on Clifford's memoir in augmenting his recollections.

Despite Truman's frequent quotations from the Bible during his presidency, scholars have not presented contemporary evidence suggesting that he understood the creation of Israel as prophetic fulfillment of biblical promises. Nor do such claims fit with what we do know about how Truman interpreted the Bible. The evidence we do have from the time period suggests that Truman understood biblical prophecy not as something to be fulfilled, but as a moral guide to a better world. The prophets, the president noted in 1952, "were the protagonists of the common man, and that is the reason they survived, and for *no other reason*."[44] Truman also questioned the very idea that Jews were a chosen people. In a private note from June 1945, penned after a "dull" church service had allowed Truman "the chance to do some thinking," he wrote, "The Jews claim God Almighty picked 'em out for special privilege. Well, I'm sure He had better judgment. Fact is I never thought God picked any favorites."[45] The claim that Truman viewed the creation of Israel as somehow a fulfillment of biblical promises thus depends completely on the testimony of Clifford, who made no such claim in 1977, noted that Truman "would refer from time to time to Isaiah" and "to other prophets and their views and their commitments" in 1984, and claimed very specifically Truman's fondness for Deuteronomy 1:8 in 1991.[46] Until earlier corroborating evidence is found, Clifford's late recollections remain questionable—as do the arguments that have depended on them.[47]

Gary Smith relatedly contends that Truman sought and took seriously the advice of J. Frank Norris in shaping his Palestine policy. Smith's evidence of this occurrence is the October 2, 1947, letter from Norris to the president (examined in chapter 8) in which the fundamentalist rabble-rouser made the case for Zionism based on his reading of the Bible and international law.[48] While Norris certainly was an influential pastor—and while he was persistent and successful in his efforts to correspond and rub elbows with powerful people—his own suggestions of having influence over the president should not be taken seriously. Neither is there any reason that Truman's politely dismissive reply should be accepted as suggesting that Truman gave the pastor's letter serious consideration, as Smith suggests.[49] Indeed, quoting Truman's letter in full is probably enough to demonstrate that Truman was merely trying to placate the fundamentalist: "I am most grateful for your thoughtful letter of October second. I deeply appreciate having the benefit of this expression of your views because I know that you have given long and extensive study to the Jewish Palestinian question."[50] Though the fundamentalist gloried in the president's attention, printing Truman's response in both the *Fundamentalist* and *My Fifth Trip to Palestine*, it was a tepid acknowledgment at best.

Paul Merkley argues that Truman self-consciously modeled his policy on the biblical example of Cyrus the Great. Two anecdotes figure prominently in this claim. One comes from Eliahu Elath (formerly Epstein), Israel's first ambassador to the United States. About one year after the Israeli proclamation of statehood and Truman's subsequent recognition, the president met with the ambassador and Rabbi Isaac Herzog, the Ashkenazi Chief Rabbi of Israel. According to Elath, the chief rabbi drew a parallel between Truman and Cyrus and claimed "that when the President was still in his mother's womb and before he had seen the light of the world, the Lord had bestowed upon him the mission of helping His Chosen People at a time of despair and aiding in the fulfillment of His promise of Return to the Holy Land." Upon hearing Herzog's words, Truman apparently rose from his chair and, "with great emotion, tears glistening in his eyes," asked the rabbi "if his actions for the sake of the Jewish people were indeed to be interpreted thus and the hand of the Almighty was in the matter."[51] A second anecdote comes from scholar Moshe Davis, about a 1953 meeting with Truman at Jewish Theological Seminary in New York. Truman's longtime friend Eddie Jacobson had escorted the former president to the meeting and introduced him to the gathered scholars as "the man who helped create the State of Israel."[52] According to Davis, the remark caused Truman to turn to his friend and say, "What do you mean 'helped create?' I am Cyrus. I am Cyrus."

To Merkley, these episodes suggest that Truman consciously claimed the "mantle of Cyrus." In *American Presidents, Religion, and Israel* (2004), Merkley describes the president's 1953 quip thusly: "Truman pondered resolutely on the extraordinary circumstances that had made him president. He studied soberly his own strengths and weakness. And he came to the perfectly calm conclusion that he was Cyrus. It was not a manner of speaking, but the largest possible sort of truth, that someone, someday, would be called upon to play the role of Cyrus on behalf of the whole generation of Jews in their time of greatest need."[53] In an earlier work, Merkley likewise advised, "These words of Truman's—'I am Cyrus'—were uttered neither casually nor ironically. We must take them with the fullest seriousness, and when we do, we will have the key to understanding Truman's constant pro-Zionism."[54] While Truman certainly contemplated the examples of the great men of history, including Cyrus, and was conversant with Cyrus's role in the Bible, there is neither any evidence that Truman underwent the process of prophetic self-reflection described in the first quote nor any evidence that his words were spoken as seriously as suggested in the second. While it is of course possible that Truman had privately weighed the prophetic significance of his decision or had privately viewed Cyrus as a model, scholars have not shown that Truman entertained such thoughts prior to the aforementioned meeting with Herzog in 1949—in which it was Herzog who suggested the parallel to a tearful Truman. Even after the fact, Truman seems to have expressed these thoughts only a handful of times, to particular Jewish or Israeli audiences, while never making clear what he meant by the parallel. In his interviews with William Hillman (in the 1950s), his memoirs (in the 1950s), and his interactions with Merle Miller (in the 1960s), all of which at points touched on both the Bible and Israel, Truman never made the comparison and never cited Cyrus in explaining his policy. Two explanations of Truman's Cyrus parallels, it seems, can be argued from the evidence. The first is that Herzog's comments did inspire Truman to increasingly reflect on his decision in biblical terms and that the president only saw fit to reveal these reflections to Jewish audiences.[55] The second is that the parallel that Truman drew between himself and Cyrus was indeed, contra Merkley, uttered casually and ironically—that the biblically literate Truman liked to joke about it. Either way, these expressions only came after Truman's most important decisions involving the Palestine question.

Also important in weighing these claims is that their significance depends on teleological assumptions about Truman's policy. In other words, they have been made to explain why the President supported partition in 1947 or recognized Israel in 1948. However, Truman was never committed to a particular political resolution to the Palestine question. Indeed, at several points, he despaired of the possibility of a solution. Beyond that, Truman was quite willing to entertain policy proposals that stopped short of creating a Jewish state. He was particularly fond of the 1946 Morrison-Grady Plan, which called for the creation of a federated state with semiautonomous Arab and Jewish provinces under the authority of a central government controlled by the British.[56] Truman was alternately vexed and infuriated when the Zionists rejected it, and he even expressed regret *after the establishment of Israel* that it had not been implemented.[57] All this is to say that the evidence itself depends on the outcome it is supposed to explain: if Truman's favored policy had been enacted and an independent Jewish state had not been created, it is unlikely that scholars would argue that his interpretation of biblical prophecy or that the model of Cyrus had inclined him towards it.[58]

Truman's Faith and His Palestine Policies

Truman's vacillations were a result of the many forces that pulled on him as he sought to forge his Palestine policy as president. Coming into office upon the death of Franklin Delano Roosevelt, he had to take into account the private assurances that Roosevelt had given to both the Zionists (that he supported the creation of a Jewish commonwealth) and the Saudis (that he would consult the Arabs before implementing any policy on Palestine). He had to respect the perspective of Britain, the United States' primary ally and the ruling power in Palestine, which wanted Truman to either back its Palestine policy or back off, as well as the recommendations of the US State Department, which feared that support for Zionism would alienate the Arab world, harming access to its oil and sending the Arab states into the arms of the USSR. After the United Nations came to be involved in 1947, he had to consider the United States' investment in the organization's success. And, of course, he had to weigh urgent domestic political demands, not only in relation to the Zionist lobby or the Jewish vote in New York, but to the standing commitments of the Democratic Party and the widespread bipartisan support for the establishment of a Jewish state among the American population in general. Not to be forgotten, either, were conditions on the ground in Palestine, the broader geopolitical environment, and the continuing crisis in Europe.

Truman's religious background did not predispose him toward a particular Palestine policy as he entered this fray, but it did in several ways prepare him to be amenable to the arguments of the Zionists and their supporters within and without his administration. First, Truman's understanding of Palestine's history, informed by his reading of the Bible, led him to recognize the Jewish people's historical connection to the land. Truman may not have believed that Jews had a God-given right to Palestine, but he did believe that Palestine was the ancestral home of the Jewish people, whether or not that conveyed any contemporary political rights. As former Israeli ambassador Eliahu Elath recalled in 1977, the Bible was Truman's "main source of knowledge of the history of Palestine in ancient times."[59] Truman's knowledge of the Bible, according to Clifford's recollections that same year, led him to believe "in the historic justification for a Jewish homeland."[60] This historical reading of the Bible demonstrated for Truman the longstanding Jewish connection to the land. While these claims, like those of the previous section, come from decades after the fact, they do accord with Truman's general approach to the Bible. They also can be fit into Truman's recollections of his engagement with the Palestine question as recorded in his earlier memoirs. For while he made no mention of the Bible in his three chapters on Palestine, he did claim, "For many years I have been interested in the history of that great region."[61] The Bible certainly formed part of this historical interest, leading him to believe that the desire of Jews to immigrate to Palestine was in some sense appropriate, as his speechwriter Samuel Rosenman suggested.[62]

The president's understanding of Palestine's history also contributed to an Orientalist certainty that the Zionists would make better use of the land than would the Arabs.[63] "Except for a short period," he wrote in his memoirs, "the Arabs had never brought the area back to the position of influence and power it had once had."[64] These views derived from both the Bible, which led him to believe that Palestine had flourished in the biblical era, and history, which led him to believe that "the Arabs have just never seemed to take any interest in developing it."[65] Of course, as this study has shown, such views were widespread among Southern Baptists, as they were among Americans more broadly. Indeed, if there was anything that was characteristically—though not uniquely—"Baptist" about Truman's understanding of the Holy Land, it was the Orientalist distinctions that he drew between Jews and Arabs. Zionist leaders were attentive to this Orientalist inclination. On the eve of the UN General Assembly vote for the partition plan, for example, Zionist statesman Chaim Weizmann successfully appealed to Truman to support the inclusion of the Negev Desert and Port of Eilat in the territory allotted to the Jewish state by arguing that only the Zionists could revive and modernize the Negev and that it would remain a waste under the Arabs.[66] As Truman wrote of the Holy Land in his memoirs, the "whole region waits to be developed"—something that he believed was most likely to happen "under the Jews."[67]

Most important, though, was that supporters of Zionism successfully appealed to Truman's sense of moral duty—to Truman, the essence of religion—in pushing him to support opening Palestine as a safe haven for Jewish survivors of the Holocaust. While Truman's sense of moral duty was not the driving force behind his policy, the very real crisis facing Jews in Europe and the moral appeals of the Zionists spoke to Truman's religious sensibilities as he weighed different policy proposals, giving a moral imprimatur to the most politically advantageous course in the face of State Department arguments against it.[68] As Michael Cohen has argued, Truman was a refugee Zionist. His policy toward Palestine, which only reluctantly came to embrace Zionist goals, evolved out of his policy toward the Jewish refugees of Europe.[69] Truman gave his first public comments on the matter as a senator in 1939, when he excoriated the British government's white paper of the same year as making "a scrap of paper out of Lord Balfour's promise to the Jews."[70] He wrote those remarks in entering a *Wash-*

ington Post article into the congressional record that condemned the British government for cutting off "one of the few places on earth to which refugees could go" amid the "Nazi terror in central Europe."[71] In 1941, Truman joined the APC, which at that point prioritized the opening of Palestine to Jewish refugees from Europe.[72] Two years later, he gave a speech in Chicago calling for the creation of a safe haven for persecuted Jews, exclaiming, "Today—not tomorrow—we must do all that is humanly possible to provide a haven and place of safety for all of those who can be grasped from the hands of the Nazi butchers."[73]

While Truman believed that Palestine should be that safe haven, he did not support the Zionist program—especially after Zionists openly embraced the cause of Jewish statehood in 1942. Though a member of the APC, Truman did not support a proposed 1944 congressional resolution, promoted by the organization, that called for the creation of a Jewish commonwealth in Palestine. "I don't want to throw any bricks to upset the apple cart," he wrote supporters of the resolution, "although when the right time comes I am willing to help make the fight for a Jewish homeland in Palestine."[74] Though Truman promised to fight for a Jewish homeland, his form letter studiously avoided the resolution's *commonwealth* terminology. However, that same year, Truman was on the Democratic presidential ticket, running on a platform that called for the "opening of Palestine to unrestricted Jewish immigration and colonization, and such a policy as to result in the establishment there of a free and democratic Jewish commonwealth."[75] Truman walked back his support for the commonwealth the following year. In explaining his reversal, he expressed concern over creating a state on a religious basis—a concern that betrayed his confusion over what the Zionists were even trying to achieve.[76] Though he of course changed his mind again, these vacillations show that Truman was no committed Zionist.

Truman's refugee Zionism is also clear from the policies that he supported as president, which entailed a variety of political solutions to the Palestine question but which were consistent—if not always urgent—on the matter of refugees. His first major intervention in the question came in summer 1945, when he called on the British to allow Jewish displaced persons (DPs) to enter Palestine. After former immigration commissioner Earl Harrison submitted his bombshell report on the condition of nonrepatriable Jewish DPs in Allied-held camps in Europe, Truman wrote to British prime minister Clement Attlee in support of a Jewish Agency proposal that one hundred thousand emergency visas be issued to refugees seeking entry to Palestine.[77] The following year, he reiterated his call in endorsing the recommendation of a joint Anglo-American Committee of Inquiry for the immediate and unconditional issuance of the visas.[78] As noted in the preceding section, he was enthusiastic about the subsequent Morrison-Grady Plan for a federated, binational state under overall British rule, believing that it was fair and that it addressed his primary concern—providing for the admission of one hundred thousand DPs.[79] It was only when the domestic politics of Morrison-Grady proved untenable that Truman reluctantly turned to supporting the creation of a Jewish state through the partition of Palestine. Even as he articulated this turn—on the eve of Yom Kippur and one month before the 1946 midterm elections—he did so in terms of concern for the Jewish DPs.[80]

Truman's sense of moral duty toward Jewish survivors of the Holocaust did not drive this turn toward support for partition and statehood, but it did allow him to see those policies in a moral light—a case that the Zionists and their allies within his administration were making with urgency.[81] After all, in two separate unguarded moments, the president had alternately admitted that he had to answer to "hundreds of thousands" of constituents "anxious for the success of Zionism"[82] and barked at his cabinet that he would base his policy on "what is right."[83] Undoubtedly, those hundreds of thousands shaped Truman's initial, halting support for partition during the midterms of 1946 and his recognition of Israel in the presidential election year of 1948. Undoubtedly, too, Truman came to understand these politically advantageous policies as a way to do what was right in solving a vexing global problem. This concern for doing right by Jewish refugees was how he introduced the issue in his memoirs: "The fate of the Jewish victims of Hitlerism was a matter of deep personal concern to me. I have always been disturbed by the tragedy of people who have been made victims of intolerance and fanaticism because of their race, color, or religion. These things should not be possible in a civilized society. . . . The organized brutality of the Nazis against the Jews in Germany was one of the most shocking crimes of all times. The plight of the victims who had survived the mad genocide of Hitler's Germany was a challenge to Western civilization, and as President I undertook to do something about it. One of the solutions being proposed was a national Jewish home."[84] Zionist leaders knew the power of moral appeals to Truman. Perhaps most revealing is one of the ultimate pleas that Chaim Weizmann made to Truman in April 1948, as the end of the mandate loomed and as the administration wavered in its support for partition. An experienced and effective statesman whom Truman greatly admired, Weizmann was a practiced expert in presenting the Zionist cause in terms that spoke to the most urgent concerns of potential supporters. It is thus telling that at that crucial hour, the Zionist cause hanging in the balance, Weizmann believed that his best option was to appeal to the president on moral terms that spoke to the heart of Truman's faith. "The choice for our people, Mr. President, is between statehood and extermination," he wrote. "History and providence have placed this issue in your hands, and I am confident that you will yet decide it in the spirit of the moral law."[85] Whatever the political considerations, when Truman recognized the newly founded state at 6:11 p.m. on May 14, he certainly believed that he had.

Conclusion

Scholars who focus on the role of religion in Truman's Palestine policies have tended to contrast the president's political and religious interests in the Palestine question. Gary Smith, for example, depicts Truman's "religious faith and humanitarian instincts" as pointing the president away from the "politically expedient" route.[86] In truth, these religious interests led him in the same direction as his political interests, as Truman came to believe that the politically expedient was both in keeping with American national interest and in accord with his faith and instincts. From the Bible, he knew well the Jewish attachment to the Holy Land. From his Orientalist reading of Palestine's history, he believed that it would remain a waste under the Arabs. From his desire for a moral world order, he understood that the leader of the postwar world needed to do something for Europe's suffering Jews. These convictions did not automatically point the President toward supporting Jewish statehood. But as interests and events pulled Truman in different directions, Zionist supporters and Truman's advisors found something to grab in the president's faith that, along with the clear political benefits of their cause, provided significant leverage in bringing him toward supporting partition and recognizing the State of Israel—toward, in other words, reluctantly claiming the mantle of Cyrus.

Conclusion

The delegates who gathered at the 1948 Southern Baptist Convention in Memphis had a much less consequential decision before them than President Truman had made the week before in recognizing Israel. Their most pressing Palestine question, raised by messenger E. D. Solomon of Florida, was whether to send a congratulatory telegram to Truman on his decision. Repeatedly and overwhelmingly, the delegates voted down the proffered resolution. Why? Most, like the editors of the *Western Recorder*, simply wanted the convention to avoid "getting itself into politics."[1] John Popham, reporting on the gathering for the *New York Times*, argued that the motion's defeat "stemmed entirely from a desire to rebuke President Truman for 'playing politics with the Jewish vote' during a national election year." He quoted L. E. Barton of Montgomery, Alabama, who stated plainly, "I'm not very hot for sending anything to the President for recognizing Israel. The President was not doing anything for Palestine and then he saw he had lost the Jewish vote, so he recognized Israel twenty-one minutes after it had been declared a state by the Jews. It was strictly a political measure."[2] Of course, Truman was unpopular in Dixie for reasons far removed from Zion in 1948. Southern Baptists in particular were frustrated with the president for his many overtures to the Vatican, something that might have discouraged a congratulatory message on Israel.[3] As W. Terry Lindley has argued, the fact that J. Frank Norris initially called for the message also probably helped rally the fundamentalist's many enemies against it.[4] All in all, Southern Baptists simply had too many different concerns—too many different Palestine questions—for any such resolution to pass at Israel's birth.

The Palestine question—at least as it had existed—was soon settled by war.[5] By mid-1949, Israel had militarily secured its existence within enlarged borders defined by armistice agreements. Transjordan had seized the West Bank and East Jerusalem. Egypt had taken the Gaza Strip. The Palestinian Arabs who were able to remain found themselves divided among these governments. New questions, however, were raised by the war. Would Palestinians ever have their own country? Could Israel ever find peace with the surrounding Arab states? Could the young state accommodate the hundreds of thousands of Jewish refugees pouring into the country from both Europe and the Islamic world? What would become of the hundreds of thousands of Palestinian Arabs displaced or expelled in the war? To these questions would be added dozens more, particularly after the 1967 Six-Day War, which brought the entirety of what had been Mandatory Palestine (and more) under Israeli control and brought hundreds of thousands of Palestinians under military occupation.[6] Over a half century later, many questions still linger.

Even as these complications have multiplied, for more and more Southern Baptists—as for evangelical Christians and Americans more broadly—the ongoing conflicts between Israel and the Arab states, and between Israel and the Palestinians, have become political issues, wherein categories like pro-Israel, pro-Arab, or pro-Palestinian are relevant, if frustratingly vague. Most Southern Baptists today, like most Americans, would consider themselves pro-Israel. In the most general sense, this alignment has meant identifying first with Israeli concerns in these conflicts (or, more recently, in Israel's conflicts with Hizbollah and Iran). Many Southern Baptists, too, have come to self-identify as Christian Zionists, meaning that they follow the likes of Myrtle Robinson Creasman and J. Frank Norris in viewing support for the Jewish state as a specific Christian duty. E. D. Solomon's 1948 resolution would not fail in today's SBC. Indeed, in 2008 the convention passed a resolution celebrating the sixtieth anniversary of Israel's birth.

While the story of how Southern Baptists came to be so broadly supportive of Israel since 1948 requires its own study, *Between Dixie and Zion* does have lessons for the era of Israeli statehood. First and foremost, the significance of the reality of Israeli statehood itself cannot be overstated. Nothing changed Baptist perceptions of both Jews and Palestine between the Ottoman and Mandate eras more than the actual accomplishments of the Zionist movement on the ground, however much the recognition of those accomplishments was conditioned by Orientalist presumptions. Prejudices were reshaped, and prophecies were reinterpreted, to fit the new reality. The birth and survival of Israel had a similar, albeit more lasting, effect. All of the tacit interest in the return of Jews to Palestine, all of the enthusiasm for the rehabilitation of the Holy Land, all of the passive prophetic hope, and all of the rigid dispensationalist certainty were given definable shape by the armistice agreements that fixed Israel's borders. The Jewish state was real.

As Baptist writers like Z. T. Cody had understood the Zionists in the Mandate era, Southern Baptists would see Israel as "a little patch of our Western civilization" in the "dead and dirty east."[7] While such Orientalist distinctions did not on their own translate into political support for Zionism prior to 1948, they nonetheless provided a language that Baptist supporters of Israel could draw on in making the case for supporting the Jewish state. They also proved adaptable. As the Cold War redrew the real and imaginary lines that divided the world, many Americans—guided in part by the rhetoric of Harry S. Truman—came to interpret the conflict between the United States and the USSR as a clash between Judeo-Christian civilization and godless Communism.[8] Baptist supporters of Israel followed Norris in seizing onto these new geopolitical developments and this new discourse, arguing that the United States and Israel shared values bequeathed by a common Judeo-Christian heritage and, perhaps more importantly, shared enemies inimical to those values in the Soviet Union and its Arab proxies. These claims only grew more compelling as Israel became a Cold War ally of the United States, as Egyptian ruler and pan-Arab leader Gamal Abdel Nasser increasingly aligned with the Soviet Union in the 1960s, and as the revived Palestinian national movement under Yassir Arafat adopted revolutionary terror tactics in the 1960s and 1970s. Even since the end of the Cold War, the belief that the United States and Israel are on the same side of a fundamental civilizational clash has persisted.[9] For even as the Palestine Liberation Organization publicly renounced terror and engaged Israel in the Oslo Process, and even as Arab states like Egypt and Jordan have made peace with the Jewish state, the rise of political Islam—especially the violent Islamist Palestinian nationalism of Hamas—seemed to confirm to many Southern Baptists that the enemies of Israel were the enemies of Judeo-Christian civilization.

These broader lessons should not overshadow the specific processes by which Baptists came to identify more thoroughly with Israel after statehood. Perhaps the most important of these processes was the transformation of the fundamentalist movement both within and without the SBC. The 1940s and 1950s saw the fundamentalist movement split between a radical wing led by the likes of Bob Jones Jr. and Carl McIntire, and a more moderate "new evangelical" wing led by the likes of Harold Ockenga and Southern Baptist Billy Graham.[10] Though the new evangelicals carried over their forebears' emphasis on the fundamentals of the faith, they distinguished themselves by an optimistic desire to spark revival throughout the United States that contrasted with the pessimism and separatism of the radicals. The evangelicals, in other words, wanted to engage the world and American culture—not retreat from them. As they grew in prominence and influence from the 1940s onward, their transdenominational efforts at stirring revival drew in many Southern Baptists. At the same time, separatist fundamentalists, including Independent Baptists like Bob Jones Jr. and

John R. Rice, continued to impact Southern Baptists through their periodicals and educational institutions, through their attacks on the denomination and, sometimes, through their alliances with conservatives and fundamentalists within it.[11]

Within the SBC, a growing number of pastors in the denomination's conservative wing were pairing involvement with the broader fundamentalist or evangelical movement with their denominational commitments. Exemplary of this approach was W. A. Criswell, who succeeded George Truett as the pastor of the First Baptist Church of Dallas. Criswell had grown up Southern Baptist in Oklahoma and Texas and had experienced firsthand the battles between Norris and committed denominationalists like Truett and L. R. Scarborough. His own family had been split on the issue, with his father favoring Norris and his mother adoring Truett.[12] Criswell came to embody aspects of both pastors. He was closer to Norris theologically, particularly in his dispensationalism, and he had an independent streak, founding his own Criswell College in 1970 (former FMB missionary H. Leo Eddleman served as its first president).[13] Like Truett, though, Criswell remained devoted to denominational causes. Every year, First Baptist was a major contributor to the SBC's Cooperative Program. In 1968 and 1969, Criswell was even voted president of the convention.[14] While Criswell was not the first SBC conservative with fundamentalist or evangelical associations to serve as president (M. E. Dodd and R. G. Lee had earlier held the post), his election came as convention conservatives—or denominational fundamentalists—were growing more organized within the SBC.[15]

Into the 1970s, the SBC's denominational institutions remained in the hands of convention moderates committed to the Grand Compromise—the acceptance of relative ideological diversity for the sake of building the denomination and carrying out its missionary imperative. Between the 1950s and the 1970s, however, a string of controversies stirred the convention's conservative wing toward organization. Most prominent were the controversies over Professor Ralph Elliott's 1961 *The Message of Genesis* and the 1969 *Broadman Bible Commentary* on Genesis. Both volumes incorporated the historical-critical method, by which biblical texts are interpreted as products of their historical contexts, in analyzing the biblical account of creation. This method was anathema to convention conservatives, who were particularly troubled that the denomination's press, Broadman, was forwarding such views. In reaction to these specific controversies, as well as to a growing sense that the SBC was no longer safely insulated from pernicious changes in American culture, the conservatives came together in the mid-1970s with a specific plan to secure control of the denominational machinery, using biblical inerrancy as its rallying cry.[16] The fundamentalist takeover, as its opponents called it—or the conservative resurgence, according to proponents—began in earnest with the 1979 election of Adrian Rogers as president of the SBC.[17] While denominational conservatives had served as president before, none had used the office's powers of appointment to remake the convention's institutions. Over the next decade or so, though, conservatives began purging perceived liberals and moderates—many of whom were quite conservative theologically and socially—from denominational boards and institutions, effectively ending the Grand Compromise. From the 1980s onward, the SBC was in many ways closer to J. Frank Norris than it was to George Truett.

Entwined in these developments was premillennialism. Most of the new evangelical leaders, including Billy Graham, were premillennialists. The separatist fundamentalists and independent Baptists, like their radical fundamentalist forebears, almost exclusively subscribed to premillennial dispensationalism. Within the SBC, conservative leaders like W. A. Criswell helped popularize the system, which came to be seen as intertwined with the doctrine of biblical inerrancy.[18] By the late 1980s, surveys revealed that 59 percent of Southern Baptist leaders considered themselves to be premillennialists: the marginal had become the majority.[19] Though premillennialists had expressed a range of views regarding Zionism in the Mandate era, after the establishment of Israel (and especially after Israel's victory in the Six-Day War) they grew increasingly certain that the Jewish state represented at least a partial fulfillment of the covenantal land promises of Genesis and a waypoint on the path to the second coming.[20] Increasing numbers, too, began to hold Norris's line that it was their Christian—and ever more frequently, American—duty to support the Jewish state. Among Southern Baptists, no one pushed this line harder than Criswell, who carried Norris's synthesis forward into the Cold War era, calling on Baptists to support Israel in the name of the Bible and civilization.

The Israeli government itself also began cultivating Baptist support. While Zionist organizations had recruited Christians to their cause in the Mandate era, these efforts had focused on mainline and liberal Protestants, who were seen as more politically influential (as well as less focused on evangelism). Indicative of their priorities was that Norris, who for all his controversy was an influential figure, had to go searching for Jewish organizations with which to align himself in the late 1940s. With support for Israel waning among mainline and liberal Protestants after statehood and, especially, after the 1967 Six-Day War, however, the Israeli government grew increasingly interested in connecting with conservative evangelicals.[21] Building on earlier experiences with mainline Protestants, the government used sponsored travel to cultivate these connections. Among the Israelis' earliest and most important contacts was Criswell, who, shortly after touring the country with a government-provided guide, hosted Yitzhak Rabin (then the Israeli ambassador to the United States) at the 1969 SBC Annual Meeting.[22] In 1971, the Israeli government welcomed a massive evangelical conference on biblical prophecy in Jerusalem that Criswell helped organize.[23] During the same stretch of time, the country's Ministry of Tourism invited two groups of editors of Baptist state papers to visit the country for ten-day tours, with Southern Baptist missionary Robert L. Lindsey serving as one of their hosts.[24] Glowing accounts of the journey—and of Israel itself—soon filled state Baptist periodicals. The headline for George Sheridan's travelogue in the *Christian Index* was particularly telling: "Tour Reveals Israel IS the Holy Land."[25] The Holy Land and the Jewish state had become one and the same.

Although the seeds of the relationship between the Israeli government and American evangelicals were sown under the Labor Party, which had dominated Israeli politics since 1948, it was not until the surprising 1977 electoral victory of the right-wing Likud and the simultaneous rise of the Christian right in the United States that this relationship began to blossom.[26] The Christian right, of course, was a network of political actors and organizations that sought to organize religious voters—especially white evangelicals and fundamentalists—in support of a conservative policy agenda. It is well known that Jerry Falwell, an independent Baptist and the founder of the Moral Majority, developed a friendship with Likud prime minister Menachem Begin during several trips to Israel in the late 1970s and early 1980s.[27] Falwell had grown up as a Southern Baptist and had come to interpret the Bible in a dispensationalist manner, believing that Christians had a duty to stand by the Jewish state.[28] His many trips to Israel—and his relationship with the Israeli government—only confirmed this belief. Southern Baptist Ed McAteer, founder of the Religious Roundtable, likewise placed support for Israel at the center of his political agenda. His annual National Prayer Breakfast in Honor of Israel became an important meeting ground for Christian Zionists seeking to organize on behalf of Israel, including in support of controversial actions like Israel's annexation of East Jerusalem and the construction of settlements in the occupied Palestinian territories.[29] Besides organizing evangelicals in support of Israel, pro-Israel activists in the Christian right facilitated connections between Southern Baptist leaders and the Israeli government. In 1980, Falwell introduced McAteer's pastor, SBC president (and leader in the conservative resurgence) Adrian Rogers, to Menachem Begin at a meeting in Washington. Commenting on the meeting, Rogers noted with a Norris-like mix of geopolitical and prophetic concern, "Just from our personal interests as a nation, apart from biblical prophecy, we would want Israel there as a bulwark against Russian aggression. I still believe the Scripture where it says, 'those who bless Israel, God will bless, and those that curse Israel, God will curse.'"[30]

As Southern Baptist conservatives built relationships with the Israeli government, Baptist moderates built them with American Jewish groups.[31] These efforts were part of a larger movement among American Christians to engage and dialogue with Jews in the decades following the Holocaust. Perhaps surprisingly, the SBC did so through the HMB, which in the years after Jacob Gartenhaus's tenure had folded Jewish missions into the Department of Work related to Nonevangelicals (itself reorganized in 1970 as the Department of Interfaith Witness), which was committed to programs of dialogue and witness. In 1969, the department (under the leadership of Joseph Estes), inaugurated a series of scholars' dialogues with Jewish representatives led by Marc Tanenbaum of the American Jewish Committee and, in later meetings, leaders of the ADL.[32] From the beginning, Tanenbaum placed Israel at the center of Jewish priorities in the meetings, declaring in the inaugural conference that Jews "cannot tolerate the prospect of the undermining of the State of Israel, or the weakening of the unique experiment and mission of the Jewish people and society in Israel." At stake was "the nearly 4,000 year-old mission of the people, the faith, and the land of Israel."[33] While most Baptist participants in the dialogues were not willing to go as far as Tanenbaum, they celebrated Israel's achievements, proclaimed the necessity of its existence, and acknowledged the state's significance in the relationship between Christians and Jews.[34] Reflecting in 1980 after years of meetings, Rabbi James Rudin of the American Jewish Committee would note that they had produced a shared and "abiding commitment to the security and survival of both the people and the State of Israel."[35] These conferences continued into the 1980s, even as convention conservatives moved to return the HMB to the more exclusively evangelistic direction that it had taken during the Gartenhaus era.[36]

While Baptist leaders built relationships with American Jewish groups and the Israeli government itself, an unlikely Palestinian Arab voice was beginning to be heard in Southern Baptist circles. Evangelist Anis Shorrosh had been born in Nazareth during the British mandate.[37] His father, Augustine, had been a Melkite convert of the Southern Baptists' Nazareth mission; Augustine was one of the two promising "native workers" noted in chapter 4 who moved to Haifa and trained under Roswell Owens in the 1930s (at that time, his last name was transliterated as Shirrish). Anis's family had served as the model for the happy convert family of Doreen Owens's mission study novellas, with his brother Assad serving as the protagonist in both *The Camel Bell* and *The Village Oven*. The 1948 war, however, had brought tragedy to the family. Augustine, separated from his wife and children because of an earlier traumatic brain injury, was killed trying to reach Nazareth. The rest of the family had fled Nazareth to Jordan. There, they reconnected with Southern Baptist missionaries, who eventually helped Anis to attend New Orleans Baptist Theological Seminary, where he was a classmate of Adrian Rogers. In 1959, Anis was ordained at the First Baptist Church of New Orleans and appointed by the FMB to serve in Jordanian East Jerusalem. He resigned from the post in 1966, though, to begin an evangelistic ministry with Jan Willem van der Hoeven, a dispensationalist and Christian Zionist who would later found the International Christian Embassy at Jerusalem, now the largest Christian Zionist organization in the world. The following year, Shorrosh returned to the United States, settling in Mobile, Alabama. He became a popular itinerant speaker in the South, especially among Baptists, and began leading tours of Israel twice each year. Shorrosh's primary message was that only Christ could bring lasting peace to Israelis and Arabs. It had been his own faith, after all, that had allowed him to forgive Israelis for all that had occurred to his family. Increasingly, though, Shorrosh grew more deeply enmeshed in dispensationalist thinking and came to understand the events that had torn his family apart as part of God's plan for history.[38] Thus developed the curious situation whereby the most well-known Palestinian Arab in the SBC was himself something of a Christian Zionist.[39]

Even as all of these forces brought Southern Baptists to more closely identify with Israel, though, there remained concerns over the Jewish state's treatment of missionaries and converts.[40] While the Baptist mission had shifted toward greater local control in the previous decades, American missionaries remained the most prominent spokespeople for the field within the convention.[41] From statehood onward, Robert L. Lindsey and Dwight Baker had become vocal advocates of an expansive approach to religious liberty in Israel, an approach informed by both practical missionary concerns and the historical Baptist commitment to the separation of church and state.[42] Particularly disturbing to the missionaries was a 1977 Israeli law banning the use of material inducement in encouraging people to convert. While the Baptists (along with other Christian missionaries) had repeatedly forsworn such practices, they worried that an expansive reading of the law could threaten basic missionary functions. Concern over the issue quickly spread to stateside Baptists, who at the 1978 annual meeting passed a resolution expressing the worry that the law "may inhibit religious freedom."[43] That same year, SBC president Jimmy Allen traveled to Israel to communicate his concerns to Israeli officials. In 1980, Knesset member David Glass invited Allen back to Israel to testify before the Constitution, Law, and Justice Committee on the subject of religious liberty during discussions over the adoption of a Basic (constitutional) Law concerning human rights.[44] If Baptists had concerns about religious liberty in Israel, Knesset members such as Glass made sure that they felt their voices were heard at the highest levels. The *Baptist News* report on the aforementioned 1980 meeting between Adrian Rogers and Menachem Begin noted that the assembled evangelicals "did not have a chance to address the question of religious freedom in Israel," but that even so, Rogers did feel "that Begin had a better understanding of evangelical Christians after the meeting."[45]

Also standing somewhat askance of the burgeoning Southern Baptist support for Israel was Begin's most important Southern Baptist contact, President Jimmy Carter. A committed evangelical Christian who proudly invoked his faith on public matters, Carter adhered to a progressive evangelicalism that ran counter to the emphases of the Christian right. While his faith led him to a deep interest in Israel—he even once called Israel "the fulfillment of prophecy"—it did not lead him to unquestioning political support for the Jewish state.[46] Rather, his religious investment in the country primarily manifested itself in a desire to see peace in the Holy Land, a "sacred cause" that he made a leading priority in his administration's foreign policy.[47] While Carter failed in his grand ambition to reach a comprehensive settlement of the conflict, he played a crucial role in negotiating the Camp David Accords between Begin and Egyptian president Anwar Sadat, which prepared the way for a peace treaty between Israel and Egypt in 1979. Carter remained religiously committed to the pursuit of peace between Israel and the Palestinians after leaving office, writing in 2007 that the "spilled blood in the Holy Land still cries out to God—an anguished cry for peace."[48]

Though Carter was himself an evangelical, most evangelicals rallied to his 1980 opponent Ronald Reagan, who endorsed a gathering of Christian right leaders at a National Affairs Briefing in Dallas. That gathering was a crucial moment not only in American political history but in Baptist-Jewish relations, as Adrian Rogers's successor as SBC president, H. Bailey Smith, infamously proclaimed at the meeting, "God Almighty does not hear the prayer of a Jew."[49] After the comments were publicized in the *Dallas Morning News*, condemnation poured in on Smith and the SBC. In response to the outcry, the ADL extended an invitation to Smith and other Baptist leaders to tour Israel with ADL representatives. In November and December 1981, a group of twenty visited the country, meeting with both Israeli representatives—who apparently suggested that Baptists build a study center in East Jerusalem—and Baptist missionaries, who expressed concern "that Southern Baptist leaders realize Baptists in Israel work with both Arabs and Jews and be cautious about siding with either group."[50] Increasingly, Baptist missionaries had grown worried that growing Baptist political support for Israel was harming their ability to work among Arabs.[51] Attempting to navigate every interested party's concerns, Smith said of the trip, "Everywhere we went, people talked about the survival of the state of Israel. . . . And when you talk about the state of Israel, you're talking about everyone in it, including the Arabs. . . . We realize half the people of Israel are non-Jewish. I want to underscore our support for the people. While we were there, we discerned a warmth and respect for the rights of others to live and worship as they please."[52]

Israel remained on Southern Baptists' minds at the 1982 convention (presided over by Smith), which featured another debate over a resolution expressing support for the Jewish state. James DeLoach of Houston, Texas, was the author of the resolution, which asserted, "God's prophetic program as presented in the scriptures includes the present State of Israel as part of God's completion of all things."[53] Even among fundamentalist supporters of Israel, DeLoach was something of an extremist. He would come to be involved in the Jerusalem Temple Foundation, an organization that looked forward to the building of a third temple on the site of the Dome of the Rock and the reestablishment of the Temple cult.[54] After DeLoach's resolution came to the floor, Thomas Conley of Georgia proposed an amendment stating that the resolution "in no way condones Israel's recent invasion of Lebanon" and that Southern Baptists "support peaceful means to alleviate the problems between Israel and her neighbors."[55] The amendment passed, but the resolution itself was referred to the Committee on Resolutions. Keith Parks, president of the FMB and a moderate, then took the lead in opposing the resolution. He invoked the Grand Compromise in offering three criticisms: that it expressed an eschatological viewpoint not shared by many Baptists, that it unnecessarily implicated Baptists in political questions, and that it could harm or even imperil Baptist mission workers in Israel and Arab lands. The motion was tabled. Missionary priorities had, for the moment, overcome conservative politics. However, the failure of the 1982 resolution did not mean that Southern Baptists were not broadly supportive of Israel. It meant, rather, that there remained significant enough countervailing forces within the convention—in this case, the FMB and its concerns—to prevent an official convention statement on the matter. The following decades, however, would see a winnowing of these forces. Only one example of this trend is that Parks was pushed from the FMB in the early 1990s as conservatives continued to secure control of denominational institutions.

In 2002, a resolution expressing support for the Jewish state finally passed the convention. The timing of the resolution was no accident. The year before had witnessed the September 11 attacks on the United States. At the same time, a Palestinian uprising in the West Bank (the Second Intifada) and the Israeli response to it had grown increasingly violent. Many Americans, Baptists included, came to see the United States and Israel as sharing a common enemy—Islamic terror. Then, as ever, the lines that divided the world seemed to put the United States and Israel—to put Southern Baptists and Israel—on the same side. The 2002 resolution expressed "abhorrence of all forms of terrorism as inexcusable, barbaric, and cowardly acts" and support for "the right of sovereign nations to use force to defend themselves against aggressors."[56] The priority of the resolution, though, was to express support for "the right of Israel to exist as a sovereign state." It laid out several reasons for this support, among them that the "Jewish people have an historic connection to the land of Israel, a connection that is rooted in the promises of God" and that "the international community restored land to the Jewish people in 1947 to provide a homeland for them and reestablish the nation of Israel." It also expressed love for both Israelis and Palestinians and called on both peoples "to pursue policies that promote genuine religious liberty and peace between themselves and their neighbors." In conclusion, the resolution offered a prayer "that the true peace of our Lord will reign in the lives of the Israeli and Palestinian peoples and that this peace will bring blessing to this war-torn land."[57] Though much had changed in the Southern Baptist Convention—though much had changed in Israel and Palestine—Christ, as ever, remained Southern Baptists' ultimate answer to every Palestine question.

Notes

Introduction

1. "Draft of Recognition of Israel," May 14, 1948, Ross Papers, Alphabetical Correspondence File, 1916–1950, *Harry S. Truman Library and Museum*, http://www.trumanlibrary.org/whistlestop/study_collections/israel/large/index.php.

2. Southern Baptist messengers are representatives from affiliated churches that are allowed to vote their conscience.

3. The leading biography of Norris is Barry Hankins, *God's Rascal: J. Frank Norris and the Beginnings of Southern Fundamentalism* (Lexington: University Press of Kentucky, 1996).

4. J. Frank Norris to A. B. Akein, January 22, 1948, Box 22, Folder 1010, J. Frank Norris Papers, Southern Baptist Historical Library and Archives (SBHLA), Nashville, TN.

5. J. Frank Norris, "Who Owns or Has Title to Palestine?" *Fundamentalist*, October 10, 1947, 1.

6. W. Terry Lindley, "The 1948 SBC Opposition to Israel: The J. Frank Norris Factor," *Baptist History and Heritage* 22, no. 4 (1987): 24.

7. Samantha Smith and Carroll Doherty, "5 facts about how Americans view the Israeli-Palestinian conflict," *Pew Research Center*, May 23, 2016, http://www.pewresearch.org/fact-tank/2016/05/23/5-facts-about-how-americans-view-the-israeli-palestinian-conflict/. Some Southern Baptists contest the label "evangelical," identifying it specifically with the interdenominational evangelical movement. However, Southern Baptists' main theological emphases fit within historical definitions of evangelicalism: the authority of the Bible, the personal experience of salvation by Christ, and the missionary imperative. For an example of this debate, see James Leo Garrett, Glenn Hinson, and James Tull, *Are Southern Baptists "Evangelicals"?* (Macon, GA: Mercer University Press, 1983).

8. Samuel Goldman argues that three themes have animated American Christian Zionism: covenant, prophecy, and a sense of common heritage. See Goldman, *God's Country: Christian Zionism in America* (Philadelphia: University of Pennsylvania Press, 2018), 9–10. Daniel Hummel interprets American Christian Zionism as a reconciliation movement between American evangelicals and Jews, rooted in theological transformations, institutional collaboration, and interstate relations. See Hummel, *Covenant Brothers: Evangelicals, Jews, and U.S.-Israeli Relations* (Philadelphia: University of Pennsylvania Press, 2019).

9. On early strands of Judeo-centric prophecy interpretation, see Richard Cogley, "The Fall of the Ottoman Empire and the Restoration of Israel in the 'Judeo-Centric' Strand of Puritan Millenarianism," *Church History* 72, no. 2 (2003): 304–32; and Andrew Crome, *The Restoration of the Jews: Early Modern Hermeneutics, Eschatology, and National Identity in the Works of Thomas Brightman* (New York: Springer, 2014). Works that have emphasized the role of premillennial interpretations of the Bible in inspiring American evangelical Protestant support for Zionism and Israel include: Yona Malachy, *American Fundamentalism and Israel: The Relationship of Fundamentalist Churches to Zionism and the State of Israel* (Jerusalem: Institute of Contemporary Jewry, 1978); Timothy Weber, *Living in the Shadow of the Second Coming: American Premillennialism, 1875–1982* (Grand Rapids, MI: Zondervan, 1983), 128–57; Weber, *On the Road to Armageddon: How Evangelicals Became Israel's Best Friend* (Grand Rapids, MI: Baker Academic Press, 2004); David Rausch, *Zionism within Early American Fundamentalism, 1878–1918: A Convergence of Two Traditions* (Lewiston, NY: Edwin Mellen Press, 1979); Yaakov Ariel, *On Behalf of Israel: American Fundamentalist Attitudes toward Jews, Judaism, and Zionism, 1865–1945* (Brooklyn, NY: Carlson, 1991); Ariel, *An Unusual Relationship: Evangelical Christians and Jews* (New York: New York University Press, 2013); Paul Boyer, *When Time Shall Be No More: Prophecy Belief in Modern American Culture* (Cambridge, MA: Belknap Press, 1992); Paul C. Merkley, *The Politics of Christian Zionism, 1891–1948* (Portland, OR: Cass, 1998); Victoria Clark, *Allies for Armageddon: The Rise of Christian Zionism* (New Haven, CT: Yale University Press, 2007); and Caitlin Carenen, *The Fervent Embrace: Liberal Protestants, Evangelicals, and Israel* (New York: New York University Press, 2012), 28–30, 189–211. Robert Smith sees Christian Zionism's roots in a combination of Judeo-centric (including premillennial) hermeneutics and a belief in "covenantal nationalism" in *More Desired Than Our Owne Salvation: The Roots of Christian Zionism* (New York: Oxford University Press, 2013). Shalom Goldman foregrounds the variety of ways in which different Christian individuals and groups have engaged with Zionism and Israel, while noting the importance of eschatology to certain Protestant groups, in *Zeal for Zion: Christians, Jews, and the Idea of the Promised Land* (Chapel Hill: University of North Carolina Press, 2009). Joseph Williams argues that premillennialist Pentecostal Christians have infused Christian Zionism with an experiential element in "The Pentecostalization of Christian Zionism," *Church History* 84, no. 1 (2015): 159–94. Daniel Hummel emphasizes the role of premillennialist evangelicals within Israel in building relationships between American evangelicals and the Jewish state in "A 'Practical Outlet' to Premillennial Faith: G. Douglas Young and the Evolution of Christian Zionist Activism in Israel," *Religion and American Culture* 25, no. 1 (2015): 37–81. Amy Weiss explores American Jewish Zionist organizations' outreach to evangelicals from the 1960s onward in "Between Cooperation and Competition: The Making of American Jewish Zionist Interfaith Alliances with Liberal and Evangelical Protestants, 1898–1979," (PhD diss., New York University, 2014), 300–333. Stephen Spector argues that premillennial dispensationalism accounts for only a small amount of evangelical support for Israel and that "Christian Zionist beliefs comprise a complex system of scriptural mandate, historical justification, political conviction, and empathic connection" in *Evangelicals and Is-*

rael: The Story of American Christian Zionism (New York: Oxford University Press, 2009), 26.

10. Edward Said, whose grandparents Shukri and Munira Mosa were Southern Baptist missionaries, argued that Western cultural representations and academic studies of "the Orient"—particularly in Britain, France, and later, the United States—were inexorably intertwined with the actual political and material processes of empire and colonialism. According to Said (and the postcolonial school that followed him), Western representations of the Orient helped to create habits of mind among Westerners that rendered sensible, even necessary, the imperialist and colonialist projects of the nineteenth and twentieth centuries. Said referred to these representative practices as Orientalism. See Edward Said, *Orientalism* (New York: Pantheon, 1978) and *Culture and Imperialism* (New York: Knopf, 1993). Some scholars have applied this approach to American understandings of Palestine: Hilton Obenzinger, *American Palestine: Melville, Twain, and the Holy Land Mania* (Princeton, NJ: Princeton University Press, 1999); and Lawrence Davidson, *America's Palestine: Popular and Official Perceptions from Balfour to Israeli Statehood* (Gainesville: University Press of Florida, 2001). Douglas Little uses the concept of Orientalism to frame American foreign policy in the Middle East (including toward Israel/Palestine) in *American Orientalism: The United States and the Middle East since 1945* (Chapel Hill: University of North Carolina Press, 2002). Kathleen Christison argues that American Orientalism contributed to structuring "frames-of-reference" that have inclined American policymakers toward supporting Zionism and Israel in *Perceptions of Palestine: Their Influence on U.S. Middle East Policy* (Berkeley: University of California Press, 1999). Robert MacDonald argues that American support for Zionism in the early twentieth century was characterized by the belief that Zionists were engaged in a "civilizing mission" in "'A Land without a People for a People without a Land': Civilizing Mission and American Support for Zionism, 1880s–1929" (PhD diss., Bowling Green State University, 2012). Mae Elise Cannon emphasizes how Orientalist assumptions widely permeated American Protestant attitudes toward Palestine in "Mischief Making in Palestine: American Protestant Christian Perspectives of Israel and Palestine, Pre-1916 to 1955" (PhD diss., University of California, Davis, 2014), 85–88. Eric Newberg uses a postcolonial framework to analyze the work and writings of Pentecostal missionaries in Palestine in *The Pentecostal Mission in Palestine: The Legacy of Pentecostal Zionism* (Eugene, OR: Pickwick, 2012).

11. Spector, *Evangelicals and Israel*, 113. Neil Rubin likewise notes the intermixing of geopolitical and theological motives in contemporary evangelical support for Israel in "The Relationship between American Evangelical Christians and the State of Israel," in *Israel and the United States: Six Decades of US-Israeli Relations*, ed. Robert O. Freedman (New York: Routledge, 2018), 235. Lawrence Davidson argues that American Christian Zionism has been in part an extension of American notions of Manifest Destiny into the Middle East in "Christian Zionism as a Representation of American Manifest Destiny," *Critique: Critical Middle Eastern Studies* 14, no. 2 (2005), 157–69.

12. Harry Truman, *Memoirs*, vol. 2, *Years of Trial and Hope* (New York: Doubleday, 1956), 156.

Chapter 1

1. On the concept of the Holy Land in the broader American religious culture, see Moshe Davis, "The Holy Land in American Spiritual History," in *With Eyes toward Zion*, ed. Moshe Davis (New York: Arno Press, 1977), 3–33. See also Robert Handy, "Sources for Understanding American Christian Attitudes toward the Holy Land, 1800–1950," in Davis, *With Eyes*, 34–56.

2. Yehoshua Ben-Arieh, *The Rediscovery of the Holy Land in the Nineteenth Century* (Jerusalem: Magnes Press, 1979).

3. Butrus Abu-Manneh, "The Rise of the Sanjak of Jerusalem in the Late Nineteenth Century," in *The Israel/Palestine Question: A Reader*, ed. Ilan Pappé (New York: Routledge, 2007), 41–52.

4. Justin McCarthy, *The Population of Palestine: Population Statistics of the Late Ottoman Period and the Mandate* (New York: University of Columbia Press, 1990), 8–14.

5. For introductory works on Zionism, see Arthur Hertzberg, *The Zionist Idea: A Historical Analysis and Reader* (Philadelphia: Jewish Publication Society, 1997); Shlomo Avineri, *The Making of Modern Zionism: The Intellectual Origins of the Jewish State* (New York: Basic Books, 1981); Gideon Shimoni, *The Zionist Ideology* (Waltham, MA: Brandeis University Press, 1995); and Walter Laqueur, *A History of Zionism* (New York: Schocken, 1976).

6. Within Ottoman territory, this emergence was concentrated in what would later become Syria and Lebanon, which had more developed missionary education systems.

7. The classic work on the origins of Arab nationalism is George Antonius, *The Arab Awakening: The Story of the Arab National Movement* (Philadelphia: J. B. Lippincott, 1939). Antonius's emphasis on Christian intellectuals and American missionary schools has been repeatedly challenged since. On both Arab nationalism and scholarship of it, see Rashid Khalidi, Lisa Anderson, Muhammad Muslih, and Reeva S. Simon, eds., *The Origins of Arab Nationalism* (New York: Columbia University Press, 1991).

8. Rashid Khalidi, *Palestinian Identity: The Construction of Modern National Consciousness* (New York: Columbia University Press, 2010).

9. Ottoman subjects and, later, citizens drew on a variety of identities, even into World War I: Michelle Campos, *Ottoman Brothers: Muslims, Christians, and Jews in Early Twentieth-Century Palestine* (Stanford, CA: Stanford University Press, 2011).

10. Najib Azouri, quoted in Neville Mandel, *The Arabs and Zionism before World War I* (Berkeley: University of California Press, 1976), 52.

11. SBC Annual, 1861, 18.

12. SBC Annual, 1861, 18.

13. SBC Annual, 1861, 18 (emphasis in original).

14. SBC Annual, 1873, 20.

15. SBC Annual, 1873, 35–36.

16. "Receipts for Foreign Missions," *Foreign Mission Journal* 7, no. 3 (September 1874): 12.

17. Henry Allen Tupper, "The First Baptist Church in Jerusalem," *Foreign Mission Journal* 22, no. 1 (August 1890): 9.

18. Henry Allen Tupper, "Mission to the Jews," in *The Foreign Missions of the Southern Baptist Convention*, ed. Henry Allen Tupper (Philadelphia: American Baptist Publication Society, 1880), 442–59. Though the SBC would have no specific mission to Jews until the 1920s, at times missionaries in various foreign fields hired temporary workers to work among Jewish communities.

19. Tupper, 449–50.

20. A. J. Holt, "Jerusalem No. 1," *Foreign Mission Journal* 22, no. 2 (September 1890): 41.

21. Holt, 42.

22. Holt, 43.

23. Holt, 44.

24. T. P. Bell, "Palestine for the Jews," *Foreign Mission Journal* 22, no. 10 (May 1891): 293.

25. Scraps Picked Up, *Foreign Mission Journal* 23, no. 6 (January 1892): 169; Scraps Picked Up, *Foreign Mission Journal* 23, no. 7 (February 1892): 204–5; and Scraps Picked Up, *Foreign Mission Journal* 24, no. 3 (October 1892): 71–72.

26. "Receipts for Foreign Missions," *Foreign Mission Journal* 22, no. 8 (March 1891): 255.

27. James A. Patterson, *James Robinson Graves: Staking the Boundaries of Baptist Identity* (Nashville, TN: Broadman and Holman, 2012), 75–84; James Spivey, "The Millennium," in *Has Our Theology Changed?*, ed. Paul Basden (Nashville: Broadman and Holman, 1994), 239–42; D. E. Howe, "An Analysis of Dispensationalism and Its Implications for the Theologies of James Robinson Graves, John Franklyn Norris, and Wallie Amos Criswell" (PhD diss., Southwestern Baptist Theological Seminary, 1988), 67–139.

28. Graves came to claim dispensationalism: James Robinson Graves, *The Dispensational Expositions of the Parables and Prophecies of Christ* (Memphis, TN: Graves and Mahaffy, 1887); and Graves, *The Work of Christ Consummated in Seven Dispensations* (Memphis, TN: Baptist Book House, 1883).

29. James Robinson Graves, "THE SCRIPTURES, No. 13: What Saith the Scriptures?—Will the Jews Be Restored to Palestine?" *Tennessee Baptist*, March 11, 1854, 2.

30. Graves, 2.

31. Ernest Sandeen cites premillennialism as the guiding force behind the development of the Christian fundamentalist movement in the United States in *The Roots of Fundamentalism: British and American Millenarianism, 1800–1930* (Chicago: University of Chicago Press, 1970). George M. Marsden treats premillennialism within fundamentalism in *Fundamentalism and American Culture: The Shaping of Twentieth Century Evangelicalism, 1870–1925*, 2nd ed. (New York: Oxford University Press, 2006), 48–71. See also Joel Carpenter, *Revive Us Again: The Reawakening of American Fundamentalism* (New York: Oxford University Press, 1997), 89–109. Matthew Avery Sutton sees premillennialism as the driving force within American evangelicalism in *American Apocalypse: A History of Modern Evangelicalism* (Cambridge, MA: Harvard University Press, 2014).

32. Graves's Landmarkism was marked not only by appeals to Baptist distinctiveness but by a Jacksonian emphasis on the ability of the layperson and local church to settle their own matters. His exceptionalism was thus not a devotion to denominationalism. Andrew Smith, "'Flocking by Themselves:' Fundamentalism, Fundraising, and the Bureaucratization of the Southern Baptist Convention, 1919–1925" (PhD diss., Vanderbilt University, 2011), 8–9.

33. In a 1906 article, Albert Newman noted the spread of premillennialism among Baptists broadly. Newman cited Broughton as its representative in the South. Albert Newman, "Recent Changes in the Theology of Baptists," *American Journal of Theology* 10, no. 4 (1906): 587–609. For Broughton's own explanation of his eschatology, see Leonard Broughton, *The Second Coming of Christ* (Philadelphia, PA: Pepper, 1902).

34. William Glass, *Strangers in Zion: Fundamentalists in the South, 1900–1950* (Macon, GA: Mercer University Press, 2001), 42.

35. The list included 227 names in total, stretching back to the Reformation. "Eminent Exponents of Premillennialism," *Christian Workers Magazine*, December 1913, 223–25.

36. M. E. Dodd, *Jesus Is Coming to Earth Again* (Chicago: Chicago Bible Institute Colportage Association, 1917), 59–63.

37. On travel to Palestine and travel literature in the nineteenth and early twentieth centuries, see Ben-Arieh, *Rediscovery*; Stephanie Stidham Rogers, *Inventing the Holy Land: American Protestant Pilgrimage to Palestine, 1865–1941* (Lanham, MD: Lexington Books, 2011); Nitza Rosovsky, "Nineteenth-Century Portraits through Western Eyes," in *City of the Great King*, ed. Nitza Rosovsky (Cambridge, MA: Harvard University Press, 1996), 218–40; Hilton Obenzinger, *American Palestine: Melville, Twain, and the Holy Land Mania* (Princeton, NJ: Princeton University Press), 1999; Lester I. Vogel, *To See a Promised Land: Americans and the Holy Land in the Nineteenth Century* (University Park: Penn State University Press, 2010); and Shimon Gibson, Yoni Shapira, and Rupert Chapman, eds., *Tourists, Travellers, and Hotels in Nineteenth-Century Jerusalem* (Leeds, UK: Maney, 2013).

38. This trip was immortalized in Mark Twain, *The Innocents Abroad* (Hartford, CT: American, 1869).

39. On the professionalization of Baptist clergy in the nineteenth century, see Beth Barton Schweiger, *The Gospel Working Up: Progress and the Pulpit in Nineteenth-Century Virginia* (New York: Oxford University Press, 2000); and Paul Harvey, *Redeeming the South: Religious Cultures and Racial Identities among Southern Baptists, 1865–1925* (Chapel Hill: University of North Carolina Press, 1997).

40. The story of the Broadus gavel was relayed by L. R. Scarborough at the 1939 convention. SBC Annual, 1939, 112.

41. A. T. Robertson, *Life and Letters of John Albert Broadus* (Philadelphia: American Baptist Publication Society, 1901).

42. See, for example: Joseph Marstain Fort, *The Texas Doctor and the Arab Donkey, or Palestine and Egypt as Viewed by Modern Eyes* (Chicago: Donohue and Henneberry, 1898); and Walter Andrew Whittle, *A Baptist Abroad* (New York: J. A. Hill, 1890).

43. Henry Marvin Wharton, *A Picnic in Palestine* (Baltimore, MD: Wharton and Barron, 1892).

44. Henry Allen Tupper, *Around the World with Eyes Wide Open* (New York: Christian Herald, 1898); and Tupper, *Uncle Allen's Party in Palestine* (Philadelphia: American Baptist Publication Society, 1898).

45. W. A. Hamlett, *Travels of a Father and Son* (Lebanon, PA: Sowers, 1911).

46. An itinerary for a Gaze & Sons tour organized with Baptist pastor Thomas Treadwell Eaton can be found in box 3, folder 5, Thomas Treadwell Eaton Papers, Southern Baptist Historical Library and Archives (SBHLA). For other examples, see *Programmes and Itineraries of Cook's Arrangements for Palestine Tours* (London: Thomas Cook & Son, 1876); and *Cook's Tourists' Handbook for Palestine and Syria* (London: Thomas Cook & Son, 1876).

47. Edgar Folk, "A Delightful Tour," *Baptist and Reflector*, November 14, 1907, 8.

48. Much of the humor in Mark Twain's *The Innocents Abroad* derives from Twain's accounts of pilgrims struggling to make their experiences fit the generic pilgrimage conventions already established by the late 1860s.

49. Edward Robinson and Eli Smith, *Biblical Researches in Palestine, Mount Sinai, and Arabia Petraea: A Journal of Travels in the Year 1838* (Boston: Crocker and Brewster, 1841); and Arthur Stanley, *Sinai and Palestine in Connection with Their History* (London: Murray, 1856).

50. Rolla Floyd, *Letters from Palestine: 1868–1912*, ed. Helen Palmer Parsons (n.p.: Parsons, 1981). Joseph Fort was escorted by Floyd; see Fort, *The Texas Doctor*, 277.

51. J. W. Graham, "Nazareth and Its Baptist Mission," *Baptist Standard*, September 18, 1913, 2–3.

52. Robertson, *Life and Letters*, 261.

53. Wharton, *A Picnic in Palestine*, 71.

54. Wharton, 214; and Sarah Hale, "Travels in Palestine," *Tennessee Baptist*, June 27, 1907, 3.

55. Tupper, *Around the World*, 362, 365; Tupper, *Uncle Allen's Party*, 55; and Whittle, *A Baptist Abroad*, 432–33.

56. Tupper, for example, described workers in a field outside Bethlehem as providing "a vivid picture of Ruth gleaning after the reapers," Tupper, *Around the World*, 350.

57. Wharton, *A Picnic in Palestine*, 285.

58. Hamlett, *Travels of a Father and Son*, 121; and Wharton, *A Picnic in Palestine*, 154.

59. Tupper, *Uncle Allen's Party*, 26. Baptists referred to the groups that now constitute what we would consider the Arab population by several different names. Syrian was among the most common.

60. Tupper, *Around the World*, 331, 366.

61. Hamlett, *Travels of a Father and Son*, 121.

62. Whittle, *A Baptist Abroad*, 433.

63. Whittle, 334, 417–18.

64. Wharton, *A Picnic in Palestine*, 72.

65. Wharton, 230.

66. Wharton, 197.

67. Hamlett, *Travels of a Father and Son*, 161.

68. Hamlett, 161. Such clashes between expectation and reality were extremely

common in Protestant travelers' experiences of the Holy Land in the nineteenth century. For some other examples, see Gershon Greenberg, *The Holy Land in American Religious Thought: The Symbiosis of American Religious Approaches to Scripture's Sacred Territory* (Lanham, MD: University Press of America, 1994), 87–112.

69. Robertson, *Life and Letters*, 264.

70. For an exploration of American Christian attitudes toward Islam, see Thomas S. Kidd, *American Christians and Islam: Evangelical Culture and Muslims from the Colonial Period to the Age of Terrorism* (Princeton, NJ: Princeton University Press, 2009); and Christine Leigh Heyrman, *American Apostles: When Evangelicals Entered the World of Islam* (New York: Hill and Wang, 2015).

71. Wharton, *A Picnic in Palestine*, 207. Wharton's most overtly positive statement about Islam was, "There are many good features in the Mohammedan religion, as there are in all religions which have grown out of the truth" (147).

72. Hamlett, *Travels of a Father and Son*, 160–61.

73. Wharton, *A Picnic in Palestine*, 291–92.

74. Tupper, *Uncle Allen's Party*, 17. For other references to Muslim fanaticism, see: Hamlett, *Travels of a Father and Son*, 187, 251, 275; and Tupper, *Uncle Allen's Party*, 85, 154 (referring to Muslims in Syria).

75. Hamlett, *Travels of a Father and Son*, 150, 170.

76. Millard Jenkens, "A Trip through the Holy Land," *Biblical Recorder*, April 22, 1903, 10.

77. Wharton, *A Picnic in Palestine*, 206–7.

78. Hamlett, *Travels of a Father and Son*, 256.

79. Fort, *The Texas Doctor*, 312.

80. Robertson, *Life and Letters*, 268.

81. On the Church of the Holy Sepulchre, see Tupper, *Uncle Allen's Party*, 41. Tupper was indeed impressed by the many sacrifices that Russian pilgrims made to come to Jerusalem. On this subject, see Tupper, *Uncle Allen's Party*, 30; Tupper, *Around the World*, 334; and Tupper, "Pilgrims in the Holy Land," *Baptist and Reflector*, June 18, 1896, 1.

82. Wharton, *A Picnic in Palestine*, 250.

83. Hamlett, *Travels of a Father and Son*, 188.

84. Wharton, *A Picnic in Palestine*, 120.

85. Tupper, *Around the World*, 344.

86. Hamlett, *Travels of a Father and Son*, 258.

87. Hamlett, 259–60.

88. Sarah A. Hale, "From Jerusalem, Palestine," *Baptist and Reflector*, October 18, 1906, 7.

89. Tupper, "Pilgrims in the Holy Land," *Baptist and Reflector*, June 18, 1896, 1.

90. Tupper, *Around the World*, 332; the school was Mikveh Israel at Holon.

91. Sarah A. Hale, "From Jerusalem, Palestine," *Baptist and Reflector*, October 18, 1906, 7. Hamlett did the same, while asserting that the Jews would not inherit the land until they accepted Christ: "When they turn to God and to God's Christ, then God will turn to them and give them their land and their Temple." Hamlett, *Travels*, 263.

92. Sarah A. Hale, "From Jerusalem, Palestine," *Baptist and Reflector*, October 18, 1906, 7.

93. Wharton, *A Picnic in Palestine*, 264.

94. Wharton, 264.

95. Tupper, *Uncle Allen's Party*, 22.

96. Wharton, *A Picnic in Palestine*, 237–38.

97. Wharton, 208.

98. Although it was always a minority viewpoint, the hope that Jews would help in redeeming the land from Muslims had Protestant antecedents from the sixteenth century onward. See Richard Cogley, "The Fall of the Ottoman Empire and the Restoration of Israel in the 'Judeo-Centric' Strand of Puritan Millenarianism," *Church History* 72, no. 2 (2003): 304–32.

Chapter 2

1. For a highly readable account of the Mandate era, see Tom Segev, *One Palestine, Complete: Jews and Arabs under the British Mandate* (New York: Macmillan, 2000).

2. The Balfour Declaration stated, "His Majesty's government view with favour the establishment in Palestine of a national home for the Jewish people." The formula was a softening of the original Zionist proposal that Palestine be recognized as "*the* national home *of* the Jewish people" (emphasis added). See Leonard Stein, *The Balfour Declaration* (New York: Simon and Schuster, 1961), 547; and Jehuda Reinharz, "The Balfour Declaration in Historical Perspective," in *Essential Papers on Zionism*, ed. Jehuda Reinharz and Anita Shapira (New York: New York University Press, 1996), 587–616. For the text of the mandate, see League of Nations, "The British Mandate," in *The Israel-Arab Reader*, ed. Walter Laqueur and Barry Rubin, 7th ed. (New York: Penguin, 2008), 30–35.

3. Jacob Norris, *Land of Progress: Palestine in the Age of Colonial Development, 1905–1948* (Oxford: Oxford University Press, 2013).

4. Anita Shapira, *Israel: A History*, trans. Anthony Berris (Waltham, MA: Brandeis University Press, 2012), 67–154.

5. Itamar Rabinovich and Jehuda Reinharz, eds., *Israel in the Middle East: Documents and Readings on Society, Politics, and Foreign Relations, Pre-1948 to the Present* (Waltham, MA: Brandeis University Press, 2008), 571–72.

6. Henry McMahon, "The McMahon Letter," in Laqueur and Rubin, *The Israel-Arab Reader*, 11–12.

7. Muhammad Y. Muslih, *The Origins of Palestinian Nationalism* (New York: Columbia University Press, 1988), 115–224; Baruch Kimmerling, "The Formation of Palestinian Collective Identities: The Ottoman and Mandatory Period," *Middle Eastern Studies* 36, no. 2 (2000), 61–67; and Rashid Khalidi, *Palestinian Identity: The Construction of Modern National Consciousness* (New York: Columbia University Press, 2010), 145–76.

8. Philip Mattar, "The Mufti of Jerusalem and the Politics of Palestine," *Middle East Journal* 42, no. 2 (1988): 227–40.

9. Benny Morris, *Righteous Victims: A History of the Zionist-Arab Conflict, 1881–2001* (New York: Vintage Books, 2001), 88–106.

10. Z. T. Cody, "Zionism," *Biblical Recorder*, February 4, 1920, 8.

11. "Baptists Plan Reconstruction Program," *Snyder Signal*, October 10, 1919, 2.

12. In 1939, T. W. Medearis and George Sadler, FMB secretary for Europe, Africa, and the Near East, visited the Palestine missions during a broader inspection of Baptist work abroad. For materials on this trip, see box 4, folders 65 and 66, T. W. Medearis Papers, Southern Baptist Historical Library and Archives (SBHLA).

13. Adams was there for a month and a half. Among his fellow travelers was John Bunn, who published his account of the trip in the *Biblical Recorder*; see John Bunn, "A Visit to Jerusalem," *Biblical Recorder*, March 8, 1933, 8.

14. One important party to Palestine from the 1923 Stockholm meeting was the Armstrong Party from Texas. For more on that trip, see chapter 3. In 1934, sitting SBC president M. E. Dodd and a cohort visited Palestine after the Berlin meeting.

15. Badgett Dillard and Lucy Adams, "Oral History Interview of Lucy Oliver Adams (Mrs. J. McKee Adams)," transcribed by Michele Fowler, February 14, 1980, James P. Boyce Centennial Library Digital Repository, Southern Baptist Theological Seminary, http://hdl.handle.net/10392/43. J. McKee Adams, *Biblical Backgrounds: A Geographical Survey of Bible Lands in the Light of the Scriptures and Recent Research* (Nashville, TN: Broadman Press, 1934).

16. Percy Upchurch, "Letter from Jerusalem," *Biblical Recorder*, October 4, 1933, 11.

17. W. T. Halstead, "Conflict in the Land of Peace," *Florida Baptist Witness*, n.d., box 255, folder 30, International Mission Board (IMB) Minutes and Reports, 1849–2005, SBHLA.

18. Though Shukri Mosa's mission had effectively begun in Safed in 1910 before moving to Nazareth the next year, it was under the purview of the Illinois Baptist Missionary Convention before being taken over by the FMB in 1919. During the war, it was shut down.

19. One example of the former comes from Ernest Sellers, "Where Jesus Loved to Be," *Biblical Recorder*, November 30, 1927, 4: "If the pilgrim will allow his sanctified imagination to have free reign, will overlook much that is sordid and disgusting but will recall the life and labor of Him who began His world transforming work with such simple folk as even now live in the land."

20. Coleman Craig, "What I Remember Best from a Trip abroad," *Baptist Standard*, November 8, 1923, 9. Craig evinced no particular sympathy for Zionism during his 1923 travels, however in the late 1940s he gathered petitions in support of the American Christian Palestine Committee (ACPC). File 138, ACPC Collection, Central Zionist Archives.

21. J. M. Dawson, "A Pilgrimage and Some Parables—II," *Baptist Standard*, September 11, 1924, 8.

22. Also important in the Mandate era were literary sources. For his 1927 trip (and articles about it), Hight C. Moore amassed a small collection of literature on the region. See box 22, folder 13; box 29, folder 3; and box 67, folder 11, of the Hight C. Moore Papers, SBHLA.

23. E. F. Tatum, "Beginning (Over Again) at Jerusalem." *Biblical Recorder*, January 9, 1924, 10; John Wicker, "A Thrilling Story of a Lost Bible," *Biblical Recorder*, January 20, 1926, 14; O. R. Mangum, "Baptist Work in Palestine and Syria," *Biblical Recorder*, August 11, 1926, 10; Kyle Yates, "Jerusalem and Judea," *Biblical Recorder*, June 5, 1929, 10; John Bunn, "A Visit to Jerusalem," *Biblical Recorder*, March 8, 1933, 8; Ernest Sellers, "A Modern Miracle at Cana," *Biblical Recorder*, April 26, 1933, 1;

Mrs. Charles Leonard, "By Way of Palestine," *Biblical Recorder*, May 22, 1935, 12; Wilbur Smith, "A Notable Work among Jewish Children," *Biblical Recorder*, January 4, 1939, 12; and R. T. Bryan, "From Shanghai to New York, Second Article: Jerusalem to Beirut," *Biblical Recorder*, July 9, 1930, 3.

24. Shukri Mosa, "Letter from Nazareth," *Baptist Standard*, October 4, 1924, 15.

25. Wicker, "A Thrilling Story of a Lost Bible," 14.

26. Mrs. James Washington Watts, *Palestinian Tapestries* (Richmond, VA: Foreign Mission Board, 1936), 44.

27. R. T. Bryan, "From Shanghai to New York, Second Article: Jerusalem to Beirut," *Biblical Recorder*, July 9, 1930, 3; John Bunn, "Little Journeys in Palestine: From Jerusalem to Nazareth," *Biblical Recorder*, March 29, 1933, 1; Charles Pierce, "News from Jerusalem," *Baptist Standard*, July 25, 1929, 3; Walter Alexander, *Holy Hours in the Holy Land* (Grand Rapids, MI: Eerdmans, 1946), 117.

28. R. T. Bryan, "From Shanghai to New York, Second Article: Jerusalem to Beirut," *Biblical Recorder*, July 9, 1930, 4.

29. Alexander, *Holy Hours*, 117.

30. Alexander, 117. Alexander traveled to Palestine in 1934, though he did not publish his travelogue until 1946.

31. John Bunn, "Little Journeys in Palestine: From Nazareth to Tiberias," *Biblical Recorder*, April 26, 1933, 10.

32. R. T. Bryan, "From Shanghai to New York, Second Article: Jerusalem to Beirut," *Biblical Recorder*, July 9, 1930, 4.

33. Alexander, *Holy Hours*, 17.

34. E. Norfleet Gardner, "Joppa," *Biblical Recorder*, January 30, 1935, 13.

35. R. T. Bryan, "From Shanghai to New York, Second Article: Jerusalem to Beirut," *Biblical Recorder*, July 9, 1930, 4.

36. Z. T. Cody, "Zionism," *Biblical Recorder*, February 4, 1920, 8.

37. J. M. Dawson made such observations of Arabs in northeastern Egypt, describing the "position of women in Mohammedan lands" as pathetic. Dawson, "A Pilgrimage and Some Parables—III," *Baptist Standard*, September 18, 1924, 8.

38. John Bunn, "Little Journeys in Palestine: Journeying around Jerusalem," *Biblical Recorder*, May 24, 1933, 1.

39. Bunn, 1.

40. John Bunn, "Little Journeys in Palestine: From Nazareth to Tiberias," *Biblical Recorder*, April 26, 1933, 10.

41. J. M. Dawson, "A Pilgrimage and Some Parables—IV," *Baptist Standard*, September 23, 1924, 11.

42. Z. T. Cody, "Zionism," *Biblical Recorder*, February 4, 1920, 8. The purpose of this trip, as mentioned, was to survey the European and Levantine mission fields after the war. It is entirely possible that Cody owed his change of heart to interactions with the local Baptist community.

43. Cody, 8.

44. Morris, *Righteous Victims*, 111–20; and Hillel Cohen, *Year Zero of the Arab-Israeli Conflict: 1929*, trans. Haim Watzman (Waltham, MA: Brandeis University Press, 2015).

45. Two British commissions had concluded that the underlying causes of the

riots were fears of dispossession brought on by Zionist land purchases (which often led to the displacement of Arab peasant farmworkers), Jewish immigration, and the frustration of Arab national ambitions. *Report of the Commission on the Palestine Disturbances of August, 1929* (London: His Majesty's Stationery Office, 1930); and John Hope Simpson, *Palestine: Report on Immigration, Land Settlement and Development* (London: His Majesty's Stationery Office, 1930).

46. J. McKee Adams, "The Current Situation in Palestine," *Home and Foreign Fields*, October 1929, 3; also in Adams, *The Heart of the Levant* (Richmond, VA: Foreign Mission Board, 1937), 91–92. Jewish historiography tends to refer to the events of 1929 as the Wailing (or Western) Wall Riots. Palestinian historiography sometimes refers to them as the al-Buraq Uprising.

47. J. McKee Adams, "The Current Situation in Palestine," 4; also in Adams, *The Heart of the Levant*, 93. By "aggressive wing," Adams meant the Revisionist Zionists, the main opponents of the Labor Zionists within the Yishuv. Revisionist Zionists sought an overt British commitment to the creation of a Jewish state and had led Jewish protests at the Western Wall.

48. J. McKee Adams, "The Current Situation in Palestine," 7; also in Adams, *The Heart of the Levant*, 103.

49. Morris, *Righteous Victims*, 121–60.

50. William Robert Wellesley Peel, *Palestine Royal Commission Report* (London: Her Majesty's Stationery Office, 1937).

51. Ruth Collie, "Travels in the Holy Land," n.d., box 255, folder 30, IMB Minutes and Reports, 1849–2005, SBHLA.

52. Halstead, "Conflict in the Land of Peace," *Florida Baptist Witness*, n.d., box 255, folder 30, IMB Minutes and Reports, 1849–2005, SBHLA.

53. "British White Paper of 1939," The Avalon Project, Yale Law School, Lillian Goldman Law Library, accessed April 5, 2019, http://avalon.law.yale.edu/20th_century/brwh1939.asp.

54. Morris, *Righteous Victims*, 161–79.

55. "The Biltmore Program," in Laqueur and Rubin, *The Israel-Arab Reader*, 55–56.

56. United Nations Special Committee on Palestine, "Summary Report," in Laqueur and Rubin, *The Israel-Arab Reader*, 65–68.

57. "United Nations General Assembly Resolution 181," November 29, 1947, The Avalon Project, Yale Law School, Lillian Goldman Law Library, accessed April 5, 2019, http://avalon.law.yale.edu/20th_century/res181.asp.

58. James Day, "The Jew—the Arab—and Palestine," *Florida Baptist Witness*, November 20, 1947, 6.

59. Day, 5. In Jerusalem, Day had heard Judah Magnes, president of the Hebrew University, plead the binationalist cause to the UN Special Committee on Palestine. On Magnes, see Daniel Kotzin, *Judah L. Magnes: An American Jewish Nonconformist* (Syracuse, NY: Syracuse University Press, 2010).

60. James Day, "The Jew—the Arab—and Palestine," *Florida Baptist Witness*, January 1, 1948, 5.

61. On the war, see Benny Morris, *1948: A History of the First Arab-Israeli War* (New Haven, CT: Yale University Press, 2008).

62. State of Israel, "Proclamation of Independence," in Laqueur and Rubin, *The Israel-Arab Reader*, 81–82.

63. Duke McCall, "Israel: An Immoral Miracle," *Biblical Recorder*, November 18, 1950, 2; McCall traveled to the region as part of a worldwide trip with W. A. Criswell, who would become the leading Southern Baptist supporter of Israel in the 1960s and 1970s. McCall also used the "immoral miracle" phrase in a travelogue cowritten with Criswell: W. A. Criswell and Duke McCall, *Passport to the World* (Nashville: Broadman, 1951), 54.

64. J. McKee Adams, "Palestine and Southern Baptists," *Home and Foreign Fields*, November 1929, 7.

65. Hight Moore, "The Land of the Book for the Lord of the Book," *Home and Foreign Fields*, January 1928, 4.

66. Claude Broach, "On Visiting the Holy Land," *Christian Index*, January 20, 1938, 21, box 255, folder 30, IMB Minutes and Reports, 1849–2005, SBHLA.

67. Rashid Khalidi, *The Iron Cage: The Story of the Palestinian Struggle for Statehood* (Boston, MA: Beacon Press, 2006), 13–14.

68. Jacob Norris, "Transforming the Holy Land: The Ideology of Development and the British Mandate in Palestine," *Humanity: An International Journal of Human Rights, Humanitarianism, and Development* 8, no. 2 (2017): 269–70. These concessions included rights to Dead Sea potash and the construction of the Naharayim power plant.

69. On the dual economies of Mandatory Palestine, see Jacob Metzer, *The Divided Economy of Mandatory Palestine* (New York: Cambridge University Press, 1998).

Chapter 3

1. Ussama Makdisi, *Artillery of Heaven: American Missionaries and the Failed Conversion of the Middle East* (Ithaca, NY: Cornell University Press, 2009); and A. L. Tibawi, *American Interests in Syria, 1800–1901: A Study of Educational, Literary, and Religious Work* (Oxford: Clarendon, 1966).

2. One such figure was the novelist and historian Jurji Zaidan, who was educated at the Syrian Protestant College and later moved to Egypt. See Thomas Philipp, "Language, History, and Arab National Consciousness in the Thought of Jurji Zaidan (1861–1914)," *International Journal of Middle East Studies* 4, no. 1 (1973): 3–22.

3. Joseph Grabill, "Protestant Diplomacy and Arab Nationalism, 1914–1948," *American Presbyterians* 64, no. 2 (1986): 113–24; Grabill, *Protestant Diplomacy and the Near East: Missionary Influence on American Policy, 1810–1927* (Minneapolis: University of Minnesota Press, 1971); and Ussama Makdisi, *Faith Misplaced: The Broken Promise of U.S.-Arab Relations: 1820–2001* (New York: PublicAffairs, 2010), 132–203.

4. Other Southern Baptist missions in the Middle East were likewise initiated by locals. See Melanie E. Trexler, *Evangelizing Lebanon: Baptists, Missions, and the Question of Cultures* (Waco, TX: Baylor University Press, 2016), 11–74.

5. I have chosen to transliterate Shukri and Munira's surname as "Mosa" since this is how they themselves transliterated it in corresponding with their Southern Baptist connections. It is also how their name appears in most Southern Baptist records. The family itself, though, has come to transliterate the name as "Musa."

6. According to Munira's granddaughter Jean Said Makdisi, Munira studied Old Testament, New Testament, reading, writing, arithmetic, grammar, history, and composition in 1893 as a thirteen-year-old. Munira also attended the school's teaching class, which covered criticism lessons, singing drill, drill, plain needlework, fancy needlework, and cutting out (pattern making). Jean Said Makdisi, *Teta, Mother, and Me: Three Generations of Arab Women* (New York: Norton, 2006), 182–86.

7. Shukri Mosa, "A Letter from Nazareth," *Baptist Standard*, January 2, 1919, 31.

8. J. W. Graham, "Nazareth and Its Baptist Mission," *Baptist Standard*, September 18, 1913, 3.

9. Shukri Mosa to James Marion Frost, January 27, 1913, box 25, folder 16, James Marion Frost Papers, Southern Baptist Historical Library and Archives (SBHLA).

10. Shukri Mosa, "Annual Report to Baptist Missionary Convention," April 3, 1914, 2, box 25, folder 16, Frost Papers, SBHLA.

11. Actual attendance could vary wildly. In 1912, an average of fifty-six students attended across both Sunday school classes. The following year, however, Shukri noted only thirty-three children attending regularly; Shukri Mosa to James Marion Frost, October 9, 1912, box 25, folder 16, Frost Papers, SBHLA; and S. Mosa to Frost, January 27, 1913, box 25, folder 16, Frost Papers, SBHLA.

12. Shukri Mosa, "Annual Report to Baptist Missionary Convention," April 3, 1914, 2, box 25, folder 16, Frost Papers, SBHLA.

13. Mosa, 3.

14. Eugene Rogan, *The Fall of the Ottomans: The Great War in the Middle East* (New York: Basic Books, 2015); Kristian Coates Ulrichsen, *The First World War in the Middle East* (New York: Oxford University Press, 2014), 113–18; Abigail Jacobson, "Negotiating Ottomanism in Times of War: Jerusalem during World War I through the Eyes of a Local Muslim Resident," *International Journal of Middle East Studies* 40 (2008): 69–88; Jacobson, "A City Living through Crisis: Jerusalem during World War I," *British Journal of Middle Eastern Studies* 36, no. 1 (2009): 73–92; and Donna Robinson Divine, "Palestine in World War I," in *The Middle East and North Africa: Essays in Honor of J. C. Hurewitz*, ed. Reeva S. Simon (New York: Columbia University Press, 1990), 71–94.

15. Shukri Mosa to T. B. Ray, December 6, 1919, box 355, folder 31, International Mission Board (IMB) Minutes and Reports, 1849–2005, SBHLA.

16. At the 1920 London conference, American and European Baptist mission bodies agreed to divide and coordinate an invigorated mission effort around the globe. Palestine was assigned to the SBC. J. D. Hughey, "Europe and the Middle East," in *Advance: A History of Southern Baptist Foreign Missions*, ed. J. Baker Cauthen (Nashville, TN: Broadman Press, 1970), 194–95.

17. Shukri Mosa to T. B. Ray, March 5, 1923, box 255, folder 31, IMB Minutes and Reports, 1849–2005, SBHLA.

18. Shukri Mosa to Isaac Jacobus Van Ness, February 13, 1919, box 22, folder 3, Isaac Jacobus Van Ness Papers, SBHLA.

19. Shukri Mosa to T. B. Ray, March 5, 1923, box 255, folder 31, IMB Minutes and Reports, 1849–2005, SBHLA.

20. Shukri Mosa to T. B. Ray, July 18, 1923, box 255, folder 31, IMB Minutes and Reports, 1849–2005, SBHLA.

21. L. R. Scarborough wrote a brief recollection of the trip that was published in various state periodicals. See, for example, Scarborough, "A Strong Hope in the Land of Our Lord," *Biblical Recorder*, October 3, 1923, 5.

22. Nazareth Baptist Church to the Foreign Mission Board, September 2, 1928, box 255, folder 31, IMB Minutes and Reports, 1849–2005, SBHLA.

23. Louis Hanna to J. Wash Watts, September 19, 1928, box 62, folder 5, IMB Missionary Correspondence Files, SBHLA.

24. T. B. Ray to J. Wash Watts, September 17, 1928, box 62, folder 5, IMB Missionary Correspondence Files, SBHLA.

25. Louis Hanna, "There He Could Do No Mighty Work because of Their Unbelief," *Home and Foreign Fields*, July 1932, 14–15.

26. Velora Hanna, "New Life in Old Nazareth," *Home and Foreign Fields*, December 1933, 11.

27. That the Hannas were allowed furlough was perhaps a compromise made with the FMB over their appointment as native workers. Normally, of course, native workers did not spend furlough time in the United States. Jessie Ruth Ford, "Our Missionary Family Circle," *Commission*, April 1939, 119.

28. Shukri Mosa to T. B. Ray, February 26, 1920, box 255, folder 31, IMB Minutes and Reports, 1849–2005, SBHLA.

29. Shukri Mosa to J. F. Love, September 27, 1921, box 255, folder 31, IMB Minutes and Reports, 1849–2005, SBHLA.

30. Shukri Mosa, "My Trip through Galilee," *Baptist Standard*, July 22, 1922, 6.

31. Mosa, 6.

32. Mosa, 6.

33. Shukri Mosa, "The Near East Mission at Nazareth, Palestine," *Baptist Standard*, November 20, 1924, 10.

34. Louis Hanna, "There He Could Do No Mighty Work because of Their Unbelief," *Home and Foreign Fields*, July 1932, 14.

35. J. S. Makdisi, *Teta, Mother, and Me*, 213, 231. Enaya Hammad Othman examines the interaction of mission, gender roles, and nationalism at the Friends Girls School in Ramallah during the late Ottoman and Mandate eras in *Negotiating Palestinian Womanhood: Encounters between Palestinian Women and American Missionaries, 1880s–1940s* (New York: Lexington Books, 2016).

36. Velora Hanna, "Questing in Galilee," in *Questing in Galilee* (Richmond: Foreign Mission Board, 1937), 45.

37. Louis Hanna, "There He Could Do No Mighty Work because of Their Unbelief," *Home and Foreign Fields*, July 1932, 15.

38. Louis Hanna, "Current Movement of Thought and Religion in Palestine," *Baptist Messenger*, February 6, 1930, 6.

39. Hanna, 6–7.

40. Hanna, 7.

41. Hanna, 7.

42. Many collective identities were competing for Palestinian minds and hearts at the time. The development of a distinctively Palestinian national identity, according to Baruch Kimmerling, did not really occur until after the failure of Faisal to establish his greater Syrian kingdom; see Baruch Kimmerling, "The Formation of

Palestinian Collective Identities: The Ottoman and Mandatory Periods," *Middle Eastern Studies* 36, no. 2 (2000): 48–81. On the place of Arab Christians within the nascent Palestinian national movement, see Daphne Tsimhoni, "The Arab Christians and the Palestinian Arab National Movement during the Formative Stage," in *The Palestinians and the Middle East Conflict*, ed. G. Ben-Dor (Ramat Gan, Israel: Turtledove, 1978): 73–98; see also Noah Haiduc-Dale, *Arab Christians in British Mandate Palestine: Communalism and Nationalism, 1917–1948* (Edinburgh: Edinburgh University Press, 2013); and Laura Robson, *Colonialism and Christianity in Mandate Palestine* (Austin: University of Texas Press, 2011). For more on the place of Arab Christians within Palestinian Arab society, see Anthony O'Mahoney, "Palestinian Christians: Religion, Politics, and Society, c. 1800–1948," in *Palestinian Christians: Religion, Politics and Society in the Holy Land*, ed. Anthony O'Mahoney (London: Melisende, 1999), 9–55.

43. Nazareth did not have an organized Muslim-Christian association, but Muslim and Christian community leaders did at times unite against the Zionist movement. In 1920, the heads of both religious communities submitted a shared protest letter to the military governor. See Haiduc-Dale, *Arab Christians in British Mandate Palestine*, 42–43.

44. J. S. Makdisi, *Teta, Mother, and Me*, 220.

45. Quoted in Makdisi, 250. This sense of alienation does seem to have changed over time, as the mission came to be a permanent fixture in Nazareth. Even as they stood out, the Mosas eventually came to be respected members of the Nazareth community. See Makdisi, 229–30, 267.

46. Chapters 14 and 15 of *Teta* give an insightful depiction of a variety of ways in which the Mosas' faith set them apart from the Nazareth community.

47. Z. T. Cody, "Zionism," *Biblical Recorder*, February 4, 1920, 8.

48. On contemporary Arab Baptist leaders in Israel, see Azar Ajaj and Duane Alexander Miller, "Arab Baptist Leaders in Israel: Their History and Collective Identity," in *Arab Evangelicals in Israel*, ed. Azar Ajaj, Duane Alexander Miller, and Philip Sumpter (Eugene, OR: Pickwick, 2016), 52–64.

Chapter 4

1. E. C. Miller, "The Establishment of the First Baptist Church, College, Hospital, and Orphan Asylum at Jerusalem" (Richmond, VA: Foreign Mission Board, June 8, 1921), box 110, folder 37, International Mission Board (IMB) Minutes and Reports, 1849–2005, Southern Baptist Historical Library and Archives (SBHLA).

2. In 1919, the SBC initiated the 75 Million Campaign, a massive fundraising effort with the aim of greatly expanding the denomination's institutions and mission work at home and abroad. The campaign failed to raise the actual amount pledged and resulted in large debts for the mission boards. However, it did help speed the development of the SBC's denominational infrastructure. See Thomas S. Kidd and Barry Hankins, *Baptists in America* (New York: Oxford University Press, 2015), 177–78.

3. For a historical overview of the first decades of the mission, see the chapter "Baptists in Nazareth" in Rebecca Rowden, *Baptists in Israel: The Letters of Paul and Marjorie Rowden, 1952–1957* (Nashville, TN: Fields, 2010). The divergent priorities

of foreign missionaries and native workers in the Near East Mission's Lebanese stations is a major theme in missiologist Melanie E. Trexler's *Evangelizing Lebanon: Baptists, Missions, and the Question of Cultures* (Waco, TX: Baylor University Press, 2016), 75–140.

4. Like the Nazareth mission, the Rasheya and Kfarmichky missions had been started independently and only later were supported by the SBC.

5. For an overview of the historiography of American foreign missions, see Dana Robert, "From Missions to Mission to Beyond Missions: The Historiography of American Protestant Foreign Missions since World War II," in *New Directions in American Religious History*, ed. Harry Stout and D. G. Hart (New York: Oxford University Press, 1997), 362–93. In recent decades, scholars have given increased attention to the domestic impact of the foreign missions; see, for example, Daniel H. Bays and Grant Wacker, ed., *The Foreign Missionary Enterprise at Home: Explorations in North American Cultural History* (Tuscaloosa: University of Alabama Press, 2009); and David Hollinger, *Protestants Abroad: How Missionaries Tried to Change the World but Changed America* (Princeton, NJ: Princeton University Press, 2017). Eric Newberg has argued that Pentecostal missionaries played an important role as brokers of Pentecostal Zionism in the Mandate era; see Eric Newberg, *The Pentecostal Mission in Palestine: The Legacy of Pentecostal Zionism* (Eugene, OR: Pickwick, 2012), 181–85.

6. Portions of this section have been published as Walker Robins, "The Forgotten Origins of the Southern Baptist Convention's Near East Mission: W. A. Hamlett's Month in the Holy Land," *Baptist History & Heritage* 52, no. 2 (2017): 20–31.

7. M. E. Dodd published a short premillennial dispensationalist work in 1917 that included a list of prominent premillennialists; W. A. Hamlett was one of the few Southern Baptists named. See Dodd, *Jesus Is Coming to Earth Again* (Chicago: Chicago Bible Institute Colportage Association, 1917), 59–63. Hamlett also expressed premillennial views in *Travels of a Father and Son* (Lebanon, PA: Sowers, 1911) and a work of biblical interpretation titled *The Book of Revelation* (Louisville, KY: Mordecai Ham, n.d.), which was edited from Hamlett's notes by Mordecai Ham.

8. Hamlett, *Travels of a Father and Son*, 71.

9. Hamlett, 147–48, 170.

10. Hamlett, 285.

11. Hamlett, 256.

12. Hamlett, 256.

13. W. A. Hamlett, "Baptists in the Holy Land," *Baptist Standard*, September 15, 1921, 10.

14. Shukri Mosa to J. F. Love, September 27, 1921, box 255, folder 31, IMB Minutes and Reports, 1849–2005, SBHLA.

15. Shukri Mosa to J. F. Love, January 14, 1922, box 255, folder 31, IMB Minutes and Reports, 1849–2005, SBHLA.

16. Mosa to Love (underlining in original).

17. J. F. Love to Shukri Mosa, April 13, 1922, box 255, folder 31, IMB Minutes and Reports, 1849–2005, SBHLA.

18. Hamlett briefly returned to his pastorate at the First Baptist Church in

Austin before resigning in summer 1922. A history of the congregation published in 1923 presented his tenure as pastor as unbroken between 1913 and 1922, making no mention of his time in Palestine. See V. L. Brooks, *A History of the First Baptist Church of Austin, Texas* (Austin: n.p., 1923), 13, https://texashistory.unt.edu/ark:/67531/metapth33019/.

19. J. F. Love to Shukri Mosa, April 13, 1922, box 255, folder 31, IMB Minutes and Reports, 1849–2005, SBHLA.

20. W. A. Hamlett, "The Palestine of Today," *Baptist Standard*, February 16, 1922, 10.

21. Hamlett, 15.

22. W. A. Hamlett, "The Palestine of Today," *Baptist Standard*, February 23, 1922, 38.

23. W. A. Hamlett, "Conditions in Palestine," *Baptist Standard*, March 2, 1922, 7.

24. Still, Hamlett's negative assessment of the field did make its way into the 1922 *Southern Baptist Handbook*, which offered a survey of SBC missions and mission fields. E. P. Allredge, *Southern Baptist Handbook 1922* (Nashville, TN: Baptist Sunday School Board, 1922), 231–34.

25. Fred Pearson to T. B. Ray, April 25, 1923, box 44, IMB Missionary Correspondence Files, SBHLA.

26. In summer 1922, a revival singer at the South Austin Baptist Church (a different church than Hamlett's) had unmasked an unnamed Klansman during a "visitation" to a service, resulting in a scuffle; "State Fails to Sustain Charge against Shelton," *Austin Statesman*, August 15, 1922, 1–2. Hamlett apparently informed members of First Baptist that he was leaving the church to begin a career as a traveling lecturer; it is not clear whether he informed the congregation that he would be lecturing for the Klan; see "Dr. W. A. Hamlett Resigns Baptist Pastorate; To Go upon Lecture Platform," *Austin Statesman*, July 30, 1922, 12. The week after his resignation took effect, Hamlett gave a publicized talk in Weatherford, Texas, on "The Principles of the Knights of the Ku Klux Klan." He was advertised as the pastor of the First Baptist Church of Austin: *The Weekly Herald*, August 3, 1922, 8.

27. J. Wash Watts, "China's Appeal to Me," *Home and Foreign Fields*, October 1920, 15.

28. Some biographical information is taken from "Brief Biographies of Our Newest Missionaries," *Home and Foreign Fields*, April 1923, 22. In addition, J. Wash Watts's application can be found in box 62, folder 5, IMB Missionary Correspondence Files, SBHLA; and the Pearsons' application can be found in box 44, folder 4, IMB Missionary Correspondence Files, SBHLA.

29. J. Wash Watts to J. F. Love, March 29, 1923, box 62, folder 5, IMB Missionary Correspondence Files, SBHLA.

30. Watts to Love.

31. Jacob Norris, *Land of Progress: Palestine in the Age of Colonial Development, 1905–1948* (Oxford: Oxford University Press, 2013): 99–138.

32. J. F. Love to J. Wash Watts, October 1, 1923, box 62, folder 5, IMB Missionary Correspondence Files, SBHLA.

33. Fred Pearson and J. Wash Watts, "Recommendations concerning the Near East Mission," 1923, box 44, folder 4, IMB Missionary Correspondence Files, SBHLA.

34. Fred Pearson to J. F. Love, November 19, 1923, box 44, folder 4, IMB Missionary Correspondence Files, SBHLA. See the following documents, all in the IMB Missionary Correspondence Files at the SBHLA: J. Wash Watts to J. F. Love, October 6, 1923, box 62, folder 5; J. Wash Watts to T. B. Ray, October 17, 1923, box 62, folder 5; and Fred Pearson to J. F. Love, October 19, 1923, box 44, folder 4.

35. J. F. Love to J. W. Watts, January 25, 1924, box 62, folder 5, IMB Missionary Correspondence Files, SBHLA; and T. B. Ray to Fred Pearson, June 9, 1923, box 44, folder 4, IMB Missionary Correspondence Files, SBHLA.

36. J. Wash Watts to J. F. Love, February 9, 1924, box 62, folder 5, IMB Missionary Correspondence Files, SBHLA. Joseph Klausner drew the interest of Christian missionaries and Hebrew Christians for the publication of his work *Jesus of Nazareth: His Life, Times, and Teaching*, trans. Herbert Danby (New York: Macmillan, 1925), which sought to contextualize Jesus as a Second Temple Jew.

37. J. W. Watts to J. F. Love, September 9, 1924, box 62, folder 5, IMB Missionary Correspondence Files, SBHLA. Watts described this group to Baptist readers in "Stirrings of the Spirit in Palestine," *Home and Foreign Fields*, June 1924, 9.

38. J. W. Watts to J. F. Love, November 25, 1924, box 62, folder 5, IMB Missionary Correspondence Files, SBHLA.

39. Fred Pearson and J. Wash Watts, "Recommendations concerning the Near East Mission," 1923, box 44, folder 4, IMB Missionary Correspondence Files, SBHLA.

40. Pearson and Watts.

41. J. Wash Watts, "Shall Palestine Become a Jewish State?," *Home and Foreign Fields*, April 1922, 16. The idea that the eclipse of a Jewish religious identity by the Zionist national identity presented a missionary opening would be echoed by Jacob Gartenhaus, a Hebrew Christian and the SBC's only domestic missionary to the Jews, in his *The Rebirth of a Nation: Zionism in History and Prophecy* (Nashville, TN: Broadman Press, 1936), 126.

42. J. Wash Watts, "Shall Palestine Become a Jewish State?," *Home and Foreign Fields*, April 1922, 16.

43. J. Wash Watts, "In the Valley of Jezreel," *Home and Foreign Fields*, November 1926, 12.

44. Watts, 12.

45. Watts, 13.

46. Mattie Watts, "Jesus Loves the Little Children of the World," *Home and Foreign Fields*, June 1927, 2.

47. Watts, 3.

48. J. Wash Watts, "Opportunities for Evangelical Missions in Palestine," *Review & Expositor* 28, no. 2 (1931): 151–61; Mattie [Mrs. James Washington] Watts, *Palestinian Tapestries* (Richmond, VA: Foreign Mission Board, 1936); and Mattie Watts, "Burning Lights in Jerusalem," in *Questing in Galilee* (Richmond, VA: Foreign Mission Board, 1937), 67–99.

49. Benny Morris, *Righteous Victims: A History of the Zionist-Arab Conflict, 1881–2001* (New York: Vintage Books, 2001), 121–60.

50. Matthew Hughes, "From Law and Order to Pacification: Britain's Suppression of the Arab Revolt in Palestine, 1936–1939," *Journal of Palestine Studies* 39, no. 2 (2010): 6–22.

51. SBC Annual, 1934, 237.

52. Elsie Clor, "Palestine—In Retrospect and in Prospect," *Home and Foreign Fields*, August 1936, 10.

53. Elsie Clor, circular letter, 1934, box 14, folder 3, IMB Missionary Correspondence Files, SBHLA.

54. Elsie Clor, "In Old Jerusalem," *Home and Foreign Fields*, April 1933, 10–11.

55. Elsie Clor and Eunice Fenderson to Jessie Ford, February 1939, box 14, folder 3, IMB Missionary Correspondence Files, SBHLA.

56. Doreen Hosford Owens, circular letter, January 1, 1935, box 255, folder 30, IMB Minutes and Reports, 1849–2005, SBHLA.

57. As will be seen in the conclusion, Shirrish's son Anis would come to be a prominent figure in the SBC. However, he would transliterate his name as Shorrosh.

58. Roswell Owens, "Two Timothies in Haifa," in *Questing in Galilee* (Richmond: Foreign Mission Board, 1937), 53–56.

59. Roswell Owens, "Proclaiming the 'Good News' in Palestine," *Home and Foreign Fields*, January 1932, 9.

60. Roswell Owens, "Of One Blood," *Home and Foreign Fields*, December 1932, 3.

61. Doreen Hosford Owens, "Searchlights in Palestine," *Commission*, November 1938, 230.

62. Foreign Mission Board to Clor, March 10, 1939, box 14, folder 3, IMB Missionary Correspondence Files, SBHLA.

63. H. Leo Eddleman, "The Land of Our Master," *Commission*, December 1941, 341.

64. H. Leo Eddleman and Sarah Eddleman, "From Our Missionaries in Palestine," *Baptist Record*, September 30, 1937, box 255, folder 30, IMB Minutes and Reports, 1849–2005, SBHLA.

65. H. Leo Eddleman and Sarah Eddleman, circular letter, 1938, box 255, folder 30, IMB Minutes and Reports, 1849–2005, SBHLA.

66. H. Leo Eddleman, "Jews Set a High Example in Giving," *Western Recorder*, n.d., box 255, folder 30, IMB Minutes and Reports, 1849–2005, SBHLA.

67. H. Leo Eddleman and Sarah Eddleman, "From Our Missionaries in Palestine," *Baptist Record*, September 30, 1937, box 255, folder 30, IMB Minutes and Reports, 1849–2005, SBHLA.

68. Eddleman and Eddleman. Confrontations with national movements have been a frequent challenge for missionaries in the twentieth century. On American missions in Egypt, see Heather J. Sharkey, *American Evangelicals in Egypt: Missionary Encounters in an Age of Empire* (Princeton, NJ: Princeton University Press, 2008), 96–148.

69. H. Leo Eddleman and Sarah Eddleman, "From Our Missionaries in Palestine," *Baptist Record*, September 30, 1937, box 255, folder 30, IMB Minutes and Reports, 1849–2005, SBHLA.

70. H. Leo Eddleman and Sarah Eddleman, circular letter, February 5, 1938, box 255, folder 30, IMB Minutes and Reports, 1849–2005, SBHLA.

71. It is unclear whether the mandate government or the American consulate made the request; see Gene Newton, "News Flashes," *Commission*, July 1941, 226.

72. Kate Ellen Gruver, "A Divine Promise," *Commission*, September 1940, 243.

73. Kate Ellen Gruver, "Blackout in Palestine," *Commission*, December 1942, 401.

74. Gruver, 402.

75. Kate Ellen Gruver, "Back to School," *Commission*, March 1943, 10–11.

76. SBC Annual, 1942, 187.

77. Robert L. Lindsey, "We Have a Job to Do in Palestine," *Commission*, November 1947, 9.

78. Lindsey, circular letter, October 18, 1939, box 255, folder 30, IMB Minutes and Reports, 1849–2005, SBHLA.

79. SBC Annual, 1947, 94.

80. "In Memoriam: James Henry Hagood," *Commission*, May 1946, 12–13; and Kate Ellen Gruver, "Palestine," *Commission*, April 1946, 25–26.

81. SBC Annual, 1947, 95.

82. SBC Annual, 1947, 94. Such practical considerations had long paired nicely with millenarian Christian hopes of Jewish restoration—the idea being that Jews would return, convert, and redeem the land. A specific example of this pairing was Kerem Avraham (Abraham's Vineyard), founded by British consul and Christian restorationist James Finn in the 1850s. See Ruth Kark, "Millenarism and Agricultural Settlement in the Holy Land in the Nineteenth Century," *Journal of Historical Geography* 9, no. 1 (1983): 47–62.

83. Lindsey, "Palestine," *Commission*, January 1947, 24.

84. In 1937, FMB secretary Charles Maddry published an article laying out these principles. Charles Maddry, "Changing Methods in Foreign Mission Work," *Home and Foreign Fields*, April 1937, 1.

85. Merrel Callaway, "Epistles from Today's Apostles," *Commission*, January 1948, 1.

86. In 1953, the mission's operations were consolidated into the Baptist Convention in Israel. In 1965, the Baptist churches within Israel organized into the Association of Baptist Churches.

87. Robert L. Lindsey, "Epistles from Today's Apostles," *Commission*, March 1948, 1, 22.

88. SBC Annual, 1948, 125.

89. Robert L. Lindsey, "Epistles from Today's Apostles," *Commission*, July 1948, 25.

90. Robert L. Lindsey, "Palestine Is Now Israel," *Commission*, December 1949, 10–11.

91. SBC Annual, 1949, 102.

92. All Arab members of the Jerusalem congregation were forced to flee to surrounding countries. In the 1950s, the SBC began sponsoring work in the Jordanian-held West Bank and Egyptian-held Gaza Strip. See Dwight Baker, *Baptists Golden Jubilee: 50 Years in Palestine-Israel* (n.p.: 1961), 6.

93. Robert L. Lindsey, "Epistles from Today's Apostles," *Commission*, March 1948, 22.

94. H. Leo Eddleman, "The Land of Our Master," *Commission*, December 1941, 340–42; Eddleman, "The Land of Our Master," *Commission*, January 1942, 14–15; and Eddleman, "The Land of Our Master," *Commission*, February 1942, 64–67.

95. H. Leo Eddleman, "Middle East," *Commission*, May 1945, 34.

96. Eddleman, 34.

97. H. Leo Eddleman to Harry Truman, rpt. in D. M. Giangreco and Kathryn Moore, ed., *Dear Harry: Truman's Mailroom, 1945–1953* (Mechanicsburg, PA: Stackpole Books, 1999), 148.

98. Eddleman to Truman, 148–49.

99. Robert L. Lindsey to unnamed prayer friend, October 18, 1939, box 255, folder 30, IMB Minutes and Reports, 1849–2005, SBHLA.

100. Robert L. Lindsey, "Palestine—Experiences and Expectations," *Commission*, October 1944, 11.

101. Robert L. Lindsey, "Epistles from Today's Apostles," *Commission*, March 1948, 22.

102. Robert L. Lindsey, "We Have a Job to Do in Palestine," *Commission*, November 1947, 9.

103. Robert L. Lindsey, "Palestine—Experiences and Expectations," *Commission*, October 1944, 10.

104. Lindsey, 11.

105. In a 1949 article in the *Christian Herald*, Lindsey noted, "it does seem to me that both Arab and Jewish claims have much validity." See Robert L. Lindsey, "Christianity's Chance in Palestine," *Christian Herald*, January 1949, 26–28.

106. Lindsey would continue to passionately struggle with the theological and missionary significance of Zionism and Israel for decades, his perspective continuously evolving. See, for example, Robert L. Lindsey, *Israel in Christendom: The Problem of Jewish Identity* (n.p.: n.d.). For an analysis of his thought and work in the decades after the establishment of Israel (including his pioneering biblical scholarship), see Yaakov Ariel, "The Ambiguous Missionary: Robert Lindsey in Israel, 1948–1970," in *America and Zion: Essays and Papers in Memory of Moshe Davis*, ed. Eli Lederhendler and Jonathan Sarna (Detroit, MI: Wayne State University Press, 2002), 185–200. See also Hummel, *Covenant Brothers*, 19–39. For Lindsey's biography, see Kenneth Mullican and Loren Turnage, *One Foot in Heaven: The Story of Bob Lindsey of Jerusalem* (Baltimore, MD: PublishAmerica, 2005).

107. Robert L. Lindsey, "Epistles from Today's Apostles," *Commission*, October 1949, 20.

108. Robert L. Lindsey, "Palestine Is Now Israel," *Commission*, December 1949, 10.

109. Though the Israeli government did not follow through with outright bans on missionary activity, as some in the government hoped it would, it did work in varying ways to frustrate this activity. See Uri Bialer, *Cross on the Star of David: The Christian World in Israel's Foreign Policy, 1948–1967* (Bloomington: Indiana University Press, 2005), 93–120.

Chapter 5

1. Portions of this chapter have been published in "Jacob Gartenhaus: The Southern Baptists' Jew," *Journal of Southern Religion* 19 (2017): http://jsreligion.org/vol19/robins.

2. Minutes of the Executive Committee of the Home Mission Board, April 7, 1921, 96, box 3, item 3, Home Mission Board Minutes, Southern Baptist Historical Library and Archives (SBHLA).

3. I say "effectively" because of a few short-lived exceptions, such as the hiring of Mollie Cohen in 1939 and of Lucille McKinney in 1948.

4. Jacob Gartenhaus, *What of the Jews?* (Atlanta, GA: Home Mission Board, 1948), 78.

5. Eliza McGraw, "'How to Win the Jews for Christ': Jewishness and the Southern Baptist Convention," *Mississippi Quarterly* 53, no. 2 (2000): 209–23; Daniel Goodman, "Strangers, Neighbors, and Strangers Again: The History of Southern Baptist Approaches to Jews and Judaism," *Review & Expositor* 103, no. 1 (2006): 63–89. Lee B. Spitzer's recent study of Baptist responses to the Holocaust is more attentive to Gartenhaus's role in representing Jewish issues to Baptists: Spitzer, *Baptists, Jews, and the Holocaust: The Hand of Sincere Friendship* (Valley Forge, PA: Judson Press, 2017), 286–97.

6. Jacob Gartenhaus, *The Rebirth of a Nation: Zionism in History and Prophecy* (Nashville, TN: Broadman Press, 1936), 128.

7. On the impact of nineteenth-century efforts and Jewish responses, see Jonathan Sarna, "The Impact of Nineteenth-Century Christian Missions on American Jews," in *Jewish Apostasy in the Modern World*, ed. Todd M. Endelman (New York: Holmes and Meier, 1987), 232–54. For a survey of American and British efforts, see Max Eisen, "Christian Missions to the Jews in North America and Great Britain," *Jewish Social Studies* 10, no. 1 (1948), 31–66; see also David Max Eichhorn, *Evangelizing the American Jew* (Middle Village, NY: Jonathan David, 1978). The definitive work on American evangelical missions to Jews is Yaakov Ariel, *Evangelizing the Chosen People: Missions to the Jews in America, 1880–2000* (Chapel Hill: University of North Carolina Press, 2000).

8. Yaakov Ariel, *On Behalf of Israel: American Fundamentalist Attitudes toward Jews, Judaism, and Zionism, 1865–1945* (Brooklyn, NY: Carlson, 1991), 55–96.

9. Ariel, *Evangelizing the Chosen People*, 22–37.

10. Ariel, in particular, emphasizes the dispensationalist roots of these missions in *Evangelizing the Chosen People.*

11. On Hebrew Christianity in Great Britain, see Michael R. Darby, *The Emergence of the Hebrew Christian Movement in Nineteenth-Century Britain* (Leiden, Netherlands: Brill, 2010). On connections between British Hebrew Christianity and the American movement, see B. Z. Sobel, *Hebrew Christianity: The Thirteenth Tribe* (New York: Wiley, 1974), 127–224; see also Sobel, "Legitimation and Antisemitism as Factors in the Functioning of a Hebrew-Christian Mission," *Jewish Social Studies* 23, no. 3 (1961): 170–86; and Sobel, "Protestant Evangelists and the Formulation of a Jewish Racial Mystique: The Missionary Discovery of Sociology," *Journal for the Scientific Study of Religion* 5, no. 3 (1966): 343–56. On the development of American Hebrew Christianity and the subsequent Messianic Judaism movement see: David Rausch, *Messianic Judaism: Its History, Theology, and Polity* (Lewiston, NY: Edwin Mellen Press, 1982); and Dan Cohn-Sherbok, *Messianic Judaism: A Critical Anthology* (New York: Continuum, 2000), 15–59. Ariel also discusses the movement in *Evangelizing the Chosen People*, 47–50, 80–86, 94–99.

12. Indeed, Carver, who had recommended Gartenhaus to the HMB, would become one of the SBC's leading opponents of premillennial dispensationalism.

13. Jacob Gartenhaus, *A New Emphasis on Jewish Evangelization through the Lo-*

cal Church (Atlanta: Home Mission Board, n.d.), box 1, folder 14, Jacob Gartenhaus Papers (JG), SBHLA.

14. Jacob Gartenhaus, "The Local Church and the Jews," in *Report of the First International Hebrew Christian Conference* (London: Marshall Brothers, 1925), 154–60.

15. Jacob Gartenhaus, *Pioneer Work among Southern Jews* (Birmingham, AL: Woman's Missionary Union, n.d.), 2, box 13, folder 34, Una Roberts Lawrence Papers (URL), SBHLA.

16. Gartenhaus's pamphlets included: *Who is He?* (Atlanta: Home Mission Board, n.d.), 13, box 1, folder 14, JG, SBHLA; *An Open Letter to the Jewish People of the South* (Atlanta: Home Mission Board, n.d.), 2, box 1, folder 14, JG, SBHLA; *How to Win the Jews for Christ* (Atlanta: Home Mission Board, n.d.), box 13, folder 26, URL, SBHLA; *The Virgin Birth of the Messiah* (Atlanta: Home Mission Board, n.d.), box 1, folder 14, JG, SBHLA; *The Jew's Contribution to the South* (Atlanta: Home Mission Board, n.d.), box 1, folder 13, JG, SBHLA; *A Jew, A Book, A Miracle* (Philadelphia: Million Testaments Campaign, n.d.), box 13, folder 36, URL, SBHLA; and *The Jewish Passover* (Nashville: Broadman Press, 1944). His books included: *The Jew and Jesus* (Nashville, TN: Sunday School Board, 1934); *The Influence of the Jews upon Civilization* (Grand Rapids, MI: Zondervan, 1943); *The Rebirth of a Nation*; and *What of the Jews?*

17. Roy Mason, "World's Greatest Jewish Christian Has Fiftieth Anniversary," *Grace and Life* (Tampa, FL), January 1966, box 1, folder 2, JG, SBHLA.

18. "Talks on Judaism and Christianity," *Palm Beach (FL) Post*, December 14, 1928.

19. Jacob Gartenhaus, "Work among the Jews," in SBC Annual, 1925, 343.

20. Jacob Gartenhaus, "The Gospel to the Jews," in SBC Annual, 1935, 276.

21. "Missionary Believes God Using Hitler as Tool to Weld New Jewish Nation," *Daily Current-Argus* (Carlsbad, NM), box 1, folder 2, JG, SBHLA. The cities included Albuquerque, Springer, Tucumcari, Portales, Hobbs, Tularosa, Carlsbad, Las Cruces, and Deming.

22. Jacob Gartenhaus, "The Gospel to the Jews," in SBC Annual, 1935, 276.

23. Mrs. H. C. Peelman, "Rev. Jacob Gartenhaus and the Florida Assembly," undated newspaper clipping, box 13, folder 31, URL, SBHLA.

24. "Series of Meetings Here This Week," *State* (Columbia, SC), April 27, 1930, box 1, folder 19, JG, SBHLA.

25. On Kligerman, see "Kligerman Tells His Life's Story, Gartenhaus Heard by Capacity Congregation," *State* (Columbia, SC), May 1, 1930, box 1, folder 19, JG, SBHLA. On Singer, see "Jewish Services Held Next Week," undated clipping, box 1, folder 19, JG, SBHLA. On Newman, see "Jewish-Christian Meetings," *Tennessean* (Nashville, TN), January 1931, box 1, folder 19, JG, SBHLA.

26. "Series of Meetings Here This Week," *State* (Columbia, SC), April 27, 1930, box 1, folder 19, JG, SBHLA.

27. "Annual Report of Woman's Missionary Union to Southern Baptist Convention," in SBC Annual, 1925, 106.

28. "Annual Report on Work of Woman's Missionary Union to Southern Baptist Convention," in SBC Annual, 1926, 76.

29. Jacob Gartenhaus, "Report of Jacob Gartenhaus," in SBC Annual, 1927, 294.

30. "Record of Personal Service," in SBC Annual, 1937, 392. Local chapters cir-

culated among themselves and the Jews of their communities a Hebrew Christian periodical coedited by Gartenhaus called the *Mediator*. In 1939, the Illinois, Florida, and Texas WMUs all began sponsoring female Jewish workers in their territories. "Woman's Missionary Union," in SBC Annual, 1939, 414.

31. In 1922 he reported 1,501 visits: Jacob Gartenhaus, "Work among the Jews," in SBC Annual, 1922, 346. In 1923, he reported 955: Gartenhaus, "Report of Jacob Gartenhaus," in SBC Annual, 1923, 191. In 1925, he reported 1,442: Gartenhaus, "Report of Jacob Gartenhaus," in SBC Annual, 1925, 343. In 1935, he reported 800: Gartenhaus, "The Gospel to the Jews," in SBC Annual, 1935, 276. And in 1936, he reported 750: Gartenhaus, "He Came unto His Own," in SBC Annual, 1936, 237.

32. Jacob Gartenhaus, "Work among the Jews," in SBC Annual, 1922, 346.

33. Jacob Gartenhaus, "Report of Jacob Gartenhaus," in SBC Annual, 1923, 191.

34. Jacob Gartenhaus, "The Gospel to the Jews," in SBC Annual, 1935, 276.

35. Jacob Gartenhaus, "He Came unto His Own," in SBC Annual, 1936, 236.

36. Jacob Gartenhaus, "Jewish Work," in SBC Annual, 1930, 278.

37. "Series of Meetings Here This Week," *State* (Columbia, SC), April 27, 1930, box 1, folder 19, JG, SBHLA.

38. Gartenhaus used *race* and *nation* interchangeably.

39. Jacob Gartenhaus, *Who Is He?* (Atlanta: Home Mission Board, n.d.), 13, box 1, folder 14, JG, SBHLA.

40. Jacob Gartenhaus, *An Open Letter to the Jewish People of the South* (Atlanta: Home Mission Board, n.d.), 2, box 1, folder 14, JG, SBHLA.

41. McGraw presents these claims as a rhetorical device in "How to Win the Jews for Christ," while Sobel presents the maintenance of Jewish identity as a missionary tactic in *Hebrew Christianity*, 127–224.

42. Jacob Gartenhaus, qtd. in Charles Joseph, "Random Thoughts," *American Israelite* (Cincinnati, OH), May 12, 1932, 1; the letter was also printed in Baptist periodicals: "Gartenhaus Replies to Hebrew Critic," *Baptist Messenger*, June 16, 1932, box 13, folder 22, URL, SBHLA.

43. See, respectively: Jacob Gartenhaus, "New Opportunities for Winning the Jews for Christ," *Monthly B.Y.P.U. Magazine*, June 1934, 7, box 13, folder 22, URL, SBHLA; "Christianized Austrian Jew Will Speak Sunday at the First Baptist Church," *Burlington (N.C.) Daily Times-News*, August 25, 1939, box 1, folder 19, JG, SBHLA; "The Chosen People," *Baptist Home Missions*, undated clipping, box 13, folder 22, URL, SBHLA; "Rev. Jacob Gartenhaus," *Baptist Standard*, box 13, folder 22, URL, SBHLA; and "Racial Faith Sticks: Victory for Jews Seen," newspaper clipping, May 1939, box 13, folder 25, URL, SBHLA.

44. F. M. McConnell, "The Conversion of Jews," *Baptist Standard*, January 29, 1931, 4.

45. Helen Parker, "Why I am Interested in Giving the Gospel to the Jewish People," box 1, folder 5, JG, SBHLA.

46. Ellis Fuller, preface to Gartenhaus, *The Rebirth of a Nation*, 7–8.

47. Gartenhaus, *The Rebirth of a Nation*, 26. In *Rebirth*, Gartenhaus attributed this "aloofness" both to Christian persecution and to Jewish national characteristics, particularly that which he called a "racial pride that has become a mania" (19). Gartenhaus, of course, often demonstrated his own racial pride. He also tempered his critiques of Jewish racial pride amid the worsening situation in Europe.

48. Jacob Gartenhaus, *The Jew's Contribution to the South* (Atlanta: Home Mission Board, n.d.), box 1, folder 13, JG, SBHLA; and Gartenhaus, *The Influence of the Jews upon Civilization*. Other examples include: Joseph Jacobs, *Jewish Contributions to Civilization: An Estimate* (Philadelphia: Jewish Publication Society of America, 1919); and Cecil Roth, *The Jewish Contribution to Civilization* (New York: Macmillan, 1938). Gartenhaus drew on the latter for his 1943 *The Influence of the Jews*.

49. Mark Silk, "Notes on the Judeo-Christian Tradition in America," *American Quarterly* 36, no. 1 (1984): 65–85; and Deborah Dash Moore, "Jewish GIs and the Creation of the Judeo-Christian Tradition," *Religion and American Culture* 8, no. 1 (1998): 31–53.

50. Gartenhaus, *The Influence of the Jews upon Civilization*, 20.

51. Gartenhaus, *The Jew and Jesus*, 12.

52. Gartenhaus, *An Urgent Call on Behalf of the Jews of the South* (Atlanta: Home Mission Board, 1921), 3, box 1, folder 14, JG, SBHLA.

53. Gartenhaus, 4.

54. Jacob Gartenhaus, *How to Win the Jews for Christ* (Atlanta: Home Mission Board, n.d.), 4, box 13, folder 26, URL, SBHLA.

55. Gartenhaus, *What of the Jews?*, 31.

56. "Eyes of World on Jew Today," *Lexington (KY) Herald*, August 8, 1927, box 1, folder 19, JG, SBHLA.

57. Gartenhaus, *The Rebirth of a Nation*, 22.

58. Gartenhaus, 22.

59. Gartenhaus, *What of the Jews?*, 21–22.

60. "Missionary Believes God Using Hitler as Tool to Weld New Jewish Nation," *Daily Current-Argus* (Carlsbad, NM), box 1, folder 2, JG, SBHLA.

61. "Eyes of World on Jew Today," *Lexington (KY) Herald*, August 8, 1927, box 1, folder 19, JG, SBHLA.

62. Jacob Gartenhaus, "Thy People Israel," *Royal Service*, December 1925, 27.

63. Hyman Appelman to Jacob Gartenhaus, May 2, 1934, box 1, folder 4, JG, SBHLA.

64. "World in Ignorance of Nazi Killing of Jews, Asserts Minister Here," *Atlanta Constitution*, September 3, 1934, 5.

65. Robert Ross mines the Northern and Southern Baptist Conventions' annual reports to examine Baptist responses to Nazism and the Holocaust. See his chapter, "Baptists, Jews, Nazis: 1933–1947," in *Bearing Witness to the Holocaust, 1939–1989*, ed. Alan Berger (Lewiston, NY: Edwin Mellen Press, 1991), 207–26. For a comprehensive examination of Baptist responses to the Holocaust, see Spitzer, *Baptists, Jews, and the Holocaust*.

66. M. E. Dodd, *Girdling the Globe for God* (Shreveport, LA: John S. Ramond, 1935), 29–38.

67. Ben Bridges, "Baptists, Hitler, and the Jews," *Arkansas Baptist*, March 29, 1934, 16.

68. Jacob Gartenhaus, "Israel Needs Prayers," *Hebrew Christian Alliance Quarterly* 23, no. 3 (1938): 14.

69. Jacob Gartenhaus to Una Roberts Lawrence, October 10, 1938, box 13, folder 25, URL, SBHLA.

70. SBC Annual, 1938, 292.

71. Associated Press, "Mission Board Leader Hails Baptist 'Loyalty, Generosity,'" *Washington Post*, November 8, 1940, 19.

72. Jacob Gartenhaus to Una Roberts Lawrence, October 29, 1945, box 3, folder 25, URL, SBHLA.

73. Jacob Gartenhaus, "Resolution concerning the Jews," in *Seventh Baptist World Congress: Official Report*, ed. Walter Lewis (London: Baptist World Alliance, 1948), 99.

74. SBC Annual, 1942, 274.

75. SBC Annual, 1938, 292.

76. SBC Annual, 1938, 293.

77. "Missionary Believes God Using Hitler as Tool to Weld New Jewish Nation," *Daily Current-Argus* (Carlsbad, NM), box 1, folder 2, JG, SBHLA.

78. SBC Annual, 1944, 304.

79. Gartenhaus, *The Rebirth of a Nation*, 39.

80. Gartenhaus, 31.

81. Gartenhaus, 39–40.

82. Gartenhaus, 51.

83. Gartenhaus, 39.

84. Gartenhaus, 128.

85. Gartenhaus, 34.

86. Gartenhaus, *What of the Jews?*, 36.

87. Chaim Weizmann, qtd. in Gartenhaus, *The Rebirth of a Nation*, 86.

88. Yitzhak Conforti, "'The New Jew' in the Zionist Movement: Ideology and Historiography," *Australian Journal for Jewish Studies* 25 (2011): 87–118.

89. Gartenhaus, *The Rebirth of a Nation*, 117.

90. Gartenhaus, 126.

91. Gartenhaus, 90.

92. Gartenhaus, 94.

93. Gartenhaus, 93.

94. Gartenhaus, 107.

95. Gartenhaus, 94–105.

96. Gartenhaus, *What of the Jews?*, 40.

97. Gartenhaus, 41.

98. Gartenhaus, 44.

99. Gartenhaus, 47.

100. Gartenhaus, *Traitor?* (Chattanooga, TN: International Board of Jewish Missions, 1980), 211.

101. "Minutes of the Executive Committee of the Home Mission Board," March 3, 1949, 182, box 8, item 3, Home Mission Board Minutes, SBHLA.

102. Rogers to J. B. Lawrence, May 26, 1938, box 3, folder 8, Home Mission Board Executive Office Files, SBHLA.

103. "Minutes of the Executive Committee of the Home Mission Board," November 28, 1952, 121, box 8, item 9, Home Mission Board Minutes, SBHLA.

104. For more on Gartenhaus's role in embodying the boundaries between faiths, see Robins, "Jacob Gartenhaus"; and Robins, "A Meshummad in Dixie:

Jacob Gartenhaus as a Convert Missionary in the Southern Baptist Convention, 1921–1949," in *Konversion in Räumen jüdischer Geschichte*, ed. Carsten Schapkow and Martin Przybilski (Wiesbaden, Germany: Dr. Ludwig Reichert Academic Press, 2014), 135–49.

105. John L. Hill, foreword to Gartenhaus, *The Jew and Jesus*, 5.

106. Mark K. Bauman, *A New Vision of Southern Jewish History: Studies in Institution Building, Leadership, Interaction, and Mobility* (Tuscaloosa: University of Alabama Press, 2019), 34–35.

Chapter 6

1. The national WMU was preceded by local organizations. On the early WMU, see Catherine Allen, *A Century to Celebrate: History of Woman's Missionary Union* (Birmingham: Woman's Missionary Union, 1987), 189–210.

2. *Encyclopedia of Southern Baptists*, ed. Norman Cox and Lynn May, 4 vols. (Nashville: Broadman Press, 1958–82), s.v. "Woman's Missionary Union."

3. SBC Annual, 1926, 76.

4. SBC Annual, 1922, 80.

5. *Encyclopedia of Southern Baptists*, s.v. "Woman's Missionary Union."

6. *Encyclopedia of Southern Baptists*, s.v. "Creasman, Myrtle Robinson."

7. Myrtle Robinson (Mrs. C. D.) Creasman, "Program for January," *Royal Service*, January 1935, 23.

8. Creasman, 29.

9. Elizabeth Brower (Mrs. W. R.) Nimmo, "Program for November," *Royal Service*, November 1926, 19; of course, Jesus is actually a prophet in Islam, well known to "Hagars."

10. Doreen Hosford Owens, qtd. in Myrtle Robinson (Mrs. C. D.) Creasman, "Program for August: Topic—The Return of the Word to Europe and Palestine," *Royal Service*, August 1933, 24.

11. Creasman, 24.

12. Elizabeth Brower (Mrs. W. R.) Nimmo, "Program for November," *Royal Service*, November 1926, 21.

13. Myrtle Robinson (Mrs. C. D.) Creasman, "Program for July: Topic: Debtor to the Jew," *Royal Service*, July 1932, 25.

14. Creasman, 23.

15. Myrtle Robinson (Mrs. C. D.) Creasman, "Program for January," *Royal Service*, January 1935, 29.

16. Inna Belle Coleman, the FMB's first secretary of publicity, was tasked with preparing "a graded series and cycle of mission study literature for children and young people" in 1934. SBC Annual, 1934, 163. At the end of the decade, the FMB also published a graded series on world missions that included some materials on Palestine. See, for example, Florence Boston Decker, *World Airways for the King* (Nashville, TN: Broadman Press, 1941).

17. Doreen Hosford Owens, *The Camel Bell* (Richmond, VA: Foreign Mission Board, 1937); and Owens, *The Village Oven* (Richmond, VA: Foreign Mission Board, 1937).

18. *Questing in Galilee* (Richmond, VA: Foreign Mission Board, 1937).

19. Mattie (Mrs. James Washington) Watts, *Palestinian Tapestries* (Richmond, VA: Foreign Mission Board, 1936).

20. J. McKee Adams, *The Heart of the Levant* (Richmond, VA: Foreign Mission Board, 1937).

21. Adams, 143. See also Owens, *The Camel Bell*, 42: "[The land] is precious to us because so many people live here who have never heard of God's love and of our Saviour."

22. Watts, *Palestinian Tapestries*, 79.

23. Owens, *The Village Oven*, 17.

24. Owens, *The Camel Bell*, 14. Watts urged the same: *Palestinian Tapestries*, 28.

25. Owens, *The Village Oven*, 44.

26. Owens, 62.

27. Adams, *The Heart of the Levant*, 53.

28. Owens, *The Camel Bell*, 22.

29. Owens, 25. The belief that Muslims worshipped Muhammad was widespread among Southern Baptists.

30. Watts, *Palestinian Tapestries*, 13.

31. J. Wash Watts, qtd. in M. Watts, *Palestinian Tapestries*, 39.

32. For some ritualistic practices concerning the evil eye in Greater Syria at the turn of the twentieth century, see Ghosn el-Howie, "The Evil Eye," *Palestine Exploration Quarterly* 36, no. 2 (1904): 148–50. On the evil eye in Islam, see *Encyclopaedia of Islam*, 2nd ed., s.v. "ʿAyn," by Ph. Marçais, accessed December 10, 2014, http://referenceworks.brillonline.com/. On the evil eye in Judaism, see *Encyclopaedia of Judaism*, s.v. "Evil Eye in Judaism," by Rivka Ulmer, accessed December 10, 2014, http://referenceworks.brillonline.com/.

33. Owens, *The Camel Bell*, 4.

34. Watts, *Palestinian Tapestries*, 36.

35. Owens, *The Village Oven*, 63.

36. Owens, *The Camel Bell*, 16.

37. Owens, 71. Such sentiments are echoed in Watts's *Palestinian Tapestries*, 35.

38. Hanna, "Questing in Galilee," in *Questing in Galilee*, 26.

39. Hanna, 35.

40. Watts, *Palestinian Tapestries*, 30.

41. Watts, 31.

42. Adams, *The Heart of the Levant*, 124.

43. Adams, 126.

44. Adams, 142: "Whether Zionism succeeds or fails is a secondary question: *the Jews* will never succeed until they receive their rejected Messiah!"; and Watts, *Palestinian Tapestries*, 83: "Restoration to the Promised Land may be a means to an end in God's providence, but never an end in itself."

45. William Robert Wellesley Peel, *Palestine Royal Commission Report* (London: Her Majesty's Stationery Office, 1937).

46. Owens, *The Village Oven*, 53.

47. Watts, *Palestinian Tapestries*, 5.

48. *Questing in Galilee*, 18.

49. Watts, *Palestinian Tapestries*, 31.

50. Watts, 83.

51. Adams, *The Heart of the Levant*, 109.

52. Adams, 92.

53. Adams, 110–11.

54. Adams, 112.

55. Adams, 95 (emphasis in original).

56. Owens, *The Village Oven*, 125.

57. Everett Gill, "Modern Palestine and Zionism," in *Questing in Galilee*, 120.

58. Adams, *The Heart of the Levant*, 142.

59. "Business Woman's Circles," *Royal Service*, February 1947, 16. *Author's note:* The 1947 issues use the singular ("Woman's"), but the preceding issues use the plural ("Women's"). For consistency, I switched the earlier reference to the plural.

60. Myrtle Robinson (Mrs. C. D.) Creasman, "Program for February," *Royal Service*, February 1937, 26.

61. Creasman, 27.

62. Myrtle Robinson (Mrs. C. D.) Creasman, "Program Material," *Royal Service*, February 1947, 20.

63. Myrtle Robinson (Mrs. C. D.) Creasman, "Program Material," *Royal Service*, August 1943, 26.

64. Myrtle Robinson (Mrs. C. D.) Creasman, "Program Material," *Royal Service*, October 1938, 19–28.

65. Myrtle Robinson (Mrs. C. D.) Creasman, "Program Material," *Royal Service*, September 1940, 24.

66. Myrtle Robinson (Mrs. C. D.) Creasman, "Program Material," *Royal Service*, February 1947, 18.

67. Creasman, 19.

68. Creasman, 21.

69. Myrtle Robinson (Mrs. C. D.) Creasman, "Program for October," *Royal Service*, October 1938, 23.

70. Myrtle Robinson (Mrs. C. D.) Creasman, "Program Material," *Royal Service*, September 1940, 24.

71. Myrtle Robinson (Mrs. C. D.) Creasman, "Program Material," *Royal Service*, April 1944, 14.

72. Myrtle Robinson (Mrs. C. D.) Creasman, "Program for October," *Royal Service*, October 1938, 26.

73. Mrs. Charles Mullins, "Business Women's Circles," *Royal Service*, April 1944, 11.

74. Myrtle Robinson (Mrs. C. D.) Creasman, "Program for October," *Royal Service*, October 1938, 23.

Chapter 7

1. "Building a Denomination—Our Organized Work," *Baptist Messenger*, June 23, 1920.

2. On SBC responses to the northern split, see Andrew Smith, *Fundamentalism, Fundraising, and the Southern Baptist Convention, 1919–1925* (Knoxville: University of Tennessee Press, 2016). On Southern Baptists' engagement with the broader

fundamentalist-modernist split, see James Thompson, *Tried as by Fire: Southern Baptists and the Religious Controversies of the 1920s* (Macon, GA: Mercer University Press, 1982), 61–82.

3. L. R. Scarborough, "Two Kinds of Fundamentalism," *Baptist Standard*, November 2, 1922, 13.

4. Barry Hankins offers a full-length study of Norris's career in *God's Rascal: J. Frank Norris and the Beginnings of Southern Fundamentalism* (Lexington: University Press of Kentucky, 1996). See also: Thompson, *Tried as by Fire*, 137–66; and William Glass, *Strangers in Zion: Fundamentalists in the South, 1900–1950* (Macon, GA: Mercer University Press, 2001), 64, 76–77.

5. Bill J. Leonard, *God's Last and Only Hope: The Fragmentation of the Southern Baptist Convention* (Grand Rapids, MI: Eerdmans, 1990), 6.

6. Thompson, *Tried as by Fire*, 43–60.

7. "A Divisive Movement," *Biblical Recorder*, April 18, 1923, 1.

8. Wayne Flynt has argued that much of the SBC imbibed "fundamentalism by osmosis." See Flynt, *Alabama Baptists: Southern Baptists in the Heart of Dixie* (Tuscaloosa: University of Alabama Press, 1998), 408.

9. W. A. Criswell, "In Memory of Mother," May 8, 1977, W. A. Criswell Sermon Library, accessed April 24, 2019, https://www.wacriswell.com/sermons/1977/in-memory-of-mother1-2/.

10. A memoir by a grandson of Rice also includes large historical and biographical sections on the fundamentalist leader. See Andrew Himes, *The Sword of the Lord: The Roots of Fundamentalism in an American Family* (Seattle: Chiara Press, 2011).

11. Mordecai Ham, *The Second Coming of Christ* (Louisville, KY: printed by the author, 1943).

12. Hyman Appelman, *Appelman's Sermon Outlines and Illustrations* (Grand Rapids, MI: Zondervan, 1944), 51; Appelman, *From Jewish Lawyer to Baptist Preacher* (Fairfield, AL: Faith of Our Fathers, 1944); and Appelman, *The Battle of Armageddon* (Grand Rapids, MI: Zondervan, 1944).

13. Some splinter groups like the Orthodox Baptists of Oklahoma, led by W. Lee Rector, were premillennialist. However, premillennialism was not the determining factor in this group's 1931 split from the SBC. *Encyclopedia of Southern Baptists*, ed. Norman Cox and Lynn May, 4 vols. (Nashville: Broadman Press, 1958–82), s.v. "Oklahoma Fundamentalism."

14. "The Fundamentals," *Biblical Recorder*, January 21, 1920, 1.

15. E. Y. Mullins, "Great Doctrines of the Bible," *Biblical Recorder*, May 2, 1923, 4. Mullins himself had advocated for premillennialism earlier in his career.

16. As Flynt has noted of Alabama Baptists near the mid-century, most were a "mixture of pre-, post-, and amillennialist, or they were simply evangelicals with no strong opinion one way or the other about the timing of Christ's return": *Alabama Baptists*, 408. For a general overview of millennialism within the SBC, see William Pitts, "Southern Baptists and Millennialism, 1900-2000: Conceptual Patterns and Historical Expressions," *Baptist History and Heritage* 34, no. 2 (1999): 7-27.

17. E. Y. Mullins, "Great Doctrines of the Bible," *Biblical Recorder*, May 2, 1923, 4.

18. "Book Reviews," *Baptist Standard*, September 11, 1929, 15.

19. For a thorough look at Carver's disagreements with premillennialists, see Mark Wilson, *William Owen Carver's Controversies in the Baptist South* (Macon, GA: Mercer University Press, 2010), 108–18.

20. W. O. Carver to F. V. McFatridge, quoted in Wilson, *William Owen Carver's Controversies*, 112.

21. W. O. Carver (managing editor), "Life Factors and Tendencies: Millennial Pentecostalism," *Review & Expositor* 37, no. 2 (April 1940): 195.

22. W. O. Carver, "Facts and Factors in History Making," *Pastor's Periscope*, August 1940, 6.

23. William Glass, "From Southern Baptist to Fundamentalist: The Case of I. W. Rogers and *The Faith*, 1945–57," *American Baptist Quarterly* 14 (1995): 241–59.

24. *Encyclopedia of Southern Baptists*, s.v. "Premillennial Baptist Groups."

25. W. A. Hamlett, *Travels of a Father and Son* (Lebanon, PA: Sowers, 1911), 263.

26. W. A. Hamlett, "The Palestine Question," *Florida Baptist Witness*, May 27, 1948, 3.

27. M. E. Dodd, *Jesus Is Coming to Earth Again* (Chicago: Chicago Bible Institute Colportage Association), 55.

28. Dodd, 56.

29. M. E. Dodd, *Girdling the Globe for God* (Shreveport, LA): John S. Ramond, 40–51.

30. Austin Tucker, "Monroe Elmon Dodd and His Preaching," (ThD diss., Southwestern Baptist Theological Seminary, 1971), 117–40. It is possible that Dodd sought to downplay his premillennialism while sitting as SBC president.

31. T. T. Martin, "The Second Coming of Christ," *Western Recorder*, November 15, 1917, 3; see also Martin, *The Second Coming of Christ* (n.p.: n.p., n.d.), Southern Baptist Theological Seminary.

32. Martin, *The Second Coming of Christ*, 20.

33. W. E. Tynes, "III. The Second Coming," *Baptist Chronicle*, January 24, 1918, 4.

34. Jacob Gartenhaus, *The Rebirth of a Nation: Zionism in History and Prophecy* (Nashville, TN: Broadman Press, 1936), 128.

35. John R. Rice, *World-Wide War and the Bible* (Wheaton, IL: Sword of the Lord, 1940), 117.

36. Rice, 100.

37. John R. Rice, *Jewish Persecution and Bible Prophecies* (Wheaton, IL: Sword of the Lord, 1941), 33–34, 39.

38. John R. Rice, *The Coming Kingdom of Christ* (Wheaton, IL: Sword of the Lord, 1945), 29.

39. Rice, 28.

40. Rice, 36.

41. Rice, 37.

42. W. O. Carver (managing editor), "Life Factors and Tendencies: Millennial Pentecostalism," *Review & Expositor* 37, no. 2 (April 1940): 193–195.

43. W. O. Carver, "Facts and Factors in History Making," *Pastor's Periscope*, February 1940, 4.

44. H. Cornell Goerner, "Zionism and the Scriptures," *Review & Expositor* 34, no. 3 (July 1937): 302.

45. Goerner, 303.
46. Goerner, 304.
47. Goerner, 313.
48. Goerner, 313–14.
49. Goerner, 313.

Chapter 8

1. Barry Hankins, *God's Rascal: J. Frank Norris and the Beginnings of Southern Fundamentalism* (Lexington: University Press of Kentucky), 74–89. As Hankins notes, Norris eventually evolved his own variations on dispensationalist doctrines and later even declaimed the system. See also D. E. Howe, "An Analysis of Dispensationalism and Its Implications for the Theologies of James Robinson Graves, John Franklyn Norris, and Wallie Amos Criswell," (PhD diss., Southwestern Baptist Theological Seminary, 1988), 140–201.

2. J. Frank Norris, "Jesus Is Coming" *Searchlight*, March 2, 1917, 1.

3. "The Allenbys," *Searchlight*, March 13, 1919, 2. The teacher of the class, Mr. Collins, declared "that as General Allenby had rescued Jerusalem from the reign of the Turk it is the purpose of the Allenby Class to rescue young men from the reign and domination of Satan."

4. J. Frank Norris, "World War Needed to Fulfill Word of Bible, Says Norris," *Searchlight*, July 3, 1919, 3–4.

5. Norris, 3.

6. Stephen Spector, *Evangelicals and Israel: The Story of American Christian Zionism* (New York: Oxford University Press, 2009), 113.

7. J. Frank Norris, "From the Pastor: Sunday Service on Ship in Mediterranean," *Searchlight*, October 7, 1920, 2.

8. J. Frank Norris, "Palestine Restored to the Jews," *Searchlight*, October 21, 1920, 1.

9. Norris, 2.

10. Norris, 1.

11. Norris, 1.

12. Norris, 2.

13. J. Frank Norris, "Jerusalem," *Searchlight*, October 28, 1920, 2.

14. "Unprecedented since Abraham's Time!" *Searchlight*, November 11, 1920, 1.

15. Advertisement titled "The First Baptist Church," *Fort Worth (TX) Star-Telegram*, November 28, 1920, 4.

16. "The Pastor Speaks for the Jews," *Searchlight*, November 25, 1920, 2.

17. J. Frank Norris, "Jerusalem," *Searchlight*, December 2, 1920, 1.

18. J. Frank Norris, "But for the British Soldiers We Would Both Have Been Cruelly Murdered," *Fundamentalist*, September 3, 1937, 1.

19. Norris, 7.

20. J. Frank Norris, "Will the Next and Final War Break Out in Palestine?," *Fundamentalist*, September 17, 1937, 5.

21. J. Frank Norris, "Why the Jews and Not the Arabs Will Control Palestine," *Fundamentalist*, September 24, 1937, 1.

22. Norris, 1.

23. J. Frank Norris, "Will the Next and Final War Break Out in Palestine?," *Fundamentalist*, September 17, 1937, 5.

24. J. Frank Norris, "The 'Swastika' an Ancient Jewish Emblem, and 'Nazi' a Jewish Title?," *Fundamentalist*, September 1, 1939, 2.

25. J. Frank Norris, "Great Britain and Palestine—Will There Be Another Munich?," *Fundamentalist*, October 6, 1939, 3.

26. J. Frank Norris, "The Persecution of the Jews in Germany," *Fundamentalist*, April 7, 1933, 3.

27. J. Frank Norris, "Will the Next and Final War Break Out in Palestine?," *Fundamentalist*, September 17, 1937, 5. Norris publicly clashed with his mentor, William Bell Riley, over the authenticity of the 1903 *Protocols of the Elders of Zion* (Norris believed, rightly, that this text was an anti-Semitic fabrication). His confrontation with Riley came right after his 1937 trip: J. Frank Norris, "Protocols of the Wise Men of Zion," *Fundamentalist*, October 22, 1937, 1; and Norris, *Did the Jews Write the Protocols?* (Detroit, MI: n.p., 1938).

28. J. Frank Norris, "The First Baptist Church, Jerusalem," *Fundamentalist*, September 3, 1937, 8.

29. Norris, 5.

30. J. Frank Norris, "Is 'Jacob's Trouble' Near? 'O, Jerusalem, Jerusalem,'" *Fundamentalist*, September 1, 1939, 7.

31. On Norris's habit of ingratiating himself with influential figures, see Hankins, *God's Rascal*, 8.

32. Ben Goldman to J. Frank Norris, June 10, 1947, box 22, folder 1010, J. Frank Norris Papers, Southern Baptist Historical Library and Archives (SBHLA).

33. J. Frank Norris, *My Fifth Trip to Palestine* (Fort Worth, TX: Fundamentalist Press, 1948), 9.

34. Norris, 11.

35. Norris, 10.

36. Norris, 12. On the relationship between Hajj Amin al-Husseini and the Nazis, see Norman Stillman, *The Jews of Arab Lands in Modern Times* (Philadelphia: Jewish Publication Society, 1991), 105–12, 116–17.

37. Norris, *My Fifth Trip to Palestine*, 12. He reiterated this point in the *Fundamentalist*: Norris, "And They Parted My Land," *Fundamentalist*, December 26, 1947, 2.

38. Norris, *My Fifth Trip to Palestine*, 12.

39. Norris, 13.

40. J. Frank Norris, "And They Parted My Land," *Fundamentalist*, December 26, 1947, 2.

41. Amy Weiss, "Between Cooperation and Competition: The Making of American Jewish Zionist Interfaith Alliances with Liberal and Evangelical Protestants, 1898–1979," (PhD diss., New York University, 2014), 134–35.

42. J. Frank Norris to William Kaufman, January 24, 1948, box 22, item 13575, J. Frank Norris Papers, SBHLA. Caitlin Carenen recounts an episode from two years later in which an AZEC member (Samuel Newman) reached out to Norris to recruit him for membership in ACPC: Carenen, *The Fervent Embrace: Liberal Protestants, Evangelicals, and Israel* (New York: New York University Press, 2012), 101.

43. American Christian Palestine Committee, "To The United States and the United Nations," *Fundamentalist*, February 13, 1948, 7. On the ACPC, see Caitlin Carenen, "The American Christian Palestine Committee, the Holocaust, and Mainstream Protestant Zionism, 1938–1948," *Holocaust and Genocide Studies* 24, no. 2 (2010): 272–96; and Carenen, *The Fervent Embrace*.

44. Kaufman to Norris, January 27, 1948, Box 22, Item 13576, Norris Papers.

45. Norris, *My Fifth Trip to Palestine*, 35. ACPC leaders had called for the arming of the Haganah: "Group Asks Arms for Jewish State," *New York Times*, January 19, 1948. On the United States' arms embargo, see Shlomo Slonim, "The 1948 American Embargo on Arms to Palestine," *Political Science Quarterly* 94, no. 3 (1979): 495–514.

46. John Popham, "Baptists Criticize Truman on Israel," *New York Times*, May 20, 1948, 4.

47. W. Terry Lindley, "The 1948 SBC Opposition to Israel: The J. Frank Norris Factor," *Baptist History and Heritage* 22, no. 4 (1987): 23–33.

Chapter 9

1. Naomi Wiener Cohen, *The Americanization of Zionism, 1897–1948* (Hanover, NH: Brandeis University Press, 2003), 64. On the debate, see Lawrence Davidson, *America's Palestine: Popular and Official Perceptions from Balfour to Israeli Statehood* (Gainesville: University Press of Florida), 21–39.

2. Louis Brandeis, qtd. in Jonathan Sarna, "Louis Brandeis: Zionist Leader," *Brandeis Review* 11, no. 3 (1992): 26.

3. Cohen, *The Americanization of Zionism*, 64–75.

4. A. J. Holt, "News and Views," *Florida Baptist Witness*, September 13, 1917, 8.

5. Holt, "Jerusalem Captured," *Florida Baptist Witness*, December 13, 1917, 6.

6. Holt, 6.

7. Livingston Johnson, "Current Topics," *Biblical Recorder*, December 17, 1917, 7.

8. John William Porter, "Editorial: The Fall of Jerusalem," *Western Recorder*, December 13, 1917, 8.

9. E. C. Routh, "Understanding the Times and Acting Accordingly," *Baptist Standard*, November 21, 1918, 13.

10. Cohen, *The Americanization of Zionism*, 75–94.

11. Cohen, 84.

12. Naomi Wiener Cohen, *The Year after the Riots: American Responses to the Palestine Crisis of 1929–30* (Detroit, MI: Wayne State University Press, 1988), 118.

13. "Ryland Knight," in *Veterans of the Cross*, ed. William Lunsford (Dallas, TX: Baptist Standard, 1921), 62–63.

14. Ryland Knight, "Palestine—A Problem," *Review & Expositor* 27, no. 1 (January 1930): 14–15.

15. Knight, 18.

16. Knight, 16.

17. Knight, 17.

18. Knight, 22.

19. Knight, 23.

20. "American Palestine Committee: Statement of Aims and Principles," petition, file 359, Emanuel Neumann Collection, Central Zionist Archives.

21. Rauch briefly discussed his time at SBTS in an address given at the seventy-fifth anniversary celebration of the seminary in 1934: Joseph Rauch, "Among My Alma Maters," 1934, box 5, ledger 7, Joseph Rauch Papers, American Jewish Archives (AJA).

22. Years before his publication in the *Review & Expositor*, Rauch had expressed opposition to Jewish statehood; see Rauch, "Ancient Palestine and the Modern Jew," unpublished sermon, January 17, 1915, box 1, folder 3, Joseph Rauch Papers, AJA. In 1943 he coauthored a minority report against a successful resolution from the Central Conference of American Rabbis. The resolution had urged the anti-Zionist American Council for Judaism to disband: Rauch and S. H. Goldenson, "Minority Report on Resolution II," in *Yearbook of the Central Conference of American Rabbis*, vol. 53 (Philadelphia: Jewish Publication Society, 1943), 94–98. After the creation of the State of Israel, however, he would grow to become supportive.

23. Joseph Rauch, "Contemporary Palestine," *Review & Expositor* 27, no. 1 (January 1930): 27.

24. Rauch, 27.

25. Rauch, 29.

26. Rauch, 31.

27. J. S. Farmer, "Current Topics: Jews and Arabs, by a Jew," *Biblical Recorder*, January 22, 1930, 7.

28. Frederick A. Lazin, "The Response of the American Jewish Committee to the Crisis of German Jewry, 1933–1939," *American Jewish History* 68, no. 3 (1979): 283–304; and Haim Genizi, "Interfaith Cooperation on Behalf of Refugees from Nazism, 1933–1945," *American Jewish History* 70, no. 3 (1981): 347–61.

29. Aaron Berman, *Nazism, the Jews, and American Zionism, 1933–1948* (Detroit, MI: Wayne State University Press, 1990), 23–36. See also: "American Non-Jews Publish Pro-Palestine Paper," *Jewish Telegraphic Agency*, February 16, 1932, https://www.jta.org/archive.

30. J. S. Farmer, "Current Topics: The Partition of Palestine," *Biblical Recorder*, July 28, 1937, 7.

31. J. S. Farmer, "Palestine," *Biblical Recorder*, September 16, 1936, 6.

32. J. S. Farmer, "Current Topics: The Partition of Palestine," *Biblical Recorder*, July 28, 1937, 7.

33. On persecution and the refugee crisis, see: J. S. Farmer, "Current Topics: A Place of Refuge," *Biblical Recorder*, April 6, 1938, 7; Farmer, "Religious Liberty in Austria," *Biblical Recorder*, May 11, 1938, 6; Farmer, "Current Topics: Germany Refuses to Pay," *Biblical Recorder*, June 29, 1938, 9; Farmer, "The Persecuted Jews of Germany," *Biblical Recorder*, November 23, 1938, 6; and Farmer, "Current Topics: Plain Words to Germany," *Biblical Recorder*, January 4, 1939, 10. See also William Richardson, "The Race over Whom Jesus Wept," *Biblical Recorder*, August 24, 1938, 3.

34. J. S. Farmer, "Current Topics: Great Britain in Palestine," *Biblical Recorder*, October 26, 1938, 7.

35. J. S. Farmer, "Current Topics: The Nazis and the Jews," *Biblical Recorder*, November 30, 1938, 10.

36. J. S. Farmer, "The Plight of the Jewish People," *Biblical Recorder*, February 15, 1939, 10.

37. J. S. Farmer, "Current Topics: The Refugee Jews," *Biblical Recorder*, June 14, 1939, 10.

38. J. S. Farmer, "The Jews—Refugees—and Aggressors," *Biblical Recorder*, July 27, 1938, 7.

39. W. O. Carver, "Facts and Factors in History Making," *Pastor's Periscope*, November 1938, 17–18.

40. Carver, 18.

41. On Carver and Rauch's exchange, see Mark Wilson, *William Owen Carver's Controversies in the Baptist South* (Macon, GA: Mercer University Press, 2010), 111–12.

42. W. O. Carver, "Facts and Factors in History Making," *Pastor's Periscope*, November 1938, 18.

43. W. O. Carver, "Kingdom Facts and Factors," *Commission*, July 1939, 221.

44. Leek figures prominently in Wayne Flynt's *Alabama Baptists: Southern Baptists in the Heart of Dixie* (Tuscaloosa: University of Alabama Press, 1998).

45. Dan Puckett, *In the Shadow of Hitler: Alabama's Jews, the Second World War, and the Holocaust* (Tuscaloosa: University of Alabama Press, 2014), 116–17.

46. Charles Leek, "Watching the World," *Alabama Baptist*, September 8, 1938, 4.

47. Charles Leek, "Watching the World," *Alabama Baptist*, August 11, 1938, 4.

48. Charles Leek, "Watching the World," *Alabama Baptist*, June 22, 1939, 4.

49. Charles Leek, "Watching the World," *Alabama Baptist*, July 15, 1937, 4.

50. Charles Leek, "Watching the World," *Alabama Baptist*, July 28, 1938, 4.

51. Charles Leek, "Watching the World," *Alabama Baptist*, March 18, 1937, 4.

52. Charles Leek, "Watching the World," *Alabama Baptist*, March 24, 1938, 4.

53. Emma Parker Maddry, "Women and Their Work," *Commission*, September 1940, 266.

54. Charles Edward Maddry, "World Trends," *Commission*, April 1941, 117.

55. Charles Edward Maddry, "World Trends," *Commission*, October 1942, 337.

56. Berman, *Nazism, the Jews, and American Zionism*, 85–95.

57. Cohen, *The Americanization of Zionism*, 165–88.

58. Carenen, *The Fervent Embrace*, 35–66.

59. Gwaltney is also a major focus of Flynt's *Alabama Baptists.*

60. L. L. Gwaltney, *The World's Greatest Decade* (Birmingham, AL: Baptist Book Store, 1947), 16.

61. L. L. Gwaltney, "The Editor's Page," *Alabama Baptist*, April 1, 1948, 3.

62. L. L. Gwaltney, "The Editor's Page," *Alabama Baptist*, December 11, 1947, 3.

63. L. L. Gwaltney, "The Editor's Page," *Alabama Baptist*, February 12, 1948, 3.

64. Gwaltney, *The World's Greatest Decade*, 67–68.

65. L. L. Gwaltney, "The Editor's Page," *Alabama Baptist*, February 26, 1948, 3.

66. L. L. Gwaltney, "The Editor's Page," *Alabama Baptist*, March 18, 1948, 3.

67. L. L. Gwaltney, "The Editor's Page," *Alabama Baptist*, June 24, 1948, 3.

68. L. L. Gwaltney, "The Editor's Page," *Alabama Baptist*, July 15, 1948, 16.

69. W. O. Carver, "Kingdom Facts and Factors," *Commission*, May 1947, 30.

70. Tinnin, "Editorial: A Troubled Future for Palestine," *Baptist Message*, February 26, 1948, 2.

71. Charles Wells, "Trends," *Baptist Student*, February 1948, inside front cover.

72. Charles Wells, "Trends," *Baptist Student*, June 1948, inside front cover.

73. I use the term *anti-Zionist* reluctantly here, as what could be construed as anti-Zionist changed frequently during the Mandate era.

74. Walker Robins, "Cultural Zionism and Binationalism among American Liberal Protestants," *Israel Studies* 23, no. 2 (2018): 142–67. On liberal and mainline Protestant opposition to Zionism, see Hertzel Fishman, *American Protestantism and a Jewish State* (Detroit, MI: Wayne State University Press, 1973), 41–53.

Chapter 10

1. Portions of this chapter were previously published in Walker Robins, "American Cyrus? Harry Truman, the Bible, and the Palestine Question," *Journal of Church and State* 59, no. 3 (2017): 447–65.

2. Jacob Gartenhaus, *Traitor?* (Chattanooga, TN: International Board of Jewish Missions, 1980), 199; and "Daily Appointments of Harry S. Truman (February 26, 1947)," *Harry S. Truman Presidential Library and Museum*, accessed April 14, 2019, https://www.trumanlibrary.org/calendar/.

3. H. Leo Eddleman to Harry Truman, rpt. in D. M. Giangreco and Kathryn Moore, ed., *Dear Harry: Truman's Mailroom, 1945–1953* (Mechanicsburg, PA: Stackpole Books, 1999), 149.

4. Biographies of Truman include: Alonzo Hamby, *Man of the People: A Life of Harry S. Truman* (New York: Oxford University Press, 1998); Robert Dallek, *Harry S. Truman* (New York: Times Books, 2008); David McCullough, *Truman* (New York: Simon and Schuster, 2003); and Richard Lawrence Miller, *Truman: The Rise to Power* (New York: McGraw-Hill, 1986). On Truman's presidency and foreign policy, see: Robert Donovan, *Conflict and Crisis: The Presidency of Harry S. Truman, 1945–1948* (Columbia: University of Missouri Press, 1977); Arnold Offner, *Another Such Victory: President Truman and the Cold War, 1945–1953* (Stanford, CA: Stanford University Press, 2002); and Elizabeth Spalding, *The First Cold Warrior: Harry Truman, Containment, and the Remaking of Liberal Internationalism* (Lexington: University Press of Kentucky, 2006).

5. Trygve Lie, qtd. in Michael Benson, *Harry S. Truman and the Founding of Israel* (Westport, CT: Praeger, 1997), 188.

6. Frank Brecher has argued that the State Department's (and Marshall's) fears that partition would damage the American national interest led them to use underhanded tactics in attempting to thwart its implementation: Brecher, "US Secretary of State George C. Marshall's Losing Battles against President Harry S. Truman's Palestine Policy, January–June 1948," *Middle Eastern Studies* 48, no. 2 (2012): 227–47.

7. Michael Cohen, "Truman and Palestine, 1945–1948: Revisionism, Politics and Diplomacy," *Modern Judaism* 2, no. 1 (1982): 2. Per the name, the White House school tends to reflect the perspective of Truman and others who were close to him in his administration. For Truman's account of his decision, see his *Memoirs*, vol. 2 (New York: Doubleday, 1956), chapters 10–12. Clark Clifford, special counsel to the president, recorded his account in Clifford, "Recognizing Israel," *Ameri-*

can Heritage 28, no. 3 (April 1977): 4–11; and Clifford, *Counsel to the President* (New York: Random House, 1991), 3–25. Among scholars, this school includes Ian Bickerton, "President Truman's Recognition of Israel," *American Jewish Historical Quarterly* 58, no. 2 (1968), 173–240; McCullough, *Truman*, 595–620; and Allis Radosh and Ronald Radosh, *A Safe Haven: Harry S. Truman and the Founding of Israel* (New York: HarperCollins, 2009). Bruce Evensen and Michael Ottolenghi have argued for the priority of Cold War concerns in guiding Truman's policy: Evensen, "Truman, Palestine and the Cold War," *Middle Eastern Studies* 28, no. 1 (1992): 120–56; and Ottolenghi, "Harry Truman's Recognition of Israel," *Historical Journal* 47, no. 4 (2004): 963–88.

8. The State Department school includes both figures from the State Department at the time and academics who have followed their interpretations. See, for example: Evan Wilson, "The American Interest in the Palestine Question and the Establishment of Israel," *Annals of the American Academy of Political and Social Science* 401 (1972): 64–73; and John Snetsinger, *Truman, the Jewish Vote, and the Creation of Israel* (Stanford, CA: Hoover Institution Press, 1974). A recent iteration can be found in John Judis, *Genesis: Truman, American Jews, and the Origins of the Arab/Israeli Conflict* (New York: Farrar, Straus and Giroux, 2014). Zvi Ganin emphasized Truman's humanitarian interests while acknowledging the weight of politics in his decision to support Israel. Ganin also argued that Truman never clearly understood the implications of his policy: Zvi Ganin, *Truman, American Jewry, and Israel, 1945–1948* (New York: Holmes and Meier, 1979). Michael Cohen has argued that Truman came to the Palestine question through the refugee question but that his Palestine policy was not determined by an enduring concern for the displaced persons (DPs). Ultimately, Cohen argues that Truman's policy was guided by his "aides in the White House and events": Cohen, *Truman and Israel* (Berkeley: University of California Press, 1990), 277.

9. Moshe Davis was among the earliest to call on scholars to look at Truman's possible religious motivations: Davis, "Reflections on Harry S. Truman and the State of Israel," in *Truman and the American Commitment to Israel*, ed. Allen Weinstein and Moshe Ma'oz (Jerusalem: Magnes Press, 1981), 82–85. Works that have more broadly emphasized the role of religion in Truman's foreign policy include Andrew Preston, *Sword of the Spirit, Shield of Faith: Religion in American War and Diplomacy* (New York: Anchor Books, 2012); Spalding, *The First Cold Warrior*, 199–232; and William Inboden, *Religion and American Foreign Policy, 1945–1960: The Soul of Containment* (New York: Cambridge University Press, 2008).

10. Others have rejected the idea that religion motivated Truman at all. Judis inaccurately claims that Michael Beschloss and Howard Sachar depict Truman as a Christian Zionist in their works (Judis, *Genesis*, 192–93). Beschloss mentions Truman's religion in his discussion of the Palestine question, but he does not make any specific claims about its impact on Truman's decision-making: Beschloss, *Presidential Courage: Brave Leaders and How They Changed America, 1789–1989* (New York: Simon and Schuster, 2007), 196–234. Although Sachar incorrectly depicts Truman as "pro-Zionist since his early manhood," he does not claim that Truman was any sort of Christian Zionist: Sachar, *A History of Israel: From the Rise of Zionism to Our Time*, 3rd ed. (New York: Knopf, 2004), 255.

11. Gary Smith, *Religion in the Oval Office: The Religious Lives of American Presidents* (New York: Oxford University Press, 2015), 256.

12. Benson, *Harry S. Truman and the Founding of Israel*, 7.

13. Radosh and Radosh, *A Safe Haven*, 345.

14. Paul C. Merkley, *American Presidents, Religion, and Israel: The Heirs of Cyrus* (Westport, CT: Praeger, 2004), ix; and Merkley, *The Politics of Christian Zionism, 1891–1948* (Portland, OR: Cass, 1998), 191.

15. Irvine Anderson, *Biblical Interpretation and Middle East Policy* (Gainesville: University Press of Florida, 2005), 89; Lawrence Davidson, "Truman the Politician and the Establishment of Israel," *Journal of Palestine Studies* 39, no. 4 (2010): 32; and Michelle Mart, "The 'Christianization' of Israel and Jews in 1950s America," *Religion and American Culture* 14, no. 1 (2004): 128.

16. Merlin Gustafson, "Truman as a Man of Faith," *Christian Century*, January 17, 1973, 75.

17. Harry S. Truman to Bess Wallace, February 7, 1911, box 1, Harry S. Truman Papers, Family, Business, and Personal Affairs (hereafter Truman Family Papers), Harry S. Truman Library and Museum (hereafter Truman Library), Independence, MO, accessed April 14, 2019, https://www.trumanlibrary.org/hstpaper/fbpa.htm.

18. Harry S. Truman, longhand note, August 15, 1950, box 283, Harry S. Truman Papers, President's Secretary's Files, Truman Library.

19. Miller, *Truman*, 73; Truman's quote is from William Hillman, *Mr. President: The First Publication from the Personal Diaries, Private Letters, Papers, and Revealing Interviews of Harry S. Truman, Thirty-Second President of the United States of America* (New York: Farrar, Straus, and Young, 1952), 106.

20. In a 1946 address to the Federal Council of Churches, Truman urged, "If men and nations would but live by the precepts of the ancient prophets and the teachings of the Sermon on the Mount, problems which now seem so difficult would soon disappear." Truman, "Address in Columbus at a Conference of the Federal Council of Churches," March 6, 1946, The American Presidency Project, ed. John Woolley and Gerhard Peters, accessed April 14, 2019, https://www.presidency.ucsb.edu/node/232618. The speech was written by a Jewish advisor, Samuel Rosenman, who had been carried over from the Roosevelt administration.

21. Harry S. Truman, qtd. in Gustafson, "Truman as a Man of Faith," 78.

22. Harry S. Truman, handwritten autobiographical manuscript, 1945, President's Secretary's Files, qtd. in "Harry Truman Speaks," comp. Raymond Geselbracht, Harry S. Truman Library and Museum, accessed April 14, 2019, https://www.trumanlibrary.org/speaks.htm.

23. Harry S. Truman, longhand note, April 13, 1952, box 284, President's Secretary's Files, Truman Library, accessed April 14, 2019, https://www.trumanlibrary.org/hstpaper/psf.htm.

24. Harry S. Truman to Bess Wallace, July 31, 1918, box 5, Truman Family Papers, Truman Library, accessed April 14, 2019, https://www.trumanlibrary.org/whistlestop/study_collections/ww1/index.php.

25. Harry S. Truman to Bess Truman, June 22, 1936, box 9, Truman Family Papers, Truman Library, accessed April 14, 2019, https://www.trumanlibrary.org/hstpaper/fbpa.htm.

26. See Preston, *Sword of the Spirit*, chapter 22. See also Inboden, *Religion and American Foreign Policy*, chapter 3; and Spalding, *The First Cold Warrior*, chapter 9.

27. Harry S. Truman, "Address in Columbus at a Conference of the Federal Council of Churches," March 6, 1946, The American Presidency Project, ed. John Woolley and Gerhard Peters, accessed April 14, 2019, https://www.presidency.ucsb.edu/node/232618.

28. Harry S. Truman to Bess Truman, October 2, 1947, box 16, Truman Family Papers, Truman Library, accessed April 14, 2019, https://www.trumanlibrary.org/hstpaper/fbpa.htm.

29. Harry S. Truman, handwritten manuscript, Post-Presidential Papers, qtd. in "Harry Truman Speaks," comp. Raymond Geselbracht, Harry S. Truman Library and Museum, accessed April 14, 2019. http://www.trumanlibrary.org/speaks.htm.

30. Gustafson, "Truman as a Man of Faith," 76.

31. Truman, *Memoirs*, vol. 1, 116.

32. Hillman, *Mr. President*, 169.

33. Hillman, 104. Truman added, "that is the reason they survived, and for no other reason."

34. Hillman, 105.

35. Merlin Gustafson, "The Religion of a President," *Journal of Church and State* 10, no. 3 (1968): 380.

36. Benson, *Harry S. Truman and the Founding of Israel*, 7.

37. In a 1977 interview that accompanied an article that Clifford had published in *American Heritage* about Truman's decision, interviewer Bernard Weisberger asked Clifford why he had decided to publish his recollections at that time. Clifford cited the need to combat "revisionist" accounts of the decision as well as the publication of the State Department's 1976 volume of the *Foreign Relations of the United States*, which concerned the year 1948. See Clifford, "An Exclusive Interview with Clark Clifford," interview by Bernard Weisberger, *American Heritage* 28, no. 3 (April 1977): 8.

38. 130 Cong. Rec. 11,331 (May 8, 1984) (statement of Clark Clifford); and Clifford, *Counsel to the President*, 8.

39. Clifford, "Recognizing Israel," 11.

40. Benson elides this distinction in his discussion of Truman's approach to the Bible. Benson, *Harry S. Truman and the Founding of Israel*, 54.

41. Smith, *Religion in the Oval Office*, 255.

42. Alfred Lilienthal, "Remembering General George Marshall's Clash with Clark Clifford over Premature Recognition of Israel," *Washington Report on Middle East Affairs*, June 1999, 50.

43. Alfred Lilienthal, *What Price Israel* (Chicago: Regnery, 1953); Lilienthal, *There Goes the Middle East* (New York: Devin-Adair, 1957); and Lilienthal, *The Zionist Connection* (New York: Dodd, 1978).

44. Hillman, *Mr. President*, 104 (emphasis added).

45. Harry S. Truman, longhand note, June 1, 1945, box 283, Harry S. Truman Papers, President's Secretary's Files, Truman Library, accessed April 14, 2019, https://www.trumanlibrary.org/hstpaper/psf.htm.

46. 130 Cong. Rec. 11,331 (May 8, 1984) (statement of Clark Clifford).

47. Truman was familiar with Jewish restorationist hopes from a young age. In a high school essay that Truman wrote on the character of Shylock from Shakespeare's *The Merchant of Venice*, Truman noted, "No one except the Hebrews has ruled the world, then, when they fell, remained a distinct people. After 2,000 years the Jews are a nation apart from nations, persecuted for their religion and still waiting for a leader to gather their scattered people." However, Truman added that Jews "know not that their leader has already come." Qtd. in Denis Brian, *The Elected and the Chosen: Why American Presidents Have Supported Jews and Israel* (New York: Gefen, 2012), 225; and Beschloss, *Presidential Courage*, 199–200.

48. Norris printed the letter in both the *Fundamentalist*, October 10, 1947, 1, and *My Fifth Trip to Palestine* (Fort Worth: Fundamentalist Press, 1948), 9–12.

49. Smith, *Religion in the Oval Office*, 254.

50. Qtd. in Norris, *My Fifth Trip*, 13.

51. Eliahu Elath, *Harry S. Truman: The Man and Statesman* (Jerusalem: Harry S. Truman Research Institute, 1977), 48. Truman aide David Niles likewise recalled the president's emotion at Herzog's comparison: Alfred Steinberg, *The Man from Missouri: The Life and Times of Harry S. Truman* (New York: Putnam's Sons, 1962), 308.

52. Moshe Davis, "Reflections on Harry S. Truman," 83.

53. Merkley, *American Presidents*, viii.

54. Merkley, *The Politics of Christian Zionism*, 191.

55. Radosh and Radosh argue that Truman began his biblical reflections *after* 1948: *A Safe Haven*, 344.

56. This argument is central in Judis's *Genesis*.

57. He even did so the day after recognizing the Israeli government. Cohen, *Truman and Israel*, 222.

58. Of course, Cyrus did not restore the Judeans to full sovereignty, but invocations of his model have not focused on the details of Persian tributary structures.

59. Elath, *Truman*, 49.

60. Clifford, "Recognizing Israel," 11.

61. Truman, *Memoirs*, vol. 2, 156.

62. Donovan, *Conflict and Crisis*, 386.

63. Douglass Little argues that Orientalism pervaded the administration's understanding of the Middle East: Little, *American Orientalism: The United States and the Middle East since 1945* (Chapel Hill: University of North Carolina Press, 2002), 26. William Pemberton argues for its effects on his framing of the Palestine question: Pemberton, *Harry S. Truman: Fair Dealer and Cold Warrior* (Boston: Twayne, 1989), 118–19.

64. Truman, *Memoirs*, vol. 2, 156. Truman was not, however, completely dismissive of Palestinian concerns. On Truman's policy toward the Palestinians, see Fred Lawson, "The Truman Administration and the Palestinians," *Arab Studies Quarterly* 12, no. 1/2 (1990): 43–65.

65. Merle Miller, *Plain Speaking: An Oral Biography of Harry S. Truman* (New York: Berkley, 1973), 215.

66. Chaim Weizmann, *Trial and Error: The Autobiography of Chaim Weizmann*, vol. 2 (New York: Harper and Brothers, 1949), 458.

67. Truman, *Memoirs*, vol. 2, 156.

68. Benson argues, in contrast, that Truman's sense of moral duty drove his policy. Benson, *Harry S. Truman and the Founding of Israel*, 9.

69. Cohen, *Truman and Israel*, 277.

70. 84 Cong. Rec. 2,231 (May 25, 1939) (extension of remarks of Hon. Harry S. Truman).

71. Barnet Nover, "British Surrender: A Munich for the Holy Land," *Washington Post*, May 18, 1939, 11.

72. Ganin, *Truman, American Jewry, and Israel*, 21.

73. Harry S. Truman, qtd. in Ken Hechler, "A Common Man's Perspective," in *Immigration and the Legacy of Harry S. Truman*, ed. Roger Daniels (Kirksville, MO: Truman State University Press, 2010), 52–53.

74. Harry S. Truman to Morris Feinstein, February 19, 1944, box 2259, Harry S. Truman Correspondence, American Jewish Archives (AJA).

75. "1944 Democratic Party Platform," The American Presidency Project, ed. Gerhard Peters and John T. Woolley, accessed April 14, 2019, https://www.presidency.ucsb.edu/node/273222.

76. Cohen, *Truman and Israel*, 55.

77. Harry S. Truman, "Situation of Jews in Europe," *Department of State Bulletin* 13, no. 334 (November 18, 1945): 791.

78. Anglo-American Committee of Inquiry, "Recommendations and Comments," The Avalon Project, accessed April 14, 2019, http://avalon.law.yale.edu/20th_century/angch01.asp.

79. Cohen, *Truman and Israel*, 130–37.

80. Cohen, 137–46; and Harry S. Truman, "A Decade of American Foreign Policy, 1941–1949—Immigration into Palestine—Statement by President Truman, October 4, 1946," The Avalon Project, accessed April 14, 2019, http://avalon.law.yale.edu/20th_century/decad163.asp.

81. While Benson argues overall that Truman's sense of moral duty drove his Palestine policy, he also acknowledges that the president's policy was at times guided by others, especially those "who appealed to the president in ways consistent with his beliefs": Benson, *Harry S. Truman and the Founding of Israel*, 73. David McBride has taken a similar approach in looking at the question of tensions between the national interest and Truman's political interests in the Palestine question. McBride argues that Truman's advisors convinced him that a pro-Zionist policy would ultimately not harm American interests, allowing him to take the politically advantageous course: McBride, "For All the Wrong Reasons? Re-Evaluating Truman, Domestic Influences, and the Palestine Question," *Digest of Middle East Studies* 14, no. 2 (2005): 27–51.

82. Qtd. in Michael Cohen, *Palestine and the Great Powers, 1945–1948* (Princeton, NJ: Princeton University Press, 1982), 51.

83. Radosh and Radosh, *A Safe Haven*, 178.

84. Truman, *Memoirs*, vol. 2, 132.

85. Chaim Weizmann to Harry S. Truman, April 9, 1948, in *Foreign Relations of the United States, 1948, the Near East, South Asia, and Africa*, vol. 5, part 2, Department of State: Office of the Historian, accessed April 14, 2019, https://history.state.gov/historicaldocuments/frus1948v05p2/d139.

86. Smith, *Religion in the Oval Office*, 256.

Conclusion

1. "Editorials," *Western Recorder*, March 18, 1948, 3.

2. John Popham, "Baptists Criticize Truman on Israel," *New York Times*, May 20, 1948, 4.

3. John Lee Eighmy, *Churches in Cultural Captivity: A History of the Social Attitudes of Southern Baptists* (Knoxville: University of Tennessee Press, 1972), 159.

4. W. Terry Lindley, "The 1948 SBC Opposition to Israel: The J. Frank Norris Factor," *Baptist History and Heritage* 22, no. 4 (1987): 23–33.

5. On the war, see Benny Morris, *1948: A History of the First Arab-Israeli War* (New Haven, CT: Yale University Press, 2008).

6. For a comprehensive work on the conflict, see Benny Morris, *Righteous Victims: A History of the Zionist-Arab Conflict, 1881–2001* (New York: Vintage Books, 2001).

7. Z. T. Cody, "Zionism," *Biblical Recorder*, February 4, 1920, 8.

8. It was Dwight Eisenhower who first invoked the term "Judeo-Christian" as president-elect, but Truman's civilizational and religious anti-Communist rhetoric anticipated the concept in many ways. Mark Silk, "Notes on the Judeo-Christian Tradition in America," *American Quarterly* 36, no. 1 (1984): 65–85; Michelle Mart, "The 'Christianization' of Israel and Jews in 1950s America," *Religion and American Culture* 14, no. 1 (2004): 109–47; Mart, *Eye on Israel: How America Came to View Israel as an Ally* (Albany: State University of New York Press, 2006), 85–109; and Samuel Goldman, *God's Country: Christian Zionism in America* (Philadelphia: University of Pennsylvania Press, 2018), 125–46. For an overview of American religion in the postwar era, including its ecumenical emphasis on Judeo-Christianity, see Bill J. Leonard, "Dangerous and Promising Times: American Religion in the Postwar Years," in *Cambridge History of Religions in America*, vol. 3, ed. Stephen Stein (New York: Cambridge University Press, 2012), 1–27. Andrew Warne has argued that the Christian right seized onto the language of Judeo-Christianity (and onto support for Israel) in order to performatively embrace pluralism while promoting an "exclusionary vision of who counted as an American." This language helped conservative evangelicals shed past associations with anti-Semitism and enter the political mainstream by the late 1970s: Warne, "Making a Judeo-Christian America: The Christian Right, Antisemitism, and the Politics of Religious Pluralism in the 20th Century United States" (PhD diss., Northwestern University, 2012), 11. On the archaeological and theological dimensions of Judeo-Christianity and evangelical support for Israel, see Hummel, *Covenant Brothers*, 40–58.

9. Stephen Spector has highlighted the important role that the idea of civilizational clash has played in contemporary Christian Zionism: Spector, *Evangelicals and Israel: The Story of American Christian Zionism* (New York: Oxford University Press, 2009), 50, 85–86, 89. See also Ussama Makdisi, *Faith Misplaced: The Broken Promise of U.S.-Arab Relations: 1820–2001* (New York: PublicAffairs, 2010), 230.

10. On the evangelical movement, see Joel Carpenter, *Revive Us Again: The Reawakening of American Fundamentalism* (New York: Oxford University Press, 1997); Matthew Avery Sutton, *American Apocalypse: A History of Modern Evangelicalism* (Cambridge, MA: Harvard University Press, 2014); Randall Balmer, *Blessed Assurance: A History of Evangelicalism in America* (Boston: Beacon Press, 1999); Balmer,

The Making of Evangelicalism: From Revivalism to Politics and Beyond (Waco, TX: Baylor University Press, 2010); George M. Marsden, *Reforming Fundamentalism: Fuller Seminary and the New Evangelicalism* (Grand Rapids, MI: Eerdmans, 1987); Marsden, *Understanding Fundamentalism and Evangelicalism* (Grand Rapids, MI: Eerdmans, 1991); and Barry Hankins, *American Evangelicals: A Contemporary History of a Mainstream Religious Movement* (Lanham, MD: Rowman and Littlefield, 2009). On Billy Graham, see William Martin, *Prophet with Honor: The Billy Graham Story* (New York: Morrow, 1991); and Grant Wacker, *America's Pastor: Billy Graham and the Shaping of a Nation* (Cambridge, MA: Belknap Press, 2014).

11. For a look at the varieties of Baptist fundamentalisms, see Nathan Finn, "The Development of Baptist Fundamentalism in the South, 1940–1980" (PhD diss., Southeastern Baptist Theological Seminary, 2007).

12. W. A. Criswell, "In Memory of Mother," May 8, 1977, *W. A. Criswell Sermon Library*, http://www.wacriswell.com/sermons/1977/in-memory-of-mother1/.

13. On Criswell's dispensationalism, see D. E. Howe, "An Analysis of Dispensationalism and Its Implications for the Theologies of James Robinson Graves, John Franklyn Norris, and Wallie Amos Criswell" (PhD diss., Southwestern Baptist Theological Seminary, 1988), 202–68.

14. For many of these biographical details, I have depended on C. Allyn Russell, "W. A. Criswell: A Case Study in Fundamentalism," *Review & Expositor* 44, no. 1 (1984): 107–31.

15. Finn uses the term *denominational fundamentalists*. I have chosen to follow Barry Hankins's usage of the term *conservatives*.

16. For an examination of convention conservatives and their efforts to mobilize the institutions of the SBC in a broader culture war, see Barry Hankins, *Uneasy in Babylon: Southern Baptist Conservatives and American Culture* (Tuscaloosa: University of Alabama Press, 2002).

17. Helen Lee Turner interprets the takeover/resurgence as a millenarian movement: Turner, "Fundamentalism in the Southern Baptist Convention: The Crystallization of a Millennialist Vision," (PhD diss., University of Virginia, 1990); and Turner, "Myths: Stories of This World and the World to Come," in *Southern Baptists Observed: Multiple Perspectives on a Changing Denomination*, ed. Nancy Ammerman (Knoxville: University of Tennessee Press, 1993), 98–123. For a sociological approach to the conflict, see Nancy Ammerman, *Baptist Battles: Social Change and Religious Conflict in the Southern Baptist Convention* (New Brunswick, NJ: Rutgers University Press, 1990). For a moderate's historical analysis, see Bill J. Leonard, *God's Last and Only Hope: The Fragmentation of the Southern Baptist Convention* (Grand Rapids, MI: Eerdmans, 1990). For a conservative's favorable account, see Jerry Sutton, *The Baptist Reformation: The Conservative Resurgence in the Southern Baptist Convention* (Nashville, TN: Broadman and Holman, 2000).

18. W. A. Criswell, "Why I Am a Premillennialist," October 16, 1980, W. A. Criswell Sermon Library, accessed April 15, 2019, https://www.wacriswell.com/sermons1980/why-i-am-a-premillennialist-2/; and Criswell, *The Criswell Study Bible*, ed. Paige Patterson (Nashville, TN: Thomas Nelson, 1979).

19. Ammerman, *Baptist Battles*, 75–76. Ammerman's percentages come from a survey of Baptist leaders that included pastors, deacons, and presidents of Baptist women's groups (local affiliates of the Woman's Missionary Union [WMU]).

20. Richard Land, former head of the SBC's Ethics and Religious Liberty Commission, noted in 2008, "For Southern Baptists, the return of the Jews to the land of promise in great numbers after World War II has helped promulgate premillennialism among Southern Baptists. . . . But many people with whom I went to seminary in the late 1960s and early 1970s were amillennial in their eschatological outlook. The attack on Israel helped change that, and today the majority of Southern Baptists are premillennialists." Qtd. in Greg Tomlin, "Israel Celebrates 60th Year," *Baptist Courier*, May 21, 2008.

21. Southern Baptist missionaries, including Robert Lindsey, began advising the Israeli government on cultivating evangelical tourism even prior to 1967: Hummel, *Covenant Brothers*, 106–10; Yaakov Ariel, *An Unusual Relationship: Evangelical Christians and Jews* (New York: New York University Press, 2013), 193–95.

22. Baptist missionaries in Israel facilitated these connections: Hummel, *Covenant Brothers*, 28, 96–97. On Criswell's trip, see W. A. Criswell, "Report on Israel," November 3, 1968, W. A. Criswell Sermon Library, accessed April 15, 2019, https://www.wacriswell.com/sermons/1968/report-on-israel-2/. On Rabin's visit, see SBC Annual, 1969, 56.

23. Daniel Hummel, "A 'Practical Outlet' to Premillennial Faith: G. Douglas Young and the Evolution of Christian Zionist Activism in Israel," *Religion and American Culture* 25, no. 1 (2015): 57–66; and W. A. Criswell, "The Bible and Prophecy," in *Prophecy in the Making*, ed. Carl Henry (Carol Stream, IL: Creation House, 1971), 17–34.

24. For documents related to these trips, see box 53, folder 16, William Clemont Fields Papers, Southern Baptist Historical Library and Archives (SBHLA).

25. George Sheridan, "Tour Reveals Israel IS the Holy Land," *Christian Index*, February 24, 1972, box 53, folder 16, William Clemont Fields Papers, SBHLA.

26. See Hummel, *Covenant Brothers*, 159–84. On the relationship between Likud and the Christian right, see Colin Shindler, "Likud and the Christian Dispensationalists: A Symbiotic Relationship," *Israel Studies* 5, no. 1 (2000): 153–82. On the rise of the Christian right (also called the religious right), see: *Oxford Research Encyclopedia of Religion*, s.v. "The Religious Right in America," by Michael McVicar, March 2016, https://doi.org/10.1093/acrefore/9780199340378.013.97; Angela Lahr, *Millennial Dreams and Apocalyptic Nightmares: The Cold War Origins of Political Evangelicalism* (New York: Oxford University Press, 2007); Daniel K. Williams, *God's Own Party: The Making of the Christian Right* (New York: Oxford University Press, 2010); Darren Dochuk, *From Bible Belt to Sunbelt: Plain-Folk Religion, Grassroots Politics, and the Rise of Evangelical Conservativism* (New York: Norton, 2011); Beth Moreton, *To Serve God and Wal-Mart: The Making of Christian Free Enterprise* (Cambridge, MA: Harvard University Press, 2009); Susan Friend Harding, *The Book of Jerry Falwell: Fundamentalist Language and Politics* (Princeton, NJ: Princeton University Press, 2000); William Martin, *With God on Our Side: The Rise of the Religious Right in America* (New York: Broadway Books, 1996); Lisa McGirr, *Suburban Warriors: The Origins of the New American Right* (Princeton, NJ: Princeton University Press, 2001); Steven P. Miller, *Billy Graham and the Rise of the Republican South* (Philadelphia: University of Pennsylvania Press, 2009).

27. Timothy Weber, *On the Road to Armageddon: How Evangelicals Became Israel's Best Friend* (Grand Rapids, MI: Baker Academic Press, 2004), 218–20.

28. Jerry Falwell, *Listen, America!* (New York: Bantam Books, 1980), 107–13.

29. On the growth of organized Christian Zionist groups, see Timothy Weber, "American Evangelicals and Israel: A Complicated Alliance," in *The Protestant-Jewish Conundrum*, ed. Jonathan Frankel and Ezra Mendelsohn, vol. 24 of *Studies in Contemporary Jewry* (New York: Oxford University Press, 2010): 141–57.

30. Norman Jameson, "Rogers Meets Menachem Begin, Tells of Faith," *Baptist Press*, April 18, 1980, 30–31.

31. Amy Weiss examines how American Jewish Zionist organizations began engaging more directly with evangelical Protestants after the 1967 Six-Day War in "Between Cooperation and Competition: The Making of American Jewish Zionist Interfaith Alliances with Liberal and Evangelical Protestants, 1898–1979," (PhD diss., New York University, 2014), 300–333. On dialogue between American Jewish groups and Southern Baptists, see Weiss, "Billy Graham Receives the Ten Commandments: American Jewish Interfaith Relations in the Age of Evangelicalism," *American Jewish History* 103, no. 1 (2019): 1–24.

32. Tanenbaum also built relationships with Billy Graham and Jerry Falwell. On Tanenbaum and the American Jewish Committee's engagement with evangelicals, see Daniel Hummel, "*His Land* and the Origins of the Jewish-Evangelical Israel Lobby," *Church History* 87, no. 4 (2018): 1119–51.

33. Marc Tanenbaum, "The Meaning of Israel: A Jewish View" (paper, Southern Baptist–Jewish Scholars Conference, Southern Baptist Theological Seminary, Louisville, KY, August 18–20, 1969), p. 11, box 2, folder 14, Rabbi Marc H. Tanenbaum Collection, American Jewish Archives (AJA).

34. Joseph Estes, "A Baptist Perspective of Judaism" (paper, The People of God: Jewish and Baptist Perspectives Conference, Hebrew Union College—Jewish Institute of Religion, Cincinnati, OH, June 14, 1971), box 15, folder 13, Rabbi Marc H. Tanenbaum Collection, AJA.

35. James Rudin, "A Jewish Perspective on Baptist Ecumenism," in *Baptists and Ecumenism*, ed. William Jerry Boney and Glenn A. Igleheart (Valley Forge, PA: Judson, 1980), 161, 165–66.

36. In 1982, missionary Robert L. Lindsey presented on the meaning of Israel: Lindsey, "A Baptist View of Israel" (paper, Southern Baptist–American Jewish Committee Meeting, Golden Gate Baptist Theological Seminary, Marin County, CA, February 17, 1982), box 45, folder 18, Rabbi Marc H. Tanenbaum Collection, AJA. Papers from a 1986 dialogue at the Southern Baptist Theological Seminary (SBTS) were published in the *Review & Expositor* 84, no. 2 (1987).

37. For most of Shorrosh's biographical details, I have relied on James Hefley and Marti Hefley, *The Liberated Palestinian: The Anis Shorrosh Story* (Dallas, TX: Acclaimed Books, n.d.).

38. Anis Shorrosh wrote, "The strangest thing in the world of today's politics is the fact that the Arab's [*sic*] control 3,000,000 square miles of territory, but cannot let Israel, their kinfolk, have 10,000 square miles. The hallowed parcel of land, called Palestine, has actually been in the hands of the Arabs longer than the descendants of Jacob. Yet God promised it to the Israelites." See Shorrosh, *Jesus, Prophecy, and the Middle East* (Daphne, AL: Shorrosh, 1979), 72.

39. From the late 1980s onward, Shorrosh would also establish himself as an anti-Islamic activist.

40. On Israeli efforts to restrict missionary activities prior to 1967, see Uri Bialer, *Cross on the Star of David: The Christian World in Israel's Foreign Policy, 1948–1967* (Bloomington: Indiana University Press, 2005), 93–120.

41. The ordination of Fuad Sakhnini as pastor of the Nazareth Baptist Church in 1960 was an important step toward local control. Since Louis Hanna had departed the region, the church founded by Shukri Mosa had been pastored by Americans. The 1965 formation of the Association of Baptist Churches in Israel was likewise an important institutional step towards greater local autonomy.

42. Dwight Baker, "Israel and Religious Liberty," *Journal of Church and State* 7, no. 3 (1965): 403–24.

43. SBC Annual, 1978, 67.

44. David Glass to Jimmy Allen, March 10, 1980, box 287, folder 5, International Mission Board (IMB) Minutes and Reports, 1849–2005, SBHLA.

45. Norman Jameson, "Rogers Meets Menachem Begin, Tells of Faith," *Baptist Press*, April 18, 1980, 30–31.

46. Jimmy Carter, qtd. in Paul C. Merkley, *American Presidents, Religion, and Israel: The Heirs of Cyrus* (Westport, CT: Praeger, 2004), 92.

47. Jimmy Carter, "Tel Aviv, Israel Remarks of the President and Prime Minister Begin at the Departure Ceremony," March 13, 1979, The American Presidency Project, ed. Gerhard Peters and John T. Woolley, accessed April 15, 2019, https://www.presidency.ucsb.edu/node/249005.

48. Jimmy Carter, *Blood of Abraham: Insights into the Middle East* (Fayetteville: University of Arkansas Press, 2007), 193. See also Carter, *Palestine: Peace, Not Apartheid* (New York: Simon and Schuster, 2006); and Carter, *We Can Have Peace in the Holy Land* (New York: Simon and Schuster, 2010). Carter left the SBC in 2000, after the convention revised its Faith and Message to include a statement against women pastors.

49. "Baptist Leader Claims God 'Does Not Hear the Prayer of a Jew,'" *Jewish Telegraphic Agency*, September 19, 1980. For documents on the Smith controversy, see box 1, folder 32, Bailey Smith Papers, SBHLA.

50. "Israelis Ask Baptists to Build in Jerusalem," *Baptist Press*, December 11, 1981, 4–5.

51. Finlay Graham to David King, April 8, 1983, box 3, folder 15, David King—Baptists in the Middle East Collection, SBHLA. For earlier examples, see Melanie E. Trexler, *Evangelizing Lebanon: Baptists, Missions, and the Question of Cultures* (Waco, TX: Baylor University Press, 2016), 65–67.

52. "Israelis Ask Baptists to Build in Jerusalem," *Baptist Press*, December 11, 1981, 5.

53. "Parks Takes Strong Stand against Israel Resolution," *Baptist Press*, February 9, 1983, 2.

54. Grace Halsell, *Forcing God's Hand: Why the Religious Right Wants Armageddon Now!* (Washington, DC: Crossroads, 1999), 69–70.

55. SBC Annual, 1982, 55–56.

56. SBC Annual, 2002, 74–75.

57. SBC Annual, 2002, 75.

Bibliography

Archival Materials

American Jewish Archives (AJA). Cincinnati, Ohio

Joseph Rauch Papers.
Rabbi Marc H. Tanenbaum Collection.
Truman Correspondence.

Central Zionist Archives. Jerusalem, Israel

American Christian Palestine Committee (ACPC).
Emanuel Neumann Collection.

Harry S. Truman Library and Museum (accessed through http://www.trumanlibrary.org)

Harry S. Truman Papers, Family, Business, and Personal Affairs.
President's Secretary's Files.

Southern Baptist Historical Library and Archives (SBHLA). Nashville, Tennessee

Bailey Smith Papers.
Foreign Mission Board, Historical Files.
H. C. Goerner Papers.
Hight C. Moore Papers.
Home Mission Board Executive Office Files.
Home Mission Board Minutes.
International Mission Board (IMB), Missionary Correspondence Files.
International Mission Board (IMB), Mission Minutes and Reports, 1849–2005.
Isaac Jacobus Van Ness Papers.
Jacob Gartenhaus Papers (JG).
James Marion Frost Papers.
John Franklyn Norris Papers.
Thomas Treadwell Eaton Papers.
T. W. Medearis Papers.
Una Roberts Lawrence Papers (URL).
William Clemont Fields Papers.

Online Archives

The American Presidency Project, edited by John Woolley and Gerhard Peters, http://www.presidency.ucsb.edu/.
The Avalon Project, Yale Law School, Lillian Goldman Law Library, http://avalon.law.yale.edu/default.asp.
W. A. Criswell Sermon Library, https://www.wacriswell.com/.

Published Sources

Periodicals

Alabama Baptist (Marion, AL).
Arkansas Baptist (Arkadelphia, AR).
Baptist and Reflector (Nashville, TN) (accessed through the website of the Southern Baptist Historical Library and Archives, http://www.sbhla.org/tb_archive/).
Baptist Chronicle (Shreveport, LA).
Baptist Courier (Greenville, SC).
Baptist Message (Shreveport, LA).
Baptist Messenger (Oklahoma City, OK).
Baptist Press (Nashville, TN).
Baptist Standard (Dallas, TX).
Baptist Student (Nashville, TN).
Biblical Recorder (Raleigh, NC) (accessed through the website of the Z. Smith Reynolds Library at Wake Forest University, http://digital.olivesoftware.com/Olive/APA/Wakeforest/default.aspx).
Christian Index (Atlanta, GA).
Commission (Richmond, VA) (accessed through the Solomon Databases of the International Mission Board Archives and Records Services, http://archives.imb.org/solomon.asp).
Department of State Bulletin (Washington, DC).
Florida Baptist Witness (Jacksonville, FL).
Foreign Mission Journal (Richmond, VA) (accessed through the Solomon Databases of the International Mission Board Archives and Records Services, http://archives.imb.org/solomon.asp).
Fundamentalist (Fort Worth, TX).
Hebrew Christian Alliance Quarterly (Chicago, IL).
Home and Foreign Fields (Richmond, VA) (accessed through the Solomon Databases of the International Mission Board Archives and Records Services, http://archives.imb.org/solomon.asp).
Pastor's Periscope (Nashville, TN).
Review & Expositor (Louisville, KY).
Royal Service (Birmingham, AL).
Quarterly Review (Nashville, TN).
Searchlight (Fort Worth, TX).
Snyder Signal (Snyder, TX).
Tennessee Baptist (Nashville, TN) (accessed through the website of the Southern

Baptist Historical Library and Archives, http://www.sbhla.org/sbc_annuals/index.asp).

Western Recorder (Louisville, KY).

Annuals and Minutes

Southern Baptist Convention (SBC) Annuals, 1846–present (accessed through the website of the Southern Baptist Historical Library and Archives, http://www.sbhla.org/sbc_annuals/index.asp).

Southern Baptist Convention (SBC) International Mission Board (formerly Foreign Mission Board) Minutes (accessed through the Solomon Databases of the International Mission Board Archives and Records Services, http://archives.imb.org/solomon.asp).

Primary Sources

Acheson, Dean. *Present at the Creation.* New York: Norton, 1969.

Adams, J. McKee. *Biblical Backgrounds: A Geographical Survey of Bible Lands in the Light of the Scriptures and Recent Research.* Nashville, TN: Broadman Press, 1934.

———. *The Heart of the Levant.* Richmond, VA: Foreign Mission Board, 1937.

Alexander, Walter. *Holy Hours in the Holy Land.* Grand Rapids, MI: Eerdmans, 1946.

Allredge, E. P. *Southern Baptist Handbook 1922.* Nashville, TN: Baptist Sunday School Board, 1922.

Appelman, Hyman. *Appelman's Sermon Outlines and Illustrations.* Grand Rapids, MI: Zondervan, 1944.

———. *The Battle of Armageddon.* Grand Rapids, MI: Zondervan, 1944.

———. *From Jewish Lawyer to Baptist Preacher.* Fairfield, AL: Faith of Our Fathers, 1944.

Baker, Dwight. *Baptists Golden Jubilee: 50 Years in Palestine-Israel.* n.p.: 1961.

———. "Israel and Religious Liberty." *Journal of Church and State* 7, no. 3 (1965): 403–24.

"The Biltmore Program." In *The Israel-Arab Reader*, edited by Walter Laqueur and Barry Rubin, 7th ed., 55–56. New York: Penguin, 2008.

Brooks, V. L. *A History of the First Baptist Church of Austin, Texas.* Austin: n.p., 1923. https://texashistory.unt.edu/ark:/67531/metapth33019/.

Broughton, Leonard. *The Second Coming of Christ.* Philadelphia: Pepper, 1902.

Carter, Jimmy. *Blood of Abraham: Insights into the Middle East.* Fayetteville: University of Arkansas Press, 2007.

———. *Palestine: Peace, Not Apartheid.* New York: Simon and Schuster, 2006.

———. *We Can Have Peace in the Holy Land.* New York: Simon and Schuster, 2010.

Clifford, Clark M. *Counsel to the President.* New York: Random House, 1991.

———. "An Exclusive Interview with Clark Clifford." Interview by Bernard Weisberger. *American Heritage* 28, no. 3 (April 1977).

———. "Recognizing Israel." *American Heritage* 28, no. 3 (April 1977).

Cook's Tourists' Handbook for Palestine and Syria. London: Thomas Cook & Son, 1876.

Criswell, W. A. "The Bible and Prophecy." In *Prophecy in the Making*, edited by Carl Henry, 17–34. Carol Stream, IL: Creation House, 1971.

———. *The Criswell Study Bible*. Edited by Paige Patterson. Nashville, TN: Thomas Nelson, 1979.

Criswell, W. A., and Duke McCall. *Passport to the World*. Nashville, TN: Broadman Press, 1951.

Davis, Moshe. "The Holy Land in American Spiritual History." In *With Eyes toward Zion*, edited by Moshe Davis, 3–33. New York: Arno Press, 1977.

———. "Reflections on Harry S. Truman and the State of Israel." In *Truman and the American Commitment to Israel*, edited by Allen Weinstein and Moshe Ma'oz, 82–85. Jerusalem: Magnes Press, 1981.

Decker, Florence Boston. *World Airways for the King*. Nashville, TN: Broadman Press, 1941.

Dillard, Badgett, and Lucy Adams. "Oral History Interview of Lucy Oliver Adams (Mrs. J. McKee Adams)." Transcribed by Michele Fowler, February 14, 1980. James P. Boyce Centennial Library Digital Repository, Southern Baptist Theological Seminary, http://hdl.handle.net/10392/43.

Dodd, M. E. *Girdling the Globe for God*. Shreveport, LA: John S. Ramond, 1935.

———. *Jesus Is Coming to Earth Again*. Chicago: Chicago Bible Institute Colportage Association, 1917.

Elath, Eliahu. *Harry S. Truman: The Man and Statesman*. Jerusalem: Harry S. Truman Research Institute, 1977.

Falwell, Jerry. *Listen, America!* New York: Bantam Books, 1980.

Floyd, Rolla. *Letters from Palestine: 1868–1912*. Edited by Helen Palmer Parsons. N.p.: Parsons, 1981.

Fort, Joseph Marstain. *The Texas Doctor and the Arab Donkey, or Palestine and Egypt as Viewed by Modern Eyes*. Chicago: Donohue and Henneberry, 1898.

Fosdick, Harry Emerson. *A Pilgrimage to Palestine*. New York: Macmillan, 1937.

Gartenhaus, Jacob. *The Influence of the Jews upon Civilization*. Grand Rapids, MI: Zondervan, 1943.

———. *The Jew and Jesus*. Nashville, TN: Sunday School Board, 1934.

———. *The Jewish Passover*. Nashville, TN: Broadman Press, 1944.

———. *The Rebirth of a Nation: Zionism in History and Prophecy*. Nashville, TN: Broadman Press, 1936.

———. "The Local Church and the Jews." In *Report of the First International Hebrew Christian Conference*, 154–60. London: Marshall Brothers, 1925.

———. *Traitor?* Chattanooga, TN: International Board of Jewish Missions, 1980.

———. *What of the Jews?* Atlanta, GA: Home Mission Board, 1948.

Goerner, H. Cornell. "Zionism and the Scriptures." *Review & Expositor* 34, no. 3 (1937): 302–14.

Graves, James Robinson. *The Dispensational Expositions of the Parables and Prophecies of Christ*. Memphis, TN: Graves and Mahaffy, 1887.

———. *The Work of Christ Consummated in Seven Dispensations*. Memphis, TN: Baptist Book House, 1883.

Gwaltney, L. L. *The World's Greatest Decade*. Birmingham, AL: Baptist Book Store, 1947.

Ham, Mordecai. *The Second Coming of Christ*. Louisville, KY: printed by the author, 1943.

Hamlett, W. A. *The Book of Revelation*. Louisville, KY: Mordecai Ham, n.d.

———. *Travels of a Father and Son*. Lebanon, PA: Sowers, 1911.

Handy, Robert. "Sources for Understanding American Christian Attitudes toward the Holy Land, 1800–1950." In *With Eyes toward Zion*, edited by Moshe Davis, 34–56. New York: Arno Press, 1977.

Hefley, James, and Marti Hefley. *The Liberated Palestinian: The Anis Shorrosh Story*. Dallas, TX: Acclaimed Books, n.d.

Hillman, William. *Mr. President: The First Publication from the Personal Diaries, Private Letters, Papers, and Revealing Interviews of Harry S. Truman, Thirty-Second President of the United States of America*. New York: Farrar, Straus, and Young, 1952.

Hope Simpson, John. *Palestine: Report on Immigration, Land Settlement and Development*. London: His Majesty's Stationery Office, 1930.

Howie, Ghosn el-. "The Evil Eye." *Palestine Exploration Quarterly* 36, no. 2 (1904): 148–50.

Hughey, J. D. "Europe and the Middle East." In *Advance: A History of Southern Baptist Foreign Missions*, edited by J. Baker Cauthen, 187–240. Nashville: Broadman Press, 1970.

Jacobs, Joseph. *Jewish Contributions to Civilization: An Estimate*. Philadelphia: Jewish Publication Society of America, 1919.

Klausner, Joseph. *Jesus of Nazareth: His Life, Times, and Teaching*. Translated by Herbert Danby. New York: Macmillan, 1925.

Knight, Ryland. "Palestine—A Problem." *Review & Expositor* 27, no. 1 (1930): 11–23.

League of Nations. "The British Mandate." In *The Israel-Arab Reader*, edited by Walter Laqueur and Barry Rubin, 7th ed., 30–35. New York: Penguin, 2008.

Lewis, Walter, ed. *Seventh Baptist World Congress: Official Report*. London: Baptist World Alliance, 1948.

Lilienthal, Alfred. "Remembering General George Marshall's Clash with Clark Clifford over Premature Recognition of Israel." *Washington Report on Middle East Affairs*, June 1999, 49–50.

———. *There Goes the Middle East*. New York: Devin-Adair, 1957.

———. *What Price Israel*. Chicago: Regnery, 1953.

———. *The Zionist Connection*. New York: Dodd, 1978.

Lindsey, Robert L. *Israel in Christendom: The Problem of Jewish Identity*. N.p.: n.d.

———. *Israel Seeks a Faith*. Richmond, VA: Foreign Mission Board, 1957.

Lunsford, William, ed. *Veterans of the Cross*. Dallas, TX: Baptist Standard, 1921.

Martin, T. T. *The Second Coming of Christ*. N.p.: n.d. Southern Baptist Theological Seminary.

McMahon, Henry. "The McMahon Letter." In *The Israel-Arab Reader*, edited by Walter Laqueur and Barry Rubin, 7th ed., 11–12. New York: Penguin, 2008.

Miller, Merle. *Plain Speaking: An Oral Biography of Harry S. Truman*. New York: Berkley, 1973.

Newman, Albert. "Recent Changes in the Theology of Baptists." *American Journal of Theology* 10, no. 4 (1906): 587–609.

Norris, J. Frank. *Did the Jews Write the Protocols?* Detroit, MI: n.p., 1938.

———. *My Fifth Trip to Palestine.* Fort Worth, TX: Fundamentalist Press, 1948.

Owens, Doreen Hosford. *The Camel Bell.* Richmond, VA: Foreign Mission Board, 1937.

———. *The Village Oven.* Richmond, VA: Foreign Mission Board, 1937.

Peel, William Robert Wellesley. *Palestine Royal Commission Report.* London: Her Majesty's Stationery Office, 1937.

Programmes and Itineraries of Cook's Arrangements for Palestine Tours. London: Thomas Cook & Son, 1876.

Questing in Galilee. Richmond, VA: Foreign Mission Board, 1937.

Rabinovich, Itamar, and Jehuda Reinharz, eds. *Israel in the Middle East: Documents and Readings on Society, Politics, and Foreign Relations, Pre-1948 to the Present.* Waltham, MA: Brandeis University Press, 2008.

Rauch, Joseph. "Contemporary Palestine." *Review & Expositor* 27, no. 1 (1930): 24–31.

Rauch, Joseph, and S. H. Goldenson. "Minority Report on Resolution II." In *Yearbook of the Central Conference of American Rabbis*, vol. 53, 94–98. Philadelphia: Jewish Publication Society, 1943.

Report of the Commission on the Palestine Disturbances of August, 1929. London: His Majesty's Stationery Office, 1930.

Rice, John R. *The Coming Kingdom of Christ.* Wheaton, IL: Sword of the Lord, 1945.

———. *Jewish Persecution and Bible Prophecies.* Wheaton, IL: Sword of the Lord, 1941.

———. *World-Wide War and the Bible.* Wheaton, IL: Sword of the Lord, 1940.

Robertson, A. T. *Life and Letters of John Albert Broadus.* Philadelphia: American Baptist Publication Society, 1901.

Robinson, Edward, and Eli Smith. *Biblical Researches in Palestine, Mount Sinai, and Arabia Petraea: A Journal of Travels in the Year 1838.* Boston: Crocker and Brewster, 1841.

Roth, Cecil. *The Jewish Contribution to Civilization.* New York: Macmillan, 1938.

Rudin, James. "A Jewish Perspective on Baptist Ecumenism." In *Baptists and Ecumenism*, edited by William Jerry Boney and Glenn A. Igleheart, 160–71. Valley Forge, PA: Judson, 1980.

Seay, Warren Mosby. *A Tale of Two Peoples: Gentiles and Jews.* Atlanta, GA: Home Mission Board, 1927.

Shorrosh, Anis. *Jesus, Prophecy, and the Middle East.* Daphne, AL: Shorrosh, 1979.

Stanley, Arthur. *Sinai and Palestine in Connection with Their History.* London: Murray, 1856.

State of Israel. "Proclamation of Independence." In *The Israel-Arab Reader*, edited by Walter Laqueur and Barry Rubin, 7th ed., 81–82. New York: Penguin, 2008.

Truman, Harry S. *Memoirs.* 2 vols. New York: Doubleday, 1956.

Tupper, Henry Allen. *Around the World with Eyes Wide Open.* New York: Christian Herald, 1898.

———. "Mission to the Jews." In *The Foreign Missions of the Southern Baptist Convention*, edited by Henry Allen Tupper, 442–59. Philadelphia: American Baptist Publication Society, 1880.

——. *Uncle Allen's Party in Palestine*. Philadelphia: American Baptist Publication Society, 1898.

Twain, Mark. *The Innocents Abroad*. Hartford, CT: American, 1869.

United Nations Special Committee on Palestine. "Summary Report." In *The Israel-Arab Reader*, edited by Walter Laqueur and Barry Rubin, 7th ed., 65–68. New York: Penguin, 2008.

Watts, J. Wash. "Opportunities for Evangelical Missions in Palestine." *Review & Expositor* 22, no. 2 (April 1931): 151–61.

Watts, Mrs. James Washington. *Palestinian Tapestries*. Richmond, VA: Foreign Mission Board, 1936.

Wharton, Henry Marvin. *A Picnic in Palestine*. Baltimore, MD: Wharton and Barron, 1892.

Weizmann, Chaim. *Trial and Error: The Autobiography of Chaim Weizmann*. 2 vols. New York: Harper and Brothers, 1949.

Whittle, Walter Andrew. *A Baptist Abroad*. New York: J. A. Hill, 1890.

Secondary Sources

Abu-Manneh, Butrus. "The Rise of the Sanjak of Jerusalem in the Late Nineteenth Century." In *The Israel/Palestine Question: A Reader*, edited by Ilan Pappé, 41–52. New York: Routledge, 2007.

Ajaj, Azar, and Duane Alexander Miller. "Arab Baptist Leaders in Israel: Their History and Collective Identity." In *Arab Evangelicals in Israel*, edited by Azar Ajaj, Duane Alexander Miller, and Philip Sumpter, 52–64. Eugene, OR: Pickwick, 2016.

Allen, Catherine. *A Century to Celebrate: History of Woman's Missionary Union*. Birmingham, AL: Woman's Missionary Union, 1987.

Ammerman, Nancy. *Baptist Battles: Social Change and Religious Conflict in the Southern Baptist Convention*. New Brunswick, NJ: Rutgers University Press, 1990.

Anderson, Irvine. *Biblical Interpretation and Middle East Policy*. Gainesville: University Press of Florida, 2005.

Antonius, George. *The Arab Awakening: The Story of the Arab National Movement*. Philadelphia: J. B. Lippincott, 1939.

Ariel, Yaakov. "The Ambiguous Missionary: Robert Lindsey in Israel, 1948–1970." In *America and Zion: Essays and Papers in Memory of Moshe Davis*, edited by Eli Lederhendler and Jonathan Sarna, 185–200. Detroit, MI: Wayne State University Press, 2002.

——. *Evangelizing the Chosen People: Missions to the Jews in America, 1880–2000*. Chapel Hill: University of North Carolina Press, 2000.

——. *On Behalf of Israel: American Fundamentalist Attitudes toward Jews, Judaism, and Zionism, 1865–1945*. Brooklyn, NY: Carlson, 1991.

——. *An Unusual Relationship: Evangelical Christians and Jews*. New York: New York University Press, 2013.

Avineri, Shlomo. *The Making of Modern Zionism: The Intellectual Origins of the Jewish State*. New York: Basic Books, 1981.

Baker, Robert. *The Southern Baptist Convention and Its People*. Nashville, TN: Broadman Press, 1974.

Balmer, Randall. *Blessed Assurance: A History of Evangelicalism in America*. Boston: Beacon Press, 1999.

———. *The Making of Evangelicalism: From Revivalism to Politics and Beyond*. Waco, TX: Baylor University Press, 2010.

Bauman, Mark K. *A New Vision of Southern Jewish History: Studies in Institution Building, Leadership, Interaction, and Mobility*. Tuscaloosa: University of Alabama Press, 2019.

Bays, Daniel H., and Grant Wacker, eds. *The Foreign Missionary Enterprise at Home: Explorations in North American Cultural History*. Tuscaloosa: University of Alabama Press, 2009.

Beschloss, Michael. *Presidential Courage: Brave Leaders and How They Changed America, 1789–1989*. New York: Simon and Schuster, 2007.

Ben-Arieh, Yehoshua. *The Rediscovery of the Holy Land in the Nineteenth Century*. Jerusalem: Magnes Press, 1979.

Benson, Michael. *Harry S. Truman and the Founding of Israel*. Westport, CT: Praeger, 1997.

Berman, Aaron. *Nazism, the Jews, and American Zionism, 1933–1948*. Detroit, MI: Wayne State University Press, 1990.

Bialer, Uri. *Cross on the Star of David: The Christian World in Israel's Foreign Policy, 1948–1967*. Bloomington: Indiana University Press, 2005.

Bickerton, Ian. "President Truman's Recognition of Israel." *American Jewish Historical Quarterly* 58, no. 2 (1968): 173–240.

Boyer, Paul. *When Time Shall Be No More: Prophecy Belief in Modern American Culture*. Cambridge, MA: Belknap Press, 1992.

Brecher, Frank. "US Secretary of State George C. Marshall's Losing Battles against President Harry S. Truman's Palestine Policy, January–June 1948." *Middle Eastern Studies* 48, no. 2 (2012): 227–47.

Brian, Denis. *The Elected and the Chosen: Why American Presidents Have Supported Jews and Israel*. New York: Gefen, 2012.

Campos, Michelle. *Ottoman Brothers: Muslims, Christians, and Jews in Early Twentieth-Century Palestine*. Stanford, CA: Stanford University Press, 2011.

Cannon, Mae Elise. "Mischief Making in Palestine: American Protestant Christian Perspectives of Israel and Palestine, Pre-1916 to 1955." PhD diss., University of California, Davis, 2014.

Carenen, Caitlin. "The American Christian Palestine Committee, the Holocaust, and Mainstream Protestant Zionism, 1938–1948." *Holocaust and Genocide Studies* 24, no. 2 (2010): 272–96.

———. *The Fervent Embrace: Liberal Protestants, Evangelicals, and Israel*. New York: New York University Press, 2012.

Carpenter, Joel. *Revive Us Again: The Reawakening of American Fundamentalism*. New York: Oxford University Press, 1997.

Christison, Kathleen. *Perceptions of Palestine: Their Influence on U.S. Middle East Policy*. Berkeley: University of California Press, 1999.

Clark, Victoria. *Allies for Armageddon: The Rise of Christian Zionism*. New Haven, CT: Yale University Press, 2007.

Cogley, Richard. "The Fall of the Ottoman Empire and the Restoration of Israel in the 'Judeo-Centric' Strand of Puritan Millenarianism." *Church History* 72, no. 2 (2003): 304–32.

Cohen, Hillel. *Year Zero of the Arab-Israeli Conflict: 1929*. Translated by Haim Watzman. Waltham, MA: Brandeis University Press, 2015.

Cohen, Michael. *Palestine and the Great Powers*. Princeton: Princeton University Press, 1982.

———. *Truman and Israel*. Berkeley: University of California Press, 1990.

———. "Truman and Palestine, 1945–1948: Revisionism, Politics and Diplomacy." *Modern Judaism* 2, no. 1 (1982): 1–22.

Cohen, Naomi Wiener. *The Americanization of Zionism, 1897–1948*. Hanover, NH: Brandeis University Press, 2003.

———. *The Year after the Riots: American Responses to the Palestine Crisis of 1929–30*. Detroit, MI: Wayne State University Press, 1988.

Cohn-Sherbok, Dan. *Messianic Judaism: A Critical Anthology*. New York: Continuum, 2000.

Conforti, Yitzhak. "'The New Jew' in the Zionist Movement: Ideology and Historiography." *Australian Journal for Jewish Studies* 25 (2011): 87–118.

Crome, Andrew. *The Restoration of the Jews: Early Modern Hermeneutics, Eschatology, and National Identity in the Works of Thomas Brightman*. New York: Springer, 2014.

Dallek, Robert. *Harry S. Truman*. New York: Times Books, 2008.

Darby, Michael R. *The Emergence of the Hebrew Christian Movement in Nineteenth-Century Britain*. Leiden, Netherlands: Brill, 2010.

Davidson, Lawrence. *America's Palestine: Popular and Official Perceptions from Balfour to Israeli Statehood*. Gainesville: University Press of Florida, 2001.

———. "Christian Zionism as a Representation of American Manifest Destiny." *Critique: Critical Middle Eastern Studies* 14, no. 2 (2005): 157–69.

———. "Truman the Politician and the Establishment of Israel." *Journal of Palestine Studies* 39, no. 4 (2010): 28–42.

Divine, Donna Robinson. "Palestine in World War I." In *The Middle East and North Africa: Essays in Honor of J. C. Hurewitz*, edited by Reeva S. Simon, 71–94. New York: Columbia University Press, 1990.

Dochuk, Darren. *From Bible Belt to Sunbelt: Plain-Folk Religion, Grassroots Politics, and the Rise of Evangelical Conservatism*. New York: Norton, 2011.

Donovan, Robert. *Conflict and Crisis: The Presidency of Harry S. Truman, 1945–1948*. Columbia: University of Missouri Press, 1977.

Dowty, Alan. *Israel/Palestine*. 2nd ed. Malden, MA: Polity Press, 2008.

Eichhorn, David Max. *Evangelizing the American Jew*. Middle Village, NY: Jonathan David, 1978.

Eighmy, John Lee. *Churches in Cultural Captivity: A History of the Social Attitudes of Southern Baptists*. Knoxville: University of Tennessee Press, 1972.

Eisen, Max. "Christian Missions to the Jews in North America and Great Britain." *Jewish Social Studies* 10, no. 1 (1948): 31–66.

Encyclopedia of Southern Baptists. Edited by Norman Cox and Lynn May. 4 vols. Nashville, TN: Broadman Press, 1958–82.

Epstein, Lawrence J. *Zion's Call: Christian Contributions to the Origins and Development of Israel.* Lanham, MD: University Press of America, 1984.

Evensen, Bruce. "The Limits of Presidential Leadership: Truman at War with Zionists, the Press, Public Opinion, and His Own State Department over Palestine." *Presidential Studies Quarterly* 23, no. 2 (1993): 269–87.

———. "Truman, Palestine and the Cold War." *Middle Eastern Studies* 28, no. 1 (1992): 120–56.

Feldman, Egal. *Dual Destinies: The Jewish Encounter with Protestant America.* Champaign: University of Illinois Press, 1990.

Finn, Nathan. "The Development of Baptist Fundamentalism in the South, 1940–1980." PhD diss., Southeastern Baptist Theological Seminary, 2007.

Fishman, Hertzel. *American Protestantism and a Jewish State.* Detroit, MI: Wayne State University Press, 1973.

Flynt, Wayne. *Alabama Baptists: Southern Baptists in the Heart of Dixie.* Tuscaloosa: University of Alabama Press, 1998.

Ganin, Zvi. *Truman, American Jewry, and Israel, 1945–1948.* New York: Holmes and Meier, 1979.

Garrett, James Leo. *Baptist Theology: A Four-Century Study.* Macon, GA: Mercer University Press, 2009.

Garrett, James Leo, Glenn Hinson, and James Tull. *Are Southern Baptists "Evangelicals"?* Macon, GA: Mercer University Press, 1983.

Genizi, Haim. "Interfaith Cooperation on Behalf of Refugees from Nazism, 1933–1945." *American Jewish History* 70, no. 3 (1981): 347–61.

Giangreco, D. M., and Kathryn Moore, eds. *Dear Harry: Truman's Mailroom, 1945–1953.* Mechanicsburg, PA: Stackpole Books, 1999.

Gibson, Shimon, Yoni Shapira, and Rupert Chapman. *Tourists, Travellers, and Hotels in Nineteenth-Century Jerusalem.* Leeds, UK: Maney, 2013.

Glass, William. "From Southern Baptist to Fundamentalist: The Case of I. W. Rogers and *The Faith*, 1945–57." *American Baptist Quarterly* 14 (1995): 241–59.

———. "Fundamentalism's Prophetic Vision of the Jews: The 1930s." *Jewish Social Studies* 47, no. 1 (1985): 63–76.

———. *Strangers in Zion: Fundamentalists in the South, 1900–1950.* Macon, GA: Mercer University Press, 2001.

Goldman, Samuel. *God's Country: Christian Zionism in America.* Philadelphia: University of Pennsylvania Press, 2018.

Goldman, Shalom. "Christians and Zionism: A Review Essay." *American Jewish History* 93, no. 2 (2007): 245–60.

———. *Zeal for Zion: Christians, Jews, and the Idea of the Promised Land.* Chapel Hill: University of North Carolina Press, 2009.

Goodman, Daniel. "Strangers, Neighbors, and Strangers Again: The History of Southern Baptist Approaches to Jews and Judaism." *Review & Expositor* 103, no. 1 (2006): 63–89.

Grabill, Joseph. "Protestant Diplomacy and Arab Nationalism, 1914–1948." *American Presbyterians* 64, no. 2 (1986): 113–24.

———. *Protestant Diplomacy and the Near East: Missionary Influence on American Policy, 1810–1927.* Minneapolis: University of Minnesota Press, 1971.

Greenberg, Gershon. *The Holy Land in American Religious Thought: The Symbiosis of American Religious Approaches to Scripture's Sacred Territory*. Lanham, MD: University Press of America, 1994.

Grose, Peter. *Israel in the Mind of America*. New York: Schocken Books, 1984.

Gunner, Goran, and Robert Smith, eds. *Comprehending Christian Zionism: Perspectives in Comparison*. Minneapolis, MN: Augsburg Fortress, 2014.

Gustafson, Merlin. "The Religion of a President." *Journal of Church and State* 10, no. 3 (1968): 379–87.

———. "Truman as a Man of Faith." *Christian Century*, January 17, 1973.

Haiduc-Dale, Noah. *Arab Christians in British Mandate Palestine: Communalism and Nationalism, 1917–1948*. Edinburgh: Edinburgh University Press, 2013.

Halpern, Ben. *A Clash of Heroes: Brandeis, Weizmann, and American Zionism*. New York: Oxford University Press, 1987.

Halsell, Grace. *Forcing God's Hand: Why the Religious Right Wants Armageddon Now!* Washington, DC: Crossroads, 1999.

———. *Prophecy and Politics: Militant Evangelists on the Road to Nuclear War*. Westport, CT: Lawrence Hill, 1986.

Hamby, Alonzo. *Man of the People: A Life of Harry S. Truman*. New York: Oxford University Press, 1998.

Hankins, Barry. *American Evangelicals: A Contemporary History of a Mainstream Religious Movement*. Lanham, MD: Rowman and Littlefield, 2009.

———. *God's Rascal: J. Frank Norris and the Beginnings of Southern Fundamentalism*. Lexington: University Press of Kentucky, 1996.

———. *Uneasy in Babylon: Southern Baptist Conservatives and American Culture*. Tuscaloosa: University of Alabama Press, 2002.

Harding, Susan Friend. *The Book of Jerry Falwell: Fundamentalist Language and Politics*. Princeton, NJ: Princeton University Press, 2000.

Harvey, Paul. *Redeeming the South: Religious Cultures and Racial Identities among Southern Baptists, 1865–1925*. Chapel Hill: University of North Carolina Press, 1997.

Hechler, Ken. "A Common Man's Perspective." In *Immigration and the Legacy of Harry S. Truman*, edited by Roger Daniels, 50–66. Kirksville, MO: Truman State University Press, 2010.

Hertzberg, Arthur, *The Zionist Idea: A Historical Analysis and Reader*. Philadelphia: Jewish Publication Society, 1997.

Heyrman, Christine Leigh. *American Apostles: When Evangelicals Entered the World of Islam*. New York: Hill and Wang, 2015.

Himes, Andrew. *The Sword of the Lord: The Roots of Fundamentalism in an American Family*. Seattle: Chiara Press, 2011.

Hollinger, David. *Protestants Abroad: How Missionaries Tried to Change the World but Changed America*. Princeton, NJ: Princeton University Press, 2017.

Howe, D. E. "An Analysis of Dispensationalism and Its Implications for the Theologies of James Robinson Graves, John Franklyn Norris, and Wallie Amos Criswell." PhD diss., Southwestern Baptist Theological Seminary, 1988.

Hughes, Matthew. "From Law and Order to Pacification: Britain's Suppression of the Arab Revolt in Palestine, 1936–1939." *Journal of Palestine Studies* 39, no. 2 (2010): 6–22.

Hummel, Daniel G. *Covenant Brothers: Evangelicals, Jews, and U.S.-Israeli Relations*. Philadelphia: University of Pennsylvania Press, 2019.

———. "*His Land* and the Origins of the Jewish-Evangelical Israel Lobby." *Church History* 87, no. 4 (2018): 1119–51.

———. "A 'Practical Outlet' to Premillennial Faith: G. Douglas Young and the Evolution of Christian Zionist Activism in Israel." *Religion and American Culture* 25, no. 1 (2015): 37–81.

Inboden, William. *Religion and American Foreign Policy, 1945–1960: The Soul of Containment*. New York: Cambridge University Press, 2008.

Jacobson, Abigail. "A City Living through Crisis: Jerusalem during World War I." *British Journal of Middle Eastern Studies* 36, no. 1 (2009): 73–92.

———. "Negotiating Ottomanism in Times of War: Jerusalem during World War I through the Eyes of a Local Muslim Resident." *International Journal of Middle East Studies* 40 (2008): 69–88.

Judis, John. *Genesis: Truman, American Jews, and the Origins of the Arab/Israeli Conflict*. New York: Farrar, Straus and Giroux, 2014.

Kark, Ruth. "Millenarism and Agricultural Settlement in the Holy Land in the Nineteenth Century." *Journal of Historical Geography* 9, no. 1 (1983): 47–62.

Khalidi, Rashid. *The Iron Cage: The Story of the Palestinian Struggle for Statehood*. Boston, MA: Beacon Press, 2006.

———. *Palestinian Identity: The Construction of Modern National Consciousness*. New York: Columbia University Press, 2010.

Khalidi, Rashid, Lisa Anderson, Muhammad Muslih, and Reeva S. Simon, eds. *The Origins of Arab Nationalism*. New York: Columbia University Press, 1991.

Kidd, Thomas S. *American Christians and Islam: Evangelical Culture and Muslims from the Colonial Period to the Age of Terrorism*. Princeton, NJ: Princeton University Press, 2009.

Kidd, Thomas S., and Barry Hankins. *Baptists in America: A History*. New York: Oxford University Press, 2015.

Kimmerling, Baruch. "The Formation of Palestinian Collective Identities: The Ottoman and Mandatory Periods." *Middle Eastern Studies* 36, no. 2 (2000): 48–81.

Kimmerling, Baruch, and Joel S. Migdal. *Palestinians: The Making of a People*. New York: Free Press, 1993.

Kotzin, Daniel. *Judah L. Magnes: An American Jewish Nonconformist*. Syracuse, NY: Syracuse University Press, 2010.

Lahr, Angela. *Millennial Dreams and Apocalyptic Nightmares: The Cold War Origins of Political Evangelicalism*. New York: Oxford University Press, 2007.

Laqueur, Walter. *A History of Zionism*. New York: Schocken, 1976.

Lawson, Fred. "The Truman Administration and the Palestinians." *Arab Studies Quarterly* 12, no. 1/2 (1990): 43–65.

Lazin, Frederick A. "The Response of the American Jewish Committee to the Crisis of German Jewry, 1933–1939." *American Jewish History* 68, no. 3 (1979): 283–304.

Leonard, Bill J. *Baptists in America*. New York: Columbia University Press, 2007.

———. "Dangerous and Promising Times: American Religion in the Postwar

Years." In *Cambridge History of Religions in America*, vol. 3, edited by Stephen J. Stein, 1–27. New York: Cambridge University Press, 2012.

———. *God's Last and Only Hope: The Fragmentation of the Southern Baptist Convention*. Grand Rapids, MI: Eerdmans, 1990.

Levenson, Alan. "Gentile Reception of Herzlian Zionism, a Reconsideration." *Jewish History* 16, no. 2 (2002): 187–211.

Lindley, W. Terry. "The 1948 SBC Opposition to Israel: The J. Frank Norris Factor." *Baptist History and Heritage* 22, no. 4 (1987): 23–33.

Little, Douglas. *American Orientalism: The United States and the Middle East since 1945*. Chapel Hill: University of North Carolina Press, 2002.

MacDonald, Robert. "'A Land without a People for a People without a Land': Civilizing Mission and American Support for Zionism, 1880s–1929." PhD diss., Bowling Green State University, 2012.

Makdisi, Jean Said. *Teta, Mother, and Me: Three Generations of Arab Women*. New York: Norton, 2006.

Makdisi, Ussama. *Artillery of Heaven: American Missionaries and the Failed Conversion of the Middle East*. Ithaca, NY: Cornell University Press, 2009.

———. *Faith Misplaced: The Broken Promise of U.S.-Arab Relations: 1820–2001*. New York: PublicAffairs, 2010.

Malachy, Yona. *American Fundamentalism and Israel: The Relationship of Fundamentalist Churches to Zionism and the State of Israel*. Jerusalem: Institute of Contemporary Jewry, 1978.

Mandel, Neville. *The Arabs and Zionism before World War I*. Berkeley: University of California Press, 1976.

Mansour, Bader. "A Brief Summary of Baptist History in the Holy Land: 1911–2011." Paper for the Association of Baptist Churches in Israel, 2011. http://baptist.org.il/baptistdata/en-events/d/0/0/ev107/files/100-Years-of-Baptist-Witness-in-the-Holy-Land.pdf.

Marsden, George M. *Fundamentalism and American Culture: The Shaping of Twentieth Century Evangelicalism, 1870–1925*. 2nd ed. New York: Oxford University Press, 2006.

———. *Reforming Fundamentalism: Fuller Seminary and the New Evangelicalism*. Grand Rapids, MI: Eerdmans, 1987.

———. *Understanding Fundamentalism and Evangelicalism*. Grand Rapids, MI: Eerdmans, 1991.

Mart, Michelle. "The 'Christianization' of Israel and Jews in 1950s America." *Religion and American Culture* 14. no. 1 (2004): 109–47.

———. "Constructing a Universal Ideal: Anti-Semitism, American Jews, and the Founding of Israel." *Modern Judaism* 20, no. 2 (2000): 181–208.

———. *Eye on Israel: How America Came to View Israel as an Ally*. Albany: State University of New York Press, 2006.

Martin, William. *Prophet with Honor: The Billy Graham Story*. New York: Morrow, 1991.

———. *With God on Our Side: The Rise of the Religious Right in America*. New York: Broadway Books, 1996.

Mattar, Philip. "The Mufti of Jerusalem and the Politics of Palestine." *Middle East Journal* 42, no. 2 (1988): 227–40.

McAlister, Melani. *Epic Encounters: Culture, Media, and U.S. Interests in the Middle East since 1945*. Oakland: University of California Press, 2005.

McBride, David. "For All the Wrong Reasons? Re-Evaluating Truman, Domestic Influences, and the Palestine Question." *Digest of Middle East Studies* 14, no. 2 (2005): 27–51.

McCarthy, Justin. *The Population of Palestine: Population Statistics of the Late Ottoman Period and the Mandate*. New York: University of Columbia Press, 1990.

McCullough, David. *Truman*. New York: Simon and Schuster, 2003.

McGirr, Lisa. *Suburban Warriors: The Origins of the New American Right*. Princeton, NJ: Princeton University Press, 2001.

McGraw, Eliza. "'How to Win the Jews for Christ': Jewishness and the Southern Baptist Convention." *Mississippi Quarterly* 53, no. 2 (2000): 209–23.

Merkley, Paul C. *American Presidents, Religion, and Israel: The Heirs of Cyrus*. Westport, CT: Praeger, 2004.

———. *Christian Attitudes towards the State of Israel*. Montreal: McGill-Queen's Press, 2001.

———. *The Politics of Christian Zionism, 1891–1948*. Portland, OR: Cass, 1998.

Metzer, Jacob. *The Divided Economy of Mandatory Palestine*. New York: Cambridge University Press, 1998.

Miller, Richard Lawrence. *Truman: The Rise to Power*. New York: McGraw-Hill, 1986.

Miller, Steven P. *Billy Graham and the Rise of the Republican South*. Philadelphia: University of Pennsylvania Press, 2009.

Mitelpunkt, Shaul. *Israel in the American Mind: The Cultural Politics of U.S.-Israeli Relations, 1958–1988*. New York: Cambridge University Press, 2018.

Moore, Deborah Dash. "Jewish GIs and the Creation of the Judeo-Christian Tradition." *Religion and American Culture* 8, no. 1 (1998): 31–53.

Moreton, Beth. *To Serve God and Wal-Mart: The Making of Christian Free Enterprise*. Cambridge, MA: Harvard University Press, 2009.

Morris, Benny. *1948: A History of the First Arab-Israeli War*. New Haven, CT: Yale University Press, 2008.

———. *Righteous Victims: A History of the Zionist-Arab Conflict, 1881–2001*. New York: Vintage Books, 2001.

Mullican, Kenneth, and Loren Turnage. *One Foot in Heaven: The Story of Bob Lindsey of Jerusalem*. Baltimore, MD: PublishAmerica, 2005.

Muslih, Muhammad Y. *The Origins of Palestinian Nationalism*. New York: Columbia University Press, 1988.

Newberg, Eric. *The Pentecostal Mission in Palestine: The Legacy of Pentecostal Zionism*. Eugene, OR: Pickwick, 2012.

Norris, Jacob. *Land of Progress: Palestine in the Age of Colonial Development, 1905–1948*. Oxford: Oxford University Press, 2013.

———. "Transforming the Holy Land: The Ideology of Development and the British Mandate in Palestine." *Humanity: An International Journal of Human Rights, Humanitarianism, and Development* 8, no. 2 (2017): 269–86.

Obenzinger, Hilton. *American Palestine: Melville, Twain, and the Holy Land Mania*. Princeton, NJ: Princeton University Press, 1999.

Offner, Arnold. *Another Such Victory: President Truman and the Cold War, 1945–1953*. Stanford, CA: Stanford University Press, 2002.

O'Mahoney, Anthony. "Palestinian Christians: Religion, Politics, and Society, c. 1800–1948." In *Palestinian Christians: Religion, Politics and Society in the Holy Land*, edited by Anthony O'Mahoney, 9–55. London: Melisende, 1999.

Othman, Enaya Hammad. *Negotiating Palestinian Womanhood: Encounters between Palestinian Women and American Missionaries, 1880s–1940s*. New York: Lexington Books, 2016.

Ottolenghi, Michael. "Harry Truman's Recognition of Israel." *Historical Journal* 47, no. 4 (2004): 963–88.

Patterson, James A. *James Robinson Graves: Staking the Boundaries of Baptist Identity*. Nashville, TN: Broadman and Holman, 2012.

Pemberton, William. *Harry S. Truman: Fair Dealer and Cold Warrior*. Boston: Twayne, 1989.

Phillipp, Thomas. "Language, History, and Arab National Consciousness in the Thought of Jurji Zaidan (1861–1914)." *International Journal of Middle East Studies* 4, no. 1 (1973): 3–22.

Pitts, William. "Southern Baptists and Millennialism, 1900–2000: Conceptual Patterns and Historical Expressions." *Baptist History and Heritage* 34, no. 2 (1999): 7–27.

Preston, Andrew. *Sword of the Spirit, Shield of Faith: Religion in American War and Diplomacy*. New York: Anchor Books, 2012.

Puckett, Dan. *In the Shadow of Hitler: Alabama's Jews, the Second World War, and the Holocaust*. Tuscaloosa: University of Alabama Press, 2014.

Radosh, Allis, and Ronald Radosh. *A Safe Haven: Harry S. Truman and the Founding of Israel*. New York: HarperCollins, 2009.

Rausch, David. "Fundamentalism and the Jew: An Interpretive Essay." *Journal of the Evangelical Theological Society* 23, no. 2 (1980): 105–12.

———. *Messianic Judaism: Its History, Theology, and Polity*. Lewiston, NY: Edwin Mellen Press, 1982.

———. "A Rejoinder to Timothy Weber's Reply." *Journal of the Evangelical Theological Society* 24, no. 1 (1981): 73–77.

———. *Zionism within Early American Fundamentalism, 1878–1918: A Convergence of Two Traditions*. Lewiston, NY: Edwin Mellen Press, 1979.

Reinharz, Jehuda. "The Balfour Declaration in Historical Perspective." In *Essential Papers on Zionism*, edited by Jehuda Reinharz and Anita Shapira, 587–616. New York: New York University Press, 1996.

Robert, Dana. "From Missions to Mission to Beyond Missions: The Historiography of American Protestant Foreign Missions since World War II." In *New Directions in American Religious History*, edited by Harry Stout and D. G. Hart, 362–93. New York: Oxford University Press, 1997.

Robins, Walker. "Ambiguous Witness." Master's thesis. University of Oklahoma, 2010.

———. "American Cyrus? Harry Truman, the Bible, and the Palestine Question." *Journal of Church and State* 59, no. 3 (2017): 447–65.

———. "Cultural Zionism and Binationalism among American Liberal Protestants." *Israel Studies* 23, no 2 (2018): 142–67.

———. "The Forgotten Origins of the Southern Baptist Convention's Near East Mission: W. A. Hamlett's Month in the Holy Land." *Baptist History & Heritage* 52, no. 2 (2017): 20–31.

———. "Jacob Gartenhaus: The Southern Baptists' Jew." *Journal of Southern Religion* 19 (2017): http://jsreligion.org/vol19/robins.

———. "A Meshummad in Dixie: Jacob Gartenhaus as a Convert Missionary in the Southern Baptist Convention, 1921–1949." In *Konversion in Räumen jüdischer Geschichte*, edited by Carsten Schapkow and Martin Przybilski, 135–49. Wiesbaden, Germany: Dr. Ludwig Reichert Academic Press, 2014.

Robson, Laura. *Colonialism and Christianity in Mandate Palestine*. Austin: University of Texas Press, 2011.

Rogan, Eugene. *The Fall of the Ottomans: The Great War in the Middle East*. New York: Basic Books, 2015.

Rogers, Stephanie Stidham. *Inventing the Holy Land: American Protestant Pilgrimage to Palestine, 1865–1941*. Lanham, MD: Lexington Books, 2011.

Rosovsky, Nitza. "Nineteenth-Century Portraits through Western Eyes." In *City of the Great King*, edited by Nitza Rosovsky, 218–40. Cambridge, MA: Harvard University Press, 1996.

Ross, Robert. "Baptists, Jews, Nazis: 1933–1947." In *Bearing Witness to the Holocaust, 1939–1989*, edited by Alan Berger, 207–26. Lewiston, NY: Edwin Mellen Press, 1991.

Rowden, Rebecca. *Baptists in Israel: The Letters of Paul and Marjorie Rowden, 1952–1957*. Nashville, TN: Fields, 2010.

Rubin, Neil. "The Relationship between American Evangelical Christians and the State of Israel." In *Israel and the United States: Six Decades of US-Israeli Relations*, edited by Robert O. Freedman, 232–56. New York: Routledge, 2018.

Russell, C. Allyn. "W. A. Criswell: A Case Study in Fundamentalism." *Review & Expositor* 44, no. 1 (1984): 107–31.

Sachar, Howard. *A History of Israel: From the Rise of Zionism to Our Time*. 3rd ed. New York: Knopf, 2004.

Said, Edward. *Culture and Imperialism*. New York: Knopf, 1993.

———. *Orientalism*. New York: Pantheon, 1978.

———. *Out of Place: A Memoir*. New York: Knopf, 1999.

Sandeen, Ernest. *The Roots of Fundamentalism: British and American Millenarianism, 1800–1930*. Chicago: University of Chicago Press, 1970.

Sarna, Jonathan. "The Impact of Nineteenth-Century Christian Missions on American Jews." In *Jewish Apostasy in the Modern World*, edited by Todd M. Endelman, 232–54. New York: Holmes and Meier, 1987.

———. "Louis Brandeis: Zionist Leader." *Brandeis Review* 11, no. 3 (1992): 22–27.

Scales, T. Laine. *All That Fits a Woman: Training Southern Baptist Women for Charity and Mission, 1907–1926*. Macon, GA: Mercer University Press, 2000.

Schweid, Eliezer. "The Rejection of the Diaspora in Zionist Thought: Two Approaches." *Studies in Zionism* 5, no. 1 (1984): 43–70.

Schweiger, Beth Barton. *The Gospel Working Up: Progress and the Pulpit in Nineteenth-Century Virginia*. New York: Oxford University Press, 2000.

Segev, Tom. *One Palestine, Complete: Jews and Arabs under the British Mandate*. New York: Macmillan, 2000.

Shapira, Anita. *Israel: A History*. Translated by Anthony Berris. Waltham, MA: Brandeis University Press, 2012.

Shapiro, Faydra L. *Christian Zionism: Navigating the Jewish-Christian Border*. Eugene, OR: Wipf and Stock, 2015.

Sharkey, Heather J. *American Evangelicals in Egypt: Missionary Encounters in an Age of Empire*. Princeton, NJ: Princeton University Press, 2008.

Shimoni, Gideon. *The Zionist Ideology*. Waltham, MA: Brandeis University Press, 1995.

Shindler, Colin. "Likud and the Christian Dispensationalists: A Symbiotic Relationship." *Israel Studies* 5, no. 1 (2000): 153–82.

Silk, Mark. "Notes on the Judeo-Christian Tradition in America." *American Quarterly* 36, no. 1 (1984): 65–85.

Slonim, Shlomo. "The 1948 American Embargo on Arms to Palestine." *Political Science Quarterly* 94, no. 3 (1979): 495–514.

Smith, Andrew. "'Flocking by Themselves': Fundamentalism, Fundraising, and the Bureaucratization of the Southern Baptist Convention, 1919–1925." PhD diss., Vanderbilt University, 2011.

———. *Fundamentalism, Fundraising, and the Southern Baptist Convention, 1919–1925*. Knoxville: University of Tennessee Press, 2016.

Smith, Gary. *Religion in the Oval Office: The Religious Lives of American Presidents*. New York: Oxford University Press, 2015.

Smith, Mika. "Hooded Crusaders: The Ku Klux Klan in the Panhandle and South Plains, 1921–1925." Master's thesis, Texas Tech University, 2008.

Smith, Robert. *More Desired Than Our Owne Salvation: The Roots of Christian Zionism*. New York: Oxford University Press, 2013.

Smith, Samantha, and Carroll Doherty. "5 Facts about How Americans View the Israeli-Palestinian Conflict." *Pew Research Center*. May 23, 2016. http://www.pewresearch.org/fact-tank/2016/05/23/5-facts-about-how-americans-view-the-israeli-palestinian-conflict/.

Snetsinger, John. *Truman, the Jewish Vote, and the Creation of Israel*. Stanford, CA: Hoover Institution Press, 1974.

Sobel, B. Zvi. *Hebrew Christianity: The Thirteenth Tribe*. New York: Wiley, 1974.

———. "Legitimation and Antisemitism as Factors in the Functioning of a Hebrew-Christian Mission." *Jewish Social Studies* 23, no. 3 (1961): 170–86.

———. "Protestant Evangelists and the Formulation of a Jewish Racial Mystique: The Discovery of Sociology." *Journal for the Scientific Study of Religion* 5, no. 3 (1966): 343–56.

Spain, Rufus B. *At Ease in Zion: A Social History of Southern Baptists*. Tuscaloosa: University of Alabama Press, 2003.

Spalding, Elizabeth. *The First Cold Warrior: Harry Truman, Containment, and the Remaking of Liberal Internationalism*. Lexington: University Press of Kentucky, 2006.

Spector, Stephen. *Evangelicals and Israel: The Story of American Christian Zionism*. New York: Oxford University Press, 2009.

Spitzer, Lee B. *Baptists, Jews, and the Holocaust: The Hand of Sincere Friendship*. Valley Forge, PA: Judson Press, 2017.

Spivey, James. "The Millennium." In *Has Our Theology Changed?*, edited by Paul Basden, 234–62. Nashville: Broadman and Holman, 1994.

Stein, Leonard. *The Balfour Declaration*. New York: Simon and Schuster, 1961.

Steinberg, Alfred. *The Man from Missouri: The Life and Times of Harry S. Truman*. New York: Putnam's Sons, 1962.

Stillman, Norman. *The Jews of Arab Lands in Modern Times*. Philadelphia: Jewish Publication Society, 1991.

Sutton, Jerry. *The Baptist Reformation: The Conservative Resurgence in the Southern Baptist Convention*. Nashville, TN: Broadman and Holman, 2000.

Sutton, Matthew Avery. *American Apocalypse: A History of Modern Evangelicalism*. Cambridge, MA: Harvard University Press, 2014.

Thompson, James. *Tried as by Fire: Southern Baptists and the Religious Controversies of the 1920s*. Macon, GA: Mercer University Press, 1982.

Tibawi, A. L. *American Interests in Syria, 1800–1901: A Study of Educational, Literary, and Religious Work*. Oxford: Clarendon, 1966.

Trexler, Melanie E. *Evangelizing Lebanon: Baptists, Missions, and the Question of Cultures*. Waco, TX: Baylor University Press, 2016.

Troen, S. Ilan. *Imagining Zion: Dreams, Designs, and Realities in a Century of Jewish Settlement*. New Haven, CT: Yale University Press, 2008.

Tsimhoni, Daphne. "The Arab Christians and the Palestinian Arab National Movement during the Formative Stage." In *The Palestinians and the Middle East Conflict*, edited by G. Ben-Dor, 73–98. Ramat Gan, Israel: Turtledove, 1978.

Tuchman, Barbara. *Bible and Sword: England and Palestine from the Bronze Age to Balfour*. New York: Ballantine Books, 1956.

Tucker, Austin. "Monroe Elmon Dodd and His Preaching." ThD diss., Southwestern Baptist Theological Seminary, 1971.

Turner, Helen Lee. "Fundamentalism in the Southern Baptist Convention: The Crystallization of a Millennialist Vision." PhD diss., University of Virginia, 1990.

———. "Myths: Stories of This World and the World to Come." In *Southern Baptists Observed: Multiple Perspectives on a Changing Denomination*, edited by Nancy Ammerman, 98–123. Knoxville: University of Tennessee Press, 1993.

Ulrichsen, Kristian Coates. *The First World War in the Middle East*. New York: Oxford University Press, 2014.

Urofsky, Melvin I. *American Zionism from Herzl to the Holocaust*. Garden City, NY: Anchor Press, 1976.

Vogel, Lester I. *To See a Promised Land: Americans and the Holy Land in the Nineteenth Century*. University Park: Penn State University Press, 2010.

Voss, Carl Herman, and David Rausch. "American Christians and Israel, 1948–1988." *American Jewish Archives* 40, no. 1 (1988): 41–81.

Wacker, Grant. *America's Pastor: Billy Graham and the Shaping of a Nation*. Cambridge, MA: Belknap Press, 2014.

Wagner, Donald. "Reagan and Begin, Bibi and Jerry: The Theopolitical Alliance of the Likud Party with the American Christian 'Right.'" *Arab Studies Quarterly* 20, no. 4 (1998): 33–51.

Warne, Andrew. "Making a Judeo-Christian America: The Christian Right, Anti-semitism, and the Politics of Religious Pluralism in the 20th Century United States." PhD diss., Northwestern University, 2012.

Weber, Timothy. "American Evangelicals and Israel: A Complicated Alliance." In *The Protestant-Jewish Conundrum*, edited by Jonathan Frankel and Ezra Mendelsohn, 141–57. Vol. 24 of *Studies in Contemporary Jewry*. New York: Oxford University Press, 2010.

———. *Living in the Shadow of the Second Coming: American Premillennialism, 1875–1982*. Grand Rapids, MI: Zondervan, 1983.

———. *On the Road to Armageddon: How Evangelicals Became Israel's Best Friend*. Grand Rapids, MI: Baker Academic Press, 2004.

Weiss, Amy. "Between Cooperation and Competition: The Making of American Jewish Zionist Interfaith Alliances with Liberal and Evangelical Protestants, 1898–1979." PhD diss., New York University, 2014.

———. "Billy Graham Receives the Ten Commandments: American Jewish Interfaith Relations in the Age of Evangelicalism." *American Jewish History* 103, no. 1 (2019): 1–24.

Williams, Daniel K. *God's Own Party: The Making of the Christian Right*. New York: Oxford University Press, 2010.

Williams, Joseph. "The Pentecostalization of Christian Zionism." *Church History* 84, no. 1 (2015): 159–94.

Wills, Gregory. *Southern Baptist Seminary, 1859–2009*. New York: Oxford University Press, 2010.

Wilson, Evan. "The American Interest in the Palestine Question and the Establishment of Israel." *Annals of the American Academy of Political and Social Science* 401 (1972): 64–73.

Wilson, Mark. *William Owen Carver's Controversies in the Baptist South*. Macon, GA: Mercer University Press, 2010.

Index